Harvard Business Review

Entrepreneur's Handbook

Harvard Business Review

Entrepreneur's Handbook

Everything You Need to Launch and Grow Your New Business

Harvard Business Review Press

Boston, Massachusetts

Copyright 2018 Harvard Business School Publishing Corporation
All rights reserved
Printed in the United States of America

10 9 8 7 6 5 4 3 2 1

The material in this book has been adapted and revised from works listed in the
Sources section and from *Harvard Business Essentials Entrepreneur's Toolkit:
Tools and Techniques to Launch and Grow Your New Business* (Harvard Business
School Press, 2005), subject adviser Alfred E. Osborne.

No part of this publication may be reproduced, stored in or introduced into
a retrieval system, or transmitted, in any form, or by any means (electronic,
mechanical, photocopying, recording, or otherwise), without the prior permission
of the publisher. Requests for permission should be directed to permissions@
hbsp.harvard.edu, or mailed to Permissions, Harvard Business School
Publishing, 60 Harvard Way, Boston, Massachusetts 02163.

The web addresses referenced in this book were live and correct at the time of the
book's publication but may be subject to change.

Library of Congress cataloging information is forthcoming.

Paperback ISBN: 9781633693685

Hardcover ISBN: 9781633693708

eBook ISBN: 9781633693692

The paper used in this publication meets the requirements of the American
National Standard for Permanence of Paper for Publications and Documents in
Libraries and Archives Z39.48-1992.

Contents

PART FOUR
Scaling Up

PART FIVE
Looking to the Future

Introduction

William Bygrave, a scholar and practitioner of entrepreneurship, describes an entrepreneur as someone who not only perceives an opportunity but also "creates an organization to pursue it."

That last part of Bygrave's definition is essential. Ideas are one thing, but opportunities as we generally understand them are best addressed through business organizations formed by entrepreneurs. Thomas Edison, for example, recognized the business opportunity in urban electric illumination, which he pursued through tireless laboratory experiments that eventually produced a workable incandescent light bulb. But invention was only part of Edison's genius. He also formed a company that brought together the human and financial resources needed to implement his vision of commercial and residential lighting. That company was the forerunner of the General Electric Company, one of today's largest and most powerful enterprises.

The same formula has been repeated through history: recognizing opportunity and addressing it through an organization. Some opportunities are evident and just need to be harnessed; others are created by the entrepreneur. For example, in 2007, when roommates Brian Chesky and Joe Gebbia could no longer afford the rent on their San Francisco loft, they decided to rent out space to guests. They set up a website with some photos of their apartment, quickly gaining three guests for their first weekend, at $80 each. Soon they began hearing from others who had found their site and wanted a similar offering for informal lodging in cities around the world.

The next spring, Chesky and Gebbia enlisted former roommate Nathan Blecharczyk to help them establish Airbed & Breakfast. To raise early funding, they bought cartons of breakfast cereal, repackaged it in the theme of the 2008 election, and resold it to conventioneers, raising about $30,000. Nevertheless, their site's growth stalled. While living off the extra cereal, though, they were accepted into Y Combinator's accelerator program. In the summer of 2009, they began testing their own services to better understand their users' needs. Realizing how poorly the properties were represented online, the entrepreneurs began a photography program in which hosts could have professional shots of their properties taken.

Learning and course-correcting as they went, Chesky and Gebbia saw their customer base rocket from one thousand in 2009 to over a million in 2011. Airbnb's financials are not formally disclosed, but in 2015, market reports placed its value at $25.5 billion with projected revenue of $900 million for the year, based on the company's reported three-million-plus listed properties worldwide.

Not all startup stories are so bright, of course. A complete definition of the entrepreneur must also recognize another factor: risk. In the financial world, risk contains the possibility of both gain and loss. The entrepreneur puts skin in the game—usually in the form of time and personal savings. If the venture goes badly, his or her time and hard-earned savings are lost. And indeed, 75 percent of startup ventures fail to return investors' capital, according to research by Harvard Business School's Shikhar Ghosh. But if things go well, the entrepreneur can reap a sizable profit. So if you have a business idea or an idea about how to fill a market need—or even if you just think you're interested in starting a business—how do you make sure that your venture is successful?

The same basic process applies whether your idea is the next high-growth wunderkind, a robust B2B player in a critical industry niche, or a local retail shop close to home. You recognize a potential commercial opportunity and pursue it through an organization, your own managerial or technical talents, and some combination of human and financial capital. Of course it's never quite this simple; in fact, the entrepreneurial journey often takes many twists and turns. This book will walk you through this process in more detail.

The role of entrepreneurs

Entrepreneurs play an important role in society. As described by economist Joseph Schumpeter in the 1930s, entrepreneurs act as a force for creative destruction, sweeping away established technologies, products, and ways of doing things and replacing them with others that the marketplace as a whole sees as representing greater value. In this sense, entrepreneurs are agents of change and, hopefully, progress. Thus, it was entrepreneurs who displaced home kerosene lamps with brighter and cleaner-burning gas in the middle to late 1800s. Those gas lamps, in turn, were displaced by Edison's incandescent electric light system, which provided better performance and greater safety. Fluorescent lighting came along years later, displacing many incandescent applications.

We see this pattern repeated in virtually every industry. Entrepreneurs invent or commercialize new technologies that displace the old. Photocopying, the personal computer, the World Wide Web, the spreadsheet, and new and improved drug therapies and medical devices are all products of enterprising entrepreneurs. Entrepreneurs also introduce products, services, and platforms that deliver something entirely new: the electronic calculator, next-day package delivery, crowd fund-raising, aircraft simulation software, oral contraceptives, angioplasty to open narrow heart arteries, and online marketplaces for everything from apartment rentals and ride-sharing to homemade crafts and financial payments. Entrepreneurs have given us even mundanely useful things that our parents or grandparents would not have imagined: computers we take everywhere (like our iPhones), contact lenses, milk in aseptic packaging that requires no refrigeration, online auctions that bring together buyers and sellers from every part of the world, and on and on. These products and services improve customers' lives. Many are also beneficial to society and to the planet, be they improved drug therapies, microloan systems that alleviate poverty around the globe, or drones that target pesticides to the crops that need them most, eliminating waste and pollution.

In conceiving of these new products and services and forming and running enterprises to bring them to customers and users, entrepreneurs often sweep away stagnant industries and replace them with growing ones that generate new jobs, often at higher wages. Thus they have a central role in building wealth and dynamism in the societies in which their enterprises operate.

What's ahead

This book takes a linear approach to entrepreneurship, from initial questions that you should ask yourself before you begin ("Am I the type of person who should start a business?") to the last issue that you'll need to consider as a successful business owner ("How can I cash out of the business I've built?"). Though your own experience is likely to differ from this simplified framework—the entrepreneurial process is nothing if not iterative—this book should give you a good overview of the issues you'll probably face and how to approach them.

Part 1 prepares you for your journey. In chapter 1, we describe the self-diagnosis that every prospective entrepreneur should undertake. Are you the right type of person to start up and operate a business? This chapter will help you answer that important question.

Part 2 helps you define your enterprise. The first steps in the entrepreneurial process are to identify and evaluate potential business opportunities. Chapter 2 offers five characteristics you should look for in a business opportunity, particularly focusing on the problem your business is trying to solve. It also introduces the lean-startup methodology as a way to evaluate market interest and to experiment with other hypotheses about the opportunity you've identified.

If your initial evaluation of the opportunity pans out, you'll further refine your business model and strategy. These two critical concepts are the focus of chapter 3. It describes how the business model explains the way key components of the enterprise work together to make money—and how to begin to test your business model with real customers. It also shows how strategy must be designed to differentiate the entity and confer it with a competitive advantage. Finally, the chapter offers a five-step process for formulating strategy and aligning business activities with it.

Assuming that your evaluations and experiments have given you continued confidence in your business idea, you'll need to structure your business from a legal perspective. In chapter 4, you'll learn about the various legal forms of business organization used in the United States. You'll see their pros and cons and decide which organizational structure is best for your venture: a limited-liability corporation, a sole proprietorship, a partnership, a corporation, or something else.

Chapter 5 gets you started on writing a plan for your business, incorporating many of the elements discussed previously. A business plan explains the opportunity, identifies the market to be served, and provides details about how your organization expects to pursue the opportunity. The plan also describes the unique qualifications that the management team brings to the effort, lists the resources required for success, and predicts the results over a reasonable time horizon. This chapter tells you why a business plan is necessary, gives you a format for organizing one, and offers tips for developing each section in the format. It also describes other documents similar to a business plan, such as a pitch deck.

Part 3 focuses on how to get the funding you need to finance the various stages of your enterprise. The global recession of 2008 took a big toll on entrepreneurship, a sector that has not yet recovered. In the United States, new business starts went from 525,000 in 2007 to just over 400,000 in 2014. There are many reasons for this drop-off, but small businesses tend to fare the worst in a recession because they depend heavily on bank debt, which becomes harder to obtain during economic downturns. Since the recession, some new forms of financing, such as crowdfunding, angel investing, and online banking, have appeared. This part of the book describes those new forms along with more traditional methods of raising capital.

Chapter 6 concentrates on the financing requirements that businesses typically encounter in the first phase of their life cycles. It also provides an overview of life cycles for different types of businesses.

In chapter 7, the discussion of financing continues. It addresses the next stages of a business's life cycle: that of growth and maturity.

Chapter 8 focuses on rapidly growing firms and their need for external capital specifically. Entrepreneurs can bootstrap early development from personal sources, friends, and relatives, but these enterprises usually need external infusions of capital to move to a higher level. This chapter introduces two external sources of capital—angel investors and venture capitalists or venture-capital firms (VCs)—and explains how best to approach them and win their support.

At some point, many growing firms with exceptional revenue potential seek and obtain financing through an initial public offering (IPO) of their shares to individual and institutional investors such as pension funds and mutual funds. That rare event results in a significant exchange of paper ownership shares for the hard cash the firm needs for stability and expansion. Chapter 9 describes what it takes to be an IPO candidate, the pros and cons of going public, the role of investment bankers, and eight steps for doing a deal. Because very few businesses will obtain external capital from an IPO, we also present an alternative arrangement: the private placement.

In part 4, we discuss the effects of growth on your organization. Paradoxically, success is sometimes the entrepreneurial company's greatest enemy; hierarchy, bureaucracy, and complacency frequently follow. Chapter 10 walks you through the organizational and strategic aspects of dealing with growth, while chapter 11 emphasizes that you as a leader may need to reexamine your way of working and even your own role as your business becomes larger.

As organizations grow, they tend to become more complacent about how to best serve their customers. Chapter 12 addresses how you can sustain entrepreneurial innovation and energy in your growing company even as it naturally becomes more process-driven and operations-focused. You can keep new ideas flourishing through efforts to manage your organization's culture, strategic considerations around innovation, and your own leadership involvement.

Finally, in part 5, we look to the future. In chapter 13, you learn about harvesting your investment in a private business. Founders—and the business angels and venture capitalists who support them—look forward to the day when they can turn their paper ownership into real money. This chapter describes the motivations that lead to harvesting, the primary mechanisms for doing so, and the methods you can use to answer the all-important question, "What is this business worth?"

Additional resources

The back of this book contains material you may find useful. Appendix A is a primer on financial statements. If you haven't studied accounting or haven't thought about it for a long time, this material will bring you up to speed. Go to appendix B for details of breakeven analysis not covered elsewhere in the book. Appendix C provides an overview of the methods used to determine the value of business enterprises. The appendix won't make you a master of this very technical and specialized subject, but it will teach you enough that you can deal intelligently with valuation experts. Finally, appendix D is taken directly from the US Securities and Exchange Commission site. It explains Rule 144 on the sale of restricted and control stock. Few readers will ever need to understand Rule 144, but those who do may find this useful reading.

The appendixes are followed by a glossary that provides definitions of key terms.

Finally, the book includes a "Further Reading" section. There you'll find suggestions of books and articles—both recent and classics—that provide more detailed information or unique insights into the topics covered in these chapters.

Preparing for the Journey

Is Starting a Business Right for You?

What makes entrepreneurs tick? More specifically, what are the personal traits and backgrounds of people who become successful entrepreneurs? This chapter considers those questions and helps you decide whether you have the right stuff to be a business entrepreneur.

Many books and websites include self-scoring tests that you can use to assess your fitness for entrepreneurial life. (The US Small Business Administration [SBA] provides one such test on its site at https://www .sba.gov/starting-business/how-start-business/entrepreneurship-you.) These assessments can be a good place to start as you think through what entrepreneurial work would mean for you and whether it's a good fit for your personality and goals. This self-evaluation is especially useful if you're starting with an idea for a business. Having ideas is important, but it's only one step in a process that also requires other skills and personality traits.

This and other tests typically integrate some combination or subset of the traits shown in table 1-1. Let's look at these traits in more detail.

Ideas and drive

Christopher Gergen and Gregg Vanourek, founding partners of New Mountain Ventures, an entrepreneurial leadership development company, describe the basic process of entrepreneurship as follows: "Understand a problem, grasp its full context, connect previously unconnected dots, and have the vision, courage, resourcefulness, and persistence to see the solution through to fruition."

Without those first elements—a full understanding of a problem, new connections, and a vision or direction for a solution—there is no entrepreneurial venture. Whether the problem you've identified is global or local, broad or niche, your ability to spot it and conceive new solutions is a core element of entrepreneurship. And passion about the problem you are solving might not be as important as you think—see the box "A passion for the work."

People skills

Having identified a problem or even a potential solution is one thing. But to launch a successful venture, you must also make other people see the merits of your idea and invest in it—whether they are employees, customers, or funders. Your ability to lead, persuade, take feedback, and build a network will determine whether you'll actually be able to bring your idea to fruition.

In the *HBR Guide to Buying a Small Business*, Harvard Business School professors Richard S. Ruback and Royce Yudkoff describe the people skills that entrepreneurs need first: "You need to feel comfortable reaching out to people you don't know—sellers, . . . investors, your employees—and when you do reach out, you need to project an air of confident optimism."

TABLE 1-1

Common entrepreneurial traits

Ideas and drive	People skills	Work style	Financial savvy	Entrepreneurial background
Creativity	Leadership	Goal oriented	Comfortable with finance	Family members have started businesses
Vision	Persuasion	Comfortable with uncertainty	Comfortable with financial governance	Friends have started businesses
Ability to identify opportunities	Influence	Self-challenging		You have worked at a small business or startup
Passion	Network building	Experimental mindset; OK with starting small and recognizing and moving past failures		
	Ability to excite people by vision	Perseverance in the face of adversity		
	Solitary; don't like working for others; prefer being own boss	Tendency to continuously look for a better or different way to do things		
	Rarely satisfied or complacent; can't sit still	Ability to close a deal		
	Driven to plan and be prepared	Ability to listen, trust, take advice		

Sources: Bill J. Bonnstetter, "New Research: The Skills That Make an Entrepreneur," HBR.org, December 7, 2012; Daniel Isenberg, "Should You Be an Entrepreneur? Take This Test," HBR.org, February 12, 2010; Harvard Business Review, "For Founders, Preparation Trumps Passion," *Harvard Business Review*, July–August 2015; HBS Working Knowledge, "Skills and Behaviors That Make Entrepreneur's Successful," June 6, 2016; Veroniek Collewaert and Frederik Anseel, "How Entrepreneurs Can Keep Their Passion from Fading," HBR.org, June 16, 2016.

A passion for the work

Passion, long considered an important part of entrepreneurial work, keeps entrepreneurs going when the going gets tough. It's the spark that inspires an investor to sign on; it's the vision for the change you're going to usher into the world through your new product or service. Indeed, "Follow your passion" is increasingly becoming a catchphrase as the generation that was raised with it comes of age in the professional world.

But experts caution against thinking of passion as a primary requirement for your success as an entrepreneur. Here's why:

- Research shows that passion simply doesn't correlate with success years out from the founding of a new business.

- Research also shows that passion in entrepreneurs tends to fade over time, even during the first few months of the enterprise's founding.

When it comes to funders particularly, serial entrepreneurs Evan Baehr and Evan Loomis write that "potential investors will ask themselves three simple questions during a meeting: 1) Do I like you?, 2) Do I trust you?, and 3) Do I want to do business with you?" To earn an investor's trust, you must first be appealing and interesting enough for them to get to know you well enough to trust you. To succeed in the high-pressure, fast-paced world of venture funding, you must know how to connect with people—and know when your tactics for connecting with them aren't working, and switch to a tactic that will.

But successful entrepreneurship isn't just about convincing others about the brilliance of your idea, just as networking isn't only about getting funding, and just as selling to customers isn't only about selling. These activities will also yield feedback about your business idea or how your company is operating. That information is worthless if you don't know how

- While expressing passion for your business or idea can help if you are trying to secure funding from a less experienced source—relatives or semiprofessional angel investors, for example—professional funders prefer strong preparation and a calm demeanor, which they associate with good leadership, over passion.

- As former venture capitalist and entrepreneur Dan Isenberg writes, "Passion is an emotion that blinds you." If you are too emotionally attached to your venture, you won't see its problems objectively or be able to correct course when you need to.

Sources: Cal Newport, "Solving Gen Y's Passion Problem," HBR.org, September 18, 2012; Harvard Business Review, "For Founders, Preparation Trumps Passion," *Harvard Business Review,* July–August 2015; Harvard Business Review, "How Venture Capitalists Really Assess a Pitch," *Harvard Business Review,* June 2017; Daniel Isenberg, "The Danger of Entrepreneurial Passion," HBR.org, January 6, 2010.

to listen or accept feedback. In their research of entrepreneurs around the globe, marketing professors Vincent Onyemah, Martha Rivera Pesquera, and Abdul Ali found that one of the most common mistakes in selling a new offering was entrepreneurs' failure to listen to their customers' complaints about the product: "Some realized that their passion and ego made them respond negatively to criticism and discount ideas for changes that they later saw would have increased the marketability of their offerings." Successful entrepreneurs know when to stick to their guns—and when to take the advice of others and shift course.

They also know how to recognize when they've reached the end of the road. When a project isn't working, they accept that they have to shift to something else—failing fast is better than failing long and slow. On the subject, Isenberg quotes Joseph Conrad: "Any fool can carry on, but only the wise man knows how to shorten sail."

Work style

Being your own boss may sound appealing—no one to tell you what to do!—but it also means that to succeed, you need to challenge and motivate yourself. There won't be anyone else to do it for you. Successful entrepreneurs are intrinsically motivated by the problems they see around them and the solutions that they envision; they can't sit still while there's work to be done (and there's always more work to be done).

They are also often goal oriented: they fix their eyes on a prize and impatiently and relentlessly try different ways to get there, shifting strategies quickly when necessary (see the box "Stretching the rules").

Stretching the rules

In a comprehensive study of entrepreneurial characteristics conducted between 1987 and 2002, Walter Kuemmerle, an associate professor at Harvard Business School, identified comfort with stretching the rules as a common characteristic of successful entrepreneurs. Certainly, entrepreneurs need to be creative, seeing opportunities where others don't and challenging assumptions about every part of the business. For example, LinkedIn founder Reid Hoffman maintains that "freedom from normal rules is what gives you competitive advantage," describing, for example, how Uber's use of employee referrals for hiring decisions—rather than formal screenings—helped the company scale up more quickly.

But when this outside-the-box thinking turns into disregard for legal regulations or an excuse for personal misbehavior, the consequences are more troubling. For example, Uber and Airbnb are frequently faced with scrutiny about their skirting of regulations for taxis and hotels. Harvard Business School professor Benjamin Edelman reflects on this issue: "Uber counters that [the] rules primarily benefit taxi drivers and keep prices needlessly high. That may be. But the law's unambiguous require-

Indeed, most new ventures, no matter how well planned, are experimental, and as an entrepreneur, you will benefit from an experimental mind-set. A willingness to start small gives company founders an opportunity to test and fine-tune a product or another offering before locking into a business model that will allow them to scale. They have the patience to see how customers respond to a product, its price, and the way it is served. In this way, they can course-correct before expending large amounts of capital.

The classic counterexample of this patient, experimental approach comes from Webvan, a dot-com-era company whose leaders were unwilling to take such an approach. The company's founders—including Louis

ments were duly enacted by the responsible authority. In Uber's world, a general contractor might decide building codes are too strict, then skimp on foundation or bracing. Who's to say which rules are to be followed and which to be broken?"

Meanwhile public scandals around employee mistreatment and sexual misconduct have suggested other ways that a disregard for the rules can go too far. Beyond the personal damage caused, research has shown that corporate punishment for CEO misbehavior (not necessarily outright illegal acts) can be inconsistent, but the effects on the company's reputation if such misbehavior is made public can be significant and long-lasting, and negative effects reverberate within the company as well.

Entrepreneurs, then, have a harder charge than simply "breaking the rules": they must find a way to deliver iconoclastic creativity without disregarding civil society.

Sources: Walter Kuemmerle, "A Test for the Fainthearted," *Harvard Business Review*, May 2012, 122–127; Reid Hoffman and Tim Sullivan, "Blitzscaling," *Harvard Business Review*, April 2016; Benjamin Edelman, "Digital Business Models Should Have to Follow the Law, Too," HBR.org, January 6, 2015; David Larcker and Brian Tayan, "We Studied 38 Incidents of CEO Bad Behavior and Measured Their Consequences," HBR.org, June 9, 2016.

Borders, founder of the Borders bookstore chain—envisioned a nationwide home-delivery system for groceries. Webvan began by building a monster 330,000-square-foot automated warehouse in Oakland, California. It quickly raised more than $850 million in equity capital and began work on twenty-six similar facilities in metropolitan areas across the United States. But the company never came close to breaking even. Within two years, it had burned through its cash and was forced into bankruptcy. By most estimates, Webvan had tried to do too much too fast. Instead, successful entrepreneurs are willing to shift strategies quickly.

But a good experimentation process can't eliminate all risk in an entrepreneurial venture. Unlike the more established corporate managers, you as an entrepreneur need to be comfortable with risk and must not be intimidated by a shortage of information. Compared with your corporate counterparts, you are much more likely to find yourself in a situation in which making a sale, landing a contract, or reaching an agreement with a lender means the difference between survival and bankruptcy. Entrepreneurs are so close to the edge of failure that every deal has major consequences. Whereas a corporate manager might say, "I'd like more information before I can make this decision," an entrepreneur must make the best of uncertainty and move forward. Standing still and waiting for more information isn't an option.

This kind of pressure builds particularly around deal making. Successful entrepreneurs, according to Kuemmerle, understand how to seal a deal. "However tough the market or small the transaction, they know exactly what they must give up—and what they can get away with—while finalizing deals under pressure."

Financial savvy

In ongoing research at Harvard Business School, Lynda M. Applegate, Timothy Butler, and Janet Kraus have found that HBS graduates who have gone on to start businesses tend to rate themselves as more confident with financial concepts and financial governance than do other graduates. If you're less confident with the numbers, this book includes appendixes with an overview of common financial statements and concepts like breakeven analysis. These sections can introduce you to (or refamiliarize you with) these concepts.

Entrepreneurial background

Entrepreneurship runs in families to a surprising degree. Children of business owners are more likely than others to start or purchase their own enterprises. Similarly, anecdotal data indicates that children of business owners are more likely than others to enroll in the entrepreneurship courses offered by undergraduate and MBA programs.

This connection should not be surprising. The challenges, joys, difficult choices, and rewards of business ownership are frequent topics of discussion around the dinner tables of business-owning families. The children often learn the what and how of enterprise ownership from these discussions and from many weekends and summers working in the family store or factory. Indeed, Paul Newman, whom most people think of simply as an accomplished actor, grew up in a business-owning family and has recounted in interviews the many childhood weekends he spent in his father's store. Those experiences surely had something to do with his founding of Newman's Own, a packaged-foods company whose profits are donated to charity.

Jim Koch, founder and chairman of Boston Beer Company, represents the sixth generation of brewing in his family. Similarly, Dan Bricklin, co-inventor of the first spreadsheet software VisiCalc, came from a family that owned and ran its own business. Bricklin's background surely influenced the future course of his life: "My father headed up the family printing business, Bricklin Press, which had been founded by his father in the 1930s. Afternoons spent at the printing plant and dinners devoted to the day's business problems prepared me . . . for the trials I would face in my own business ventures . . . Growing up, I never expected that some big company would eventually take care of me; instead, I was always looking for opportunities to turn some nifty ideas into a business."

No matter what your background is, an entrepreneurial venture may be right for you. Successful enterprise is a combination of personal qualities and quality planning. You don't have to be a genius with a killer idea: most successful startups begin with incremental innovations. You don't have to be totally fearless, either: entrepreneurs who prosper have a healthy aversion to risk. Nor is technical business know-how essential: you can learn as you go along, or you can enlist an experienced businessperson as a co-owner. An individual who has all the right qualities for entrepreneurial work but a poor plan will not succeed. Nor will a person with a great plan but weak motivation and a fear of uncertainty.

What you must have is a solid plan, the ability to execute it, and a high degree of motivation—motivation that makes business success an important personal goal. Do you have these qualities?

Summing up

- Ideas are an important element of success for entrepreneurs, but they're not sufficient—you also must consider your personal background, inclinations, motivation, and skills.

- Tests are available to measure a person's suitability for an entrepreneurial life, but these tests should be used only as a rough gauge.

- Entrepreneurship runs in families. Children of business owners are more likely than others to start or purchase their own enterprises.

PART TWO

Defining Your Enterprise

2.

Shaping an Opportunity

Cesar managed the service department of a large car dealership. With five years on the job as manager and many more as a mechanic, Cesar understood the economics of the auto service business, and he saw what might be an opportunity.

"We're starting to sell more electric cars," he told his sister at a family gathering. "The national organization estimates that electrics will account for 10 percent of our unit sales five years from now. And two other automakers are moving into electrics. I think that these plug-in vehicles will define the automobile market in the coming years."

"How's that going to affect your service department?" his sister asked.

"Quite a bit," Cesar responded. "We've already brought in new diagnostic machines and trained people on the electric vehicles' electronic systems—which are substantially different from those of traditional cars and even hybrids. And we'll be very busy in the years ahead, since we'll get all the repair and maintenance business on these cars for the foreseeable future, even after warranties have expired. Traditional mechanics don't know how to work on electrics, and many will never learn."

Later that day, Cesar reflected on this conversation. "There may be an opportunity here," he told himself. After new electric vehicle warranties expired, he reasoned, owners would have no options for repair and maintenance except high-priced dealer service departments like his. Neighborhood mechanics wouldn't be equipped or trained to deal with these cars for many years. Many owners would welcome a lower-priced alternative—one that specialized in the repair and maintenance of electric engine vehicles. Cesar began envisioning a service center called the Electric Car Care Center. And if that proved successful, he could foresee a chain of cloned outlets—perhaps a national franchise.

Cesar had recognized a business opportunity, a great way to begin. But before he begins to pursue it, he needs to further evaluate what he knows about the opportunity—and what he doesn't.

Identifying a problem to solve

In 2004, leading expert on entrepreneurship Jeffry Timmons described a business opportunity primarily as a product or service that creates significant value for customers and offers significant profit potential to the entrepreneur. Increasingly, entrepreneurs and those who study entrepreneurship are focusing on what creates that value to begin with, on defining and refining the problem that needs to be solved for customers and users. You need to be sure that the problem exists and be able to describe it in some detail before you begin to invest heavily in building your solution. In other words, Cesar will need to make certain that drivers of electric cars will need his specialized service. He'll also need to know the number of these drivers and understand their behavior to ensure that his solution meets an actual need that customers have.

This problem focus has come to the fore because the entrepreneurial journey is rarely a straight line between seeing a need, identifying a solution for that need, and then simply executing on that solution. In the long-accepted standard process for entrepreneurship, would-be business owners would identify an opportunity in the marketplace and, using whatever data at their disposal, create a business plan and financial forecast that would be pitched to investors. If they got the funding, then they would follow through on the long process outlined in the document to build a team, create the product, market it, and hope the plan panned out.

But more often than not, it didn't. No matter how well conceived the original product or offering, there are always major unknowns at the outset of a business venture: What is the right business model? Will it scale? What will competitors do? What will be the unexpected glitches in the supply chain? And there's the biggest questions: Is there really a market for the product or service as conceived, and if so, how big is it? Many entrepreneurs are so excited about what their new gizmo or service can do that they forget to assess its value to customers. But in the end, the business can succeed only if enough people recognize this value and are willing to pay for it.

For example, perhaps there *is* a market for service for electric cars in Cesar's town, but it's not the lower-price market he imagined. It turns out that the people who buy electric cars are wealthy and are more interested in convenience than cost savings. If Cesar can discover this marketing information before he begins building his company around the idea of a lower-cost shop, he'll have a chance to reassess how he'll differentiate his business from the existing dealers.

Whether your business idea is a local service operation or the next big thing in the tech sector, begin by asking the following customer and market questions. As you go, evaluate your confidence in your answers, and begin thinking about how you will test them. Note that the questions don't assume that the person using your offering is necessarily the customer paying for it—many businesses create a product for a user but are paid by a downstream customer like an advertiser.

- What is the problem you are trying to solve for your customers or users?

- How many people have this problem? In other words, what is the size of the market?

- Are your potential customers or users aware of this problem, or is the need latent, that is, undiscovered?

- Is the market stable or growing? If it's growing, at what annual rate?

- How will your solution benefit customers or users?

- What percentage of the total market could the product or service reasonably hope to capture over the next few years?

- Is another product or service from competitors available to fill part of this demand?

- Who exactly are the potential customers? Can you name them? Can you describe them?

- How can you reach the potential customers and make a trans-action—directly, on your own website or bricks-and-mortar loca-tion; through distributors like the Apple or Google app stores; or through already-existing retail channels?

- How does the utility of the product or service compare with substi-tutes? For example, a tablet device is easier for a customer to carry around than a laptop. But it may not have all the functionality of the full computer.

With his experience and knowledge of service department costs to guide him, Cesar begins to answer these questions and measure the breadth of his newfound business opportunity. He has industry estimates of electric vehicle sales; he knows which diagnostic and other equipment is needed—and what it costs; and he is intimately familiar with the cost of running a fully staffed service facility. When he begins putting these num-bers together, his optimism grows. But running through this exercise also helped him realize where he needs more information. Table 2-1 shows how Cesar has sized up what he knows about the problem he's trying to solve.

TABLE 2-1

Market evaluation for the Electric Car Care Center

Aspect of the market	Cesar's evaluation	Cesar's confidence and unknowns
Problem you are trying to solve	• Help customers take care of their electric vehicles.	Confident that this will be a need—but will customers see it, and what will make them choose my shop rather than their dealer?
Customer benefit from your solution	• Lower price than equivalent service at the dealer. • Greater expertise. We service only electric vehicles and have all the right equipment.	Dealers tend to be expensive, so lower price seems likely to be a good benefit—but will it be good enough to attract customers away from their dealers? It would be great to test some pricing with existing electric car owners.
Market size	• Currently over two million electric vehicles on the road worldwide.	We've been seeing more and more electric cars on the road, but it's not clear what the trajectory of growth will be. We'll want to understand this more before investing heavily.
Market growth rate	• A 32 percent compound annual rate occurred in the United States over past four years. • Industry projections differ substantially on growth projections.	Will this growth be sustained? And is the growth of electric car ownership the same in our town as nationally?
Market share	• Share of service business within a twenty-mile radius estimated at 18 percent during the first five years.	This is a guess; we'll need to test it.
Competitors	• Primary competition is dealers who get most of the business during warranty periods. • Other new electric specialty shops are likely to open to service the rising demand. • Few neighborhood garages would have the training or equipment to provide service.	These observations seem accurate or likely.
Customer awareness of need	• Will become obvious as warranty periods expire and the high cost of dealer service becomes clear.	We will definitely want to test this projection.
Customers	• All owners of electric vehicles of all makes and models.	We need to learn more about the demographics of people who buy electric cars. Most who come into the shop tend to be wealthy—early adopters. But will that change if the price of fuel rises?
Reaching customers	• Buy list of electric car owners for direct email. • Use social media. • Advertise on hyper-local sites. • Offer free informational clinics ("Understanding Your Electric Vehicle"). • Partner with local environmental groups to get the word out.	We have lots to test here—maybe start a Twitter account or Facebook page with electric car care tips and see how many people follow us? Then we'll be able to market to those customers as well.

Experimenting to test your hypotheses

Chances are that you, like Cesar, may have some good, informed thoughts about these questions, but your guesses are no more than that. Approaches to entrepreneurship coming from Silicon Valley take into consideration these unknowns at the outset of a venture and deliberately expect twists and turns—or pivots—in the entrepreneurial path. In a design-thinking approach to creating a new product or offering, innovators actively experiment with their idea to better understand the market and its needs before proposing a solution. One common formulation of this approach is the lean-startup methodology, which focuses on finding a repeatable and scalable business model for a new offering (see the box "The lean startup").

The lean startup and other similar models of entrepreneurship are iterative and nonlinear—not a step-by-step path—but they realistically reflect how companies change as they grow and learn. Taking an experimental approach from the earliest stages of your evaluation of an opportunity can reduce risk by helping you to home in on the right problem to solve, rather than jumping straight to the opportunity. And while these techniques were originally developed to help rapidly growing tech companies, the practitioners who created them see them as equally applicable to other small businesses as well.

In particular, the lean-startup approach emphasizes customer development, or working with and learning about customers from the early stages of building a solution. See the box "Agile, customer-based development" for an example of how this approach can build your understanding of the problem you are solving for customers—and how to build your solution.

Evaluating the opportunity

Especially in an experimental approach, evaluation of a business opportunity is less of a onetime event and rather a set of questions that you need to ask over and over as you experiment and learn more about your business.

The lean startup

This methodology, named by entrepreneur Eric Ries in his book *The Lean Startup*, has grown in popularity from its Silicon Valley roots to MBA classrooms. As described by serial entrepreneur and academic Steve Blank for HBR, the lean startup incorporates three elements:

- **A business-model canvas:** A business-model canvas is a one-page document that captures your hypotheses about your businesses—your guesses about what you do not and cannot know about your business plan in advance. Seeing these unknowns all on one page allows you to imagine how the different parts of your business might fit together. The standard framework for a business-model canvas was developed by Alexander Osterwalder and Yves Pigneur in their book *Business Model Generation* (figure 2-1). Blank business-model canvases are available for free in exchange for registration at Osterwalder's website, strategyzer.com. (We'll talk more about business models in the next chapter.)

- **Customer development:** To test your hypotheses, you need to interact with your customers. Gone are the days when you'd keep a product in development a secret from the world, afraid that your competitors would steal it before a big splashy launch. Instead, as Blank explains, most industries recognize that "customer feedback matters more than secrecy and . . . constant feedback yields better results than cadenced unveilings." Go out to your potential customers, vendors, and partners for feedback on the hypotheses in each part of your canvas.

- **Agile development:** To generate useful feedback from your customers, create prototypes to share with them—and do so quickly. What is the minimum viable product that you can create to test your idea? And once you get feedback, how quickly and

(continued)

incrementally can you iterate on your product design to get more feedback without wasting time on the development of unnecessary elements? (See an example in the box "Agile, customer-based development.")

Source: Steve Blank, "Why the Lean Start-Up Changes Everything," *Harvard Business Review*, May 2013.

FIGURE 2-1

The business-model canvas

Key partners	Key activities	Value propositions	Customer relationships	Customer segments
Who are our key partners? Who are our key suppliers? Which key resources are we acquiring from our partners? Which key activities do partners perform?	What key activities do our value propositions require? Our distribution channels? Customer relationships? Revenue streams?	What value do we deliver to the customer? Which one of our customers' problems are we helping to solve? What bundles of products and services are we offering to each segment?	How do we get, keep, and grow customers? Which customer relationships have we established? How are they integrated with the rest of our business model? How costly are they?	For whom are we creating value? Who are our most important customers? What are the customer archetypes?
	Key resources	Which customer needs are we satisfying?	**Channels**	
	What key resources do our value propositions require? Our distribution channels? Customer relationships? Revenue streams?	What is the minium viable product?	Through which channels do our customer segments wants to be reached? How do other companies reach them now? Which ones work best? Which ones are most cost-efficient? How are we integrating them with customer routines?	
Cost structure			**Revenue streams**	
What are the most important costs inherent to our business model? Which key resources are most expensive? Which key activities are most expensive?			For what value are our customers willing to pay? For what do they currently pay? What is the revenue model? What are the pricing tactics?	

Source: Strategyzer, "Canvases, Tools and More," accessed July 12, 2017, www.businessmodelgeneration.com/canvas. Canvas developed by Alexander Osterwalder and Yves Pigneur.

Agile, customer-based development

When Jorge Heraud and Lee Redden started Blue River Technology, they were students in my class at Stanford. They had a vision of building robotic lawn mowers for commercial spaces. After talking to over a hundred customers in ten weeks, they learned that their initial customer target—golf courses—didn't value their solution. But then they began to talk to farmers and found a huge demand for an automated way to kill weeds without chemicals. Filling this need became their new product focus, and within ten weeks, Blue River had built and tested a prototype. Nine months later, the startup had obtained more than $3 million in venture funding. The team expected to have a commercial product ready just nine months after that. By 2017, the company had successfully launched a robotic lettuce thinner and was working on using drone-based technology to add accuracy to its sensing-and-spraying products, as described on their website at http://about.bluerivert.com.

Source: Adapted and updated from Steve Blank, "Why the Lean Start-Up Changes Everything," *Harvard Business Review*, May 2013.

As you try different elements of your business model in the market, you'll learn more about the problem you're trying to solve—and your solution's viability in the marketplace. What you learn about customers will help you continually evaluate your idea.

Timmons offers the following criteria for an opportunity worth pursuing:

1. It creates significant value for customers, who are willing to pay a premium to solve a significant problem or fill an important unmet need.

2. It offers significant profit potential to the entrepreneur and investors—enough to meet their risk-versus-reward expectations.

3. It represents a good fit with the capabilities of the founder and the management team—that is, the idea is something they have the experience and skills to pursue.

4. It is durable: the opportunity for profits will persist—and, indeed, will probably grow—over a reasonable time and is not based on a momentary fad or a quickly disappearing need.

We add a fifth characteristic to this commendable list, this one suggested by Alfred E. Osborne Jr., director of UCLA's Price Center for Entrepreneurial Studies:

5. The opportunity is amenable to financing. One would think that a promising commercial idea would always find financial backing, but experience teaches us otherwise.

We explored the first criterion in the first half of this chapter; now let's examine the other segments of this definition in more detail.

Will it deliver a significant profit?

To qualify as a good opportunity, a business must offer the potential for significant profit. But what amount constitutes significant? Each person will have a different view. Some entrepreneurs and investors will look for something capable of providing a comfortable livelihood—perhaps one that can be passed on to children as they mature. Others will seek much more in terms of financial gains for themselves and their financial backers—but potentially over different periods. For example, venture capitalists typically anticipate a long time horizon before they see a return, but they have higher profit expectations than do other business investors.

Risk must play a part in every consideration of profit opportunity because the risk and return tend to go hand in hand. Corporate employees often fret about workplace insecurity: "I could lose my job if the economy doesn't improve." For the people who start new businesses, however, the risks are far higher. If things don't work out, they lose both their employment and the personal savings they've invested. Investors are similarly at risk; in the worst case, they can lose all their invested capital. Given the

high risks of entrepreneurship, there should be correspondingly high potential rewards associated with an opportunity.

There is a very real trade-off between risk and return, as shown
in figure 2-2. Point A in the figure has zero risk and a very low return.
Points B, C, and D provide the investor or entrepreneur with rewards com-
mensurate with the risk. But you should avoid opportunities at point E—in
fact, any point below the diagonal line—because they do not fully reward
the investor or entrepreneur for the risks taken. As a more concrete example, why invest in a business that promises no more than a 5 percent return
when you could do almost as well by investing in ten-year US Treasury
bonds, which have no default risk?

Every business rests on an economic structure that influences the
enterprise's ability to compete and succeed. Some businesses—such as
supermarkets—have a very low profit margin on sales, but the successful
ones have very large sales volumes. (Expressed as a percentage, profit margin is profit divided by sales revenue.) On the other end of the spectrum, we
have, for example, custom furniture makers who don't sell many items but
who generally make a large profit on each sale.

What is the profit structure of your business opportunity? Think, too,
about the cost structure of the proposed business. Some businesses operate

FIGURE 2-2

The risk-versus-return trade-off

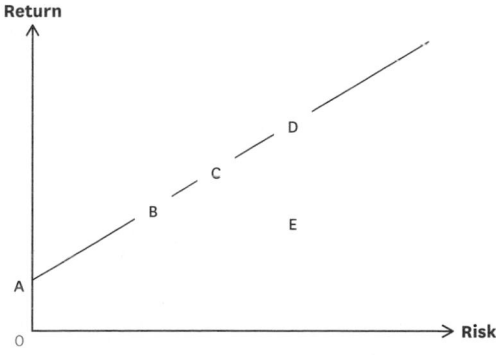

with high fixed costs and low variable costs. Fixed costs stay about the same no matter how many goods or services are produced. For example, an automobile engine plant has high fixed costs—for debt payments, insurance, specialized equipment, and salaried supervisors. These costs remain roughly the same whether the plant produces one hundred engines per year or ten thousand. Variable costs, in contrast, rise or fall with the level of output. These include the cost of materials, energy, and, often, labor. Understanding these costs will help you understand the basis of profit. And if you know the revenues you'll receive from each unit sale, you can determine the breakeven point of your operations—that is, the number of units you'll have to sell before you earn a profit. (See appendix B for an explanation of the breakeven point and how to calculate it.) Enterprises with high fixed costs and low variable costs (e.g., high-volume manufacturers) generally have high breakeven points but enjoy high profitability on sales after they get past that point. Those with low fixed costs and high variable costs (e.g., a technical service firm) have low breakeven points but relatively low profitability on sales thereafter.

A successful entrepreneur must understand the economics of a business opportunity. The next set of questions will help you think through and evaluate the economics of your opportunity. Try to provide a complete answer to each.

- Will the business be a price setter or a price taker? What are the constraints on pricing what the business sells?

- What is the supply-and-demand situation for your product or service?

- Is demand elastic or inelastic—that is, would a price increase dramatically reduce buyer demand (elastic), or would demand be only slightly affected (inelastic) in the short run?

- What substitutes do prospective customers have for your product or service?

- Will the business be dominated by fixed or variable costs?

- To what extent can suppliers and employees enforce cost increases on the proposed business?

You can begin to measure profit opportunity by means of a pro forma income statement. (If you are unfamiliar with the income statement or other financial statements used in business, see appendix A.) This kind of income statement provides a best estimate of future revenues, expenses, and taxes for one or more years. The net result shown on the statement is the anticipated profit from the entrepreneur's measure of opportunity for those years. Because lenders and investors will want to see a set of these statements, let's create a pro forma income statement using Cesar's Electric Car Care Center as an example (see table 2-2). Here, Cesar has forecast results during the first three years of operation.

In Cesar's case, the first year of operation shows a net loss of $21,000, even though he has earmarked a very small salary for himself. The magnitude of the opportunity grows substantially in succeeding years, however, as the volume of business (i.e., revenues) increases. If volume continues to build in subsequent years, a second facility—if not a regional chain—might be feasible.

Naturally, the opportunity reflected in a pro forma income statement is only as valid as the numbers it contains. A person such as Cesar, who conceives of a business that is closely or directly related to his current experience, can usually develop reliable expense numbers. Labor and benefits costs, interest expenses, rent costs per square foot, and so forth are within the scope of his experience. Revenue projections are another matter. In the absence of existing customers, Cesar has to assume revenue figures and revenue growth. And therein lies the most dangerous trap for the entrepreneur. Anything you can do to experiment to get a more realistic view of these numbers will give you a better sense of whether the opportunity is worth pursuing.

Is it a good fit for you and your team?

A good fit is a situation in which the entrepreneur and management team have the managerial, financial, and technical capabilities, along with the

TABLE 2-2

The Electric Car Care Center, pro forma income statement for years ending December 31, 2018, 2019, and 2020

	2018	2019	2020
Revenues	$450,000	$700,000	$1,000,000
Expenses:			
Owner's salary	40,000	70,000	90,000
Employee salaries	140,000	160,000	200,000
Benefits	70,000	85,000	100,000
Workers' insurance	14,000	15,000	20,000
Equipment loan 1[a]	42,000	42,000	42,000
Equipment loan 2[b]			14,000
Insurance	4,000	4,200	45,000
Shop rent	40,000	40,000	40,000
Utilities	6,000	6,200	6,400
Other	10,000	10,000	10,000
Parts & materials	100,000	185,000	250,000
Advertising	5,000	6,000	7,000
Total expenses	471,000	623,400	824,400
Profits before tax	(21,000)	76,600	175,600
Tax	0	22,980	35,400
Profits after tax	(21,000)	53,620	140,200

a. $300,000 loan at 9 percent for twelve years.
b. $100,000 loan at 9 percent for twelve years.

personal commitment, that are needed to address a business opportunity. Cesar, the fictional character in our electric car service example, appears to have a good fit with the opportunity he has identified. He already understands the technology and knows how to deal with it. He is also experienced in the management of an auto service business.

As you consider an opportunity, think about the expertise and skills it will take to run that business. Do you have those competencies? At what point will you be able to hire for them—and are they in high demand and hence very likely to require a high salary? What kind of work can you contract out versus bringing in house?

Will it last?

Some opportunities are durable—that is, they are opportunities that businesspeople can exploit over long periods. They are long-lasting and destined to grow over time. The software industry has demonstrated this durability. Other industries are too fleeting to sustain profitability over the long term. From the 1970s pet rock fad to the virtual world Second Life, most opportunities associated with fads and fashion are equally short-lived. By the time customer requirements are defined and addressed, the market has lost interest and moved on to the next new thing.

Some opportunities lack durability even though demand remains high for a long time. Low barriers to entry create these situations. A visible opportunity with low entry barriers to new competition is a deadly combination. The supply of the product or service can quickly exceed demand, resulting in price reductions and business distress all around.

As you evaluate your business idea, consider first whether the need you've identified is likely to be sustained. Sometimes, you just need to take the time to see if a new fad has staying power. It can be worth the investment of time to wait before making an investment, according to London Business School entrepreneurship professor Freek Vermeulen, even in digital industries.

But speed is often what is called for to achieve one much-lauded source of durability in many industries: network effects. Where the value of a business's offering depends on the number of users it attracts, being the first to achieve scale in a particular market can create high defensibility; users are less likely to defect to a competitor with *fewer* users, because it's less valuable to them. This means that eBay and Etsy become more valuable for sellers as they attract more buyers, and more valuable to buyers as they attract a wider variety of sellers. In these kinds of businesses, defensibility comes from growing very, very quickly, becoming the first mover at scale in your target market so that you can be the first to capture those users or customers. But effectively capitalizing on network effects isn't just about scaling your user base as quickly as you can—you also need to be aware of issues like building trust among the participants on your platform, focusing on the right kinds of users, and avoiding disintermediation. (With disintermediation, participants' trust in one another and the ease of the transactions grow so great that the participants can sidestep you as an intermediary.)

Can you defend the solution you are offering? Can you take advantage of network effects? Do other aspects of your offering make it difficult for competitors to emulate or replace?

What's the competition?

Now try to answer the next set of questions, which address your competitive landscape. If you're entering an existing market, you'll be up against competitors. Some may be entrenched and capable. If your market is new and attractive, you can be sure that it will attract other profit-seekers like you.

- How are customers currently satisfying the need you've identified (e.g., going to their auto dealer rather than seeking alternative places to get their car serviced)?

- What are the strengths and weakness of the main competitors (e.g., high quality, poor customer service, high price)?

- How would a smart competitor respond to your entering the market (e.g., by reducing price, bundling with other desirable offerings, improving customer experience)?

- Are the barriers to market entry high or low? Low barriers usually mean that competitors will continue to enter the market until returns are driven to a low level. If entry barriers are high, how will you surmount them? And will they stay high in the future?

- Have current competitors shown themselves to be agile and responsive to customer needs and technical change?

- What is the single worst thing that a competitor could do to your business prospects (e.g., drop the price 20 percent)? When you've answered this question, think about how that worst thing would affect your prospects for success and how you would respond. What strategy on pricing, positioning, service, distribution, or product features would give you a sustainable competitive advantage?

Thoroughly examine and answer each of these questions with documentation. If you will be seeking outside capital, this documentation is essential.

Is your idea amenable to financing?

A good business opportunity must be amenable to financing. You would think that any promising commercial idea would find financial backing—from the idea generator, friends, family, bankers, and so forth. But experience does not bear this out. Between 2000 and 2004, for example, entrepreneurs in the biotech industry had plenty of ideas for new vaccines and therapies. Several years earlier, these great ideas would have found the financing they needed, but they were starved for financing during the period in question because of a lack of investor confidence.

Two questions to ask yourself

After you've identified an opportunity and evaluated it in terms of the market, competition, and economic value, ask yourself two other questions:

- Is it still attractive in terms of the risk-to-return relationship described in figure 2-1?

- Is it more or less attractive than other opportunities available to you?

Don't overlook these questions. Always compare the attractiveness of an opportunity with other prospects you could pursue—including doing nothing. Leaving your capital in a money-market fund earning an anemic 2 percent interest is an alternative, one that you can follow until an opportunity with all the right characteristics appears on your radar.

Summing up

- A business opportunity (1) solves a real problem for customers, (2) offers significant risk-adjusted profit potential, (3) fits well with the capabilities of the leadership team, (4) is potentially profitable over a reasonable time span, and (5) is amenable to financing.

- Entrepreneurs often spend inadequate time considering the problem they are setting out to solve and testing how potential users and customers experience the problem.

- An experimental or lean approach to entrepreneurship lowers your risk and helps you understand customer needs and reactions to your solution before you make significant investment.

- Evaluate promising opportunities by considering the market, the current and anticipated level of competition, the underlying economics, and the resources you'll need to be successful.

3.

Building Your Business Model and Strategy

If your initial findings and experiments suggest a business opportunity, you'll want to start to solidify your business model and strategy. Ask yourself the following questions:

1. How will our new business create value for customers?

2. How will it make a profit for us and our investors?

3. How will the business differentiate itself from competitors?

4. How will the business defend its assets and position from competitors?

5. How will the business be discovered?

You should have concise answers for anyone who asks these questions. This chapter's primer on business models and strategy will help you get started.

Business executives, consultants, and the business media often use the terms *business model* and *strategy* casually and interchangeably. And indeed, various experts' definitions of the two terms do sometimes intermingle. But as an entrepreneur, you will benefit by thinking of these concepts separately. As this chapter uses the terms, a business model identifies your customers and describes how your business will profitably address their needs. Strategy, on the other hand, is about determining how you will do better than your competitors. Both a business plan and a strategy are required for your business to succeed.

Defining your business model

The term business model came into popular use when spreadsheet software first allowed entrepreneurs and analysts to easily model the costs and revenues associated with any proposed business. After the model was set up, it took only a few keystrokes to observe the impact of individual changes—for example, in unit price, profit margin, and supplier costs—on a company's bottom line. Pro forma financial statements were the primary documents of business modeling, but the emphasis was on the idea that a model could tell you something about your business *before* it launched. Now, much of the focus of the experimental approach to entrepreneurship is on business models specifically.

Understanding the power of the business model

In the most basic sense, a business model describes how an enterprise proposes to make money. Strategy expert Joan Magretta has provided a useful introduction to business models in "Why Business Models Matter," a 2002 *Harvard Business Review* article in which she views a business model as some variation of the value chain that supports every business. "Broadly speaking," she writes, "this chain has two parts. Part one includes all the activities associated with making something: designing it, purchasing raw materials, manufacturing, and so on. Part two includes all the activities associated with selling something: finding and reaching customers, transacting a sale, distributing the product or delivering the service."

She goes on to explain that unsuccessful business models fail one (or both) of two tests: the narrative test and the numbers test. Does your model tell a logical, sensible story? And if you were to represent your model on a pro forma income statement with reasonable projections of revenues and expenses, would it be profitable? (See the box "Cesar's business model" to see what this exercise looks like for our entrepreneur in electric car care.)

A useful starting point for understanding different possibilities for business models is the list of existing models assembled by Mark W. Johnson in his book on business model innovation, *Seizing the White Space* (see table 3-1). How might each of these be applied to the problem you are trying to solve?

Some of today's most powerful and profitable companies created new business models that were elegant and compelling in their logic and powerful in financial potential. See the box "Airbnb's business model" for an example.

Considering your business model

Two Harvard Business School professors, Richard Hamermesh and Paul Marshall, have refined the definition of a business model as business decisions and trade-offs that fall into four groups:

- **Revenue sources:** This money comes from sales, service fees, advertising, and so forth.

- **Cost drivers:** Examples are labor, goods purchased for resale, and energy.

- **Investment size:** Every business needs a measurable level of investment to get off the ground and, in the case of working capital, to keep it operating.

- **Critical success factors:** Depending on the business, a success factor might be the ability to roll out new products on a sustained basis, success in reaching some critical mass of business within a certain time, and so on.

Cesar's business model

As described earlier in this book, Cesar, the service manager for a dealer selling new electric cars, sees a profitable business in the repair and maintenance of these vehicles, especially after their manufacturers' warranties expire. He has some interesting ideas for testing and marketing his plan to potential customers, but otherwise, his blueprint is essentially the same one used by auto repair facilities everywhere:

1. Generate customers through local advertising and on-premises informational mini-seminars for owners of these unique but increasingly popular vehicles.

2. Have the internal capabilities to diagnose and repair damaged and malfunctioning electric engine vehicles of all major manufacturers.

3. Establish a replacement parts pipeline with several regional distributors.

4. Establish outsourcing relationships with a top-quality body shop and an auto air-conditioning service company so that personnel can concentrate on mechanical problems.

This blueprint is Cesar's model for making money. His experience with electric car repair work and with running a dealer's service department has made him an expert in the details of pricing and cost management. By modeling many types of repairs on a computer spreadsheet and factoring in known costs for labor, parts, equipment loans, rent, and overhead, he is convinced that he can break even with a crew of five employees and eight thousand service-hours per year (roughly forty weeks per year). Everything over that breakeven point should produce a profit. He has worked these figures out in a pro forma income statement.

TABLE 3-1

Business model analogies

Try adapting one of these basic forms.

Analogy	How it works	Example
Affinity club	Pay royalties to some large organization for the right to sell your product exclusively to its customers.	MBNA
Brokerage	Bring together buyers and sellers, charging a fee per transaction to one or another party.	Century 21 Orbitz
Bundling	Package related goods and services together.	Fast-food value meals iPod and iTunes
Cell phone	Charge different rates for discrete levels of a service.	Sprint Better Place
Crowdsourcing	Get a large group of people to contribute content for free in exchange for access to other people's content.	Wikipedia YouTube
Disintermediation	Sell direct, sidestepping traditional intermediaries.	Dell WebMD
Fractionalization	Sell partial use of something.	NetJets Time-shares
Freemium	Offer basic services for free, and charge for premium service.	LinkedIn
Leasing	Rent, rather than sell, high-margin, high-priced products.	Cars MachineryLink
Low-touch	Lower prices by decreasing service.	Walmart IKEA
Negative operating cycle	Lower prices by receiving payment before delivering the offering.	Amazon
Pay as you go	Charge for actual, metered usage.	Electric companies
Razor/blades	Offer the high-margin companion product (razor) below cost to increase volume sales of low-margin item (blades).	Printers and ink
Reverse razor/blades	Offer the low-margin item below cost to encourage sales of the high-margin companion product.	Kindle iPod/iTunes
Reverse auction	Set a ceiling price, and have participants bid as the price drops.	Elance.com
Product to service	Rather than sell a product, sell the service the product performs.	Zipcar
Standardization	Standardize a previously personalized service to lower costs.	MinuteClinic
Subscription	Charge a subscription fee for a service.	Netflix
User communities	Grant members access to a network, charging both membership fees and advertising.	Angie's List

Source: Adapted from Mark W. Johnson, *Seizing the White Space: Business Model Innovation for Growth and Renewal* (Boston: Harvard Business Review Press, 2010).

Airbnb's business model

Consider Airbnb, which upended the hotel industry. Founded in 2008, the company has experienced phenomenal growth: it now has more rooms than either InterContinental Hotels or Hilton Worldwide do. By 2016, Airbnb represented 19.5 percent of the hotel room supply in New York and operated in 192 countries. In these countries the company accounted for 5.4 percent of room supply (up from 3.6 percent in 2015).

The founders of Airbnb realized that platform technology allowed them to create an entirely new business model that would challenge the traditional economics of the hotel business. Unlike conventional hotel chains, Airbnb does not own or manage property. It allows users to rent any livable space (from a sofa to a mansion) through an online platform that matches individuals looking for accommodations with homeowners willing to share a room or a house. Airbnb manages the platform and takes a percentage of the rent.

How would you describe your company or business concept in terms of these model elements? Have you nailed down your revenue sources and the factors that will drive costs for your business? Do you know which costs will be fixed and which will vary with sales volume? Have you calculated the capital you'll need to launch and operate the business? What factors are essential for success? Try to answer each of these questions unambiguously, and do so before you approach any investors.

Testing your business model

Many of these questions are impossible to answer at the outset of a venture. In his work on what he calls a business-model canvas, Alexander Osterwalder and others have emphasized that many elements of a business model are not decisions but rather assumptions or hypotheses that may or may not be true—or may not always be true, depending on various conditions.

Because its income does not depend on owning or managing physical assets, Airbnb needs no large investments to scale up and thus can charge lower prices (usually 30 percent lower than what hotels charge). Moreover, since the homeowners are responsible for managing and maintaining the property and any services they may offer, Airbnb's risks (not to mention operational costs) are much lower than those of traditional hotels. On the customer side, Airbnb's model redefines the value proposition by offering a more personal service—and a cheaper one.

Before platform technology existed, there was no reason to change the hotel business in any meaningful way. But after the introduction of this technology, the dominant business model became vulnerable to attack from anyone who could take advantage of the technology to create a more compelling value proposition for customers. The new business model serves as the interface between what technology enables and what the marketplace wants.

Source: Adapted from Stelios Kavadias, Kostas Ladas, and Christoph Loch, "The 6 Elements of Truly Transformative Business Models," *Harvard Business Review,* October 2016.

Of the essential factors that you defined earlier, which are you unsure about? If you can find ways to test those factors before developing your product or service offering—or before approaching investors—you can be much more confident about your probability of success. And if you understand what might change about your hypotheses (e.g., perhaps there are no competitors in this space *now*, but there may be in the future), you'll better understand the risks inherent in your plan and be better equipped to mitigate them.

Incubators and accelerators

To begin testing your idea more formally, especially in a high-growth field, you could join a business incubator (or, if you're a bit further along, an accelerator). These programs provide support for entrepreneurial ventures in the early stages of their operation—to experiment and to test their business models and other assumptions, quickly. They give fledgling entrepreneurs the physical space and the support to learn by doing by providing coaching, mentoring, networking, funding, and educational programming.

Often the terms *incubator* and *accelerator* are used interchangeably, but while they have many similarities, they also have differences. In this book, an accelerator means a time-limited cohort program that comes with equity investment. An incubator is a less structured and less time-bound program. Incubators can be independent or connected to a bigger firm, an academic institution, a government arm, or a nonprofit. They usually either operate as a nonprofit or charge your venture for rent (you share coworking space with other young companies). Work with an incubator is not limited to the early stages of a venture's development; some incubators specialize in later-phase growth.

Accelerators, on the other hand, mostly work exclusively with early-stage businesses. They tend to be more competitive than incubators, particularly for the stronger programs. They offer funding in exchange for equity (this is described more fully in chapter 6).

A plan for discovery

A key element of your business plan is *how* your customers will find out about you. Marketing, often considered a downstream step of the original business concept, really needs to be at the center of your model from the beginning. If you don't know your customers well enough to reach them, and if you haven't built something that's a good fit for them, the rest of your model isn't going to work. That's why we focused on the problem and the market first in our discussion of the opportunity in the last chapter.

But reaching customers directly isn't always so simple, especially when you rely on others for the distribution of your product. For example, consider a new business idea that is a mobile application. There are only two ways for your customers to get your app at any kind of scale: the Apple and Android app stores. But the Apple iTunes app store has more than 2.2 million products, and Google Play more than 2.8 million. How do you get your app discovered in that busy space? You can engage in app-store optimization—understanding as much as you can about how the stores' search algorithms work. With this knowledge, you can help make sure your app is ranked high in search results (after all, one in four apps gets discovered through search). You can buy ads on Facebook or Instagram. But anyone (like your competitors) can do those things as well—they're table stakes. To be competitive, you also need to be creative about getting broader marketing, endorsements, and interactions with your customers beyond those ecosystems wherever possible.

For example, take the food-delivery app Eat24, which was acquired by Yelp for $134 million. When the founders were just starting out, they faced a market dominated by GrubHub; potential backers Benchmark, Redpoint, Excel, Insight, and Alibaba turned them down. But the founders got creative about their service and found a niche of small family restaurants that weren't well served by the behemoth GrubHub. They literally knocked on doors to get the word out and offered features of interest to potential customers: free fax machines for the restaurants wary of online ordering, no charges for very small orders, assuming the risk if a customer balked at paying. Simultaneously, the company placed relatively cheap ads on sites that were not appealing to most advertisers but that did appeal to young men. Besides being attracted to what these websites offered (we'll leave the exact nature of these offerings up to the reader to discern), these young men were also frequent users of online food delivery services.

As you develop your company's business plan, you need to be thinking about these kinds of unique features and approaches that will allow your product or service to best connect with your customers.

Defining your strategy

A business model will help you—and anyone you approach for funding—to understand what your business will do and how all its key parts fit together. But a well-conceived and promising business model is only half the equation for success, because it doesn't take into account the market competition. Dealing with competition is the job of strategy. Strategy is a plan to differentiate the enterprise and give it a competitive advantage. A successful business has both a solid business model and a good strategy. Some have argued against the present emphasis on the lean startup. They say that a strong strategy goes further to help a business than does an excess of validating tests.

Bruce Henderson, founder of Boston Consulting Group, has written that competitive advantage is found in differences: "The differences between you and your competitors are the basis of your advantage." Henderson believes that no two competitors could coexist if they sought to do business in the same way. They must differentiate themselves to survive. He writes: "Each must be different enough to have a unique advantage." For example, two men's clothing stores on the same block—one featuring formal attire and the other focusing on leisure wear—can potentially survive and prosper. However, if the same two stores sold the same things under the same terms, one or the other would perish. More likely, the one that differentiated itself through price, product mix, or ambiance would have the greater likelihood of survival. Harvard Business School professor and strategy expert Michael Porter concurs: "Competitive strategy is about being different. It means deliberately choosing a different set of activities to deliver a unique mix of value." Consider these examples:

- Southwest Airlines became the most profitable air carrier in North America, but not by copying its rivals. It differentiated itself with low fares, frequent departures, point-to-point flights, and customer-pleasing service.

- Toyota's strategy in developing the hybrid engine Prius was to create a competitive advantage within an important segment of auto buyers: people who want a vehicle that is either environmentally benign, cheap to operate, or the latest thing in auto engineering. The company also hoped that the learning associated with the Prius would give the company the lead in a technology with huge future potential.

- Apple wasn't the first company to build a digital music player and bring it to market. But it created a new business model that combined its capabilities in hardware, software, and service to create a new kind of ecosystem for customers to purchase digital music and seamlessly listen to it on their devices. iTunes made the iPod a success where the Rio and Cabo failed.

Strategies can be based on low-cost leadership, technical differentiation, or focus. They can also be understood in terms of strategic position. Porter has postulated that strategic positions emerge from three, sometimes overlapping, sources:

- **Variety-based positioning:** Here, a company chooses a narrow subset of product or service offerings from within the wider set offered in its industry. It can succeed with this strategy if it delivers faster, better, or at lower cost than competitors can deliver. For example, Starbucks offers premium coffee products and places its outlets in locations that are convenient for potential customers. But when it started, it didn't serve breakfast or sell sandwiches. Customers could get those products elsewhere; its focus was on coffee.

- **Need-based positioning:** Companies that follow this need-based approach, according to Porter, aim to serve all or most of the needs of an identifiable set of customers. These customers may be price sensitive, may demand a high level of personal attention and service, or may want products or services that are uniquely tailored (customized) to their needs. For example, financial services company USAA caters exclusively to active-duty and retired military officers and their families. After decades of serving this population, USAA understands its unique banking, insurance, and retirement needs. And it knows how to deal with the frequent transfers of military from post to post around the world and military assignments to remote locations for extended periods during which the officers are unable to respond to monthly billings.

- **Access-based positioning:** Some strategies can be based on access to customers. A discount merchandise chain, for example, might locate its stores exclusively in low-income neighborhoods.

This positioning reduces competition from suburban shopping malls and provides easy access for its target market of low-income shoppers, many of whom do not have automobiles. Cracker Barrel Old Country Store, in contrast, locates its restaurant and gift store combinations along the US expressway system, where it caters to travelers. Its website even includes a trip planner that identifies the locations of all Cracker Barrel outlets along any driving route.

What is your strategy for gaining competitive advantage? Will it differentiate your company in ways that attract customers from rivals? Will it draw new customers into the market? Will it give you a tangible advantage?

Simply being different, of course, will not keep you in business; something that is different must be perceived as valuable. And customers define value in different ways: lower cost, greater convenience, greater reliability, faster delivery, or more aesthetic appeal. The list of customer-pleasing values is extremely long. What value does your strategy aim to provide? Can it deliver?

Steps for formulating strategy

Strategy formulation is a large and deep subject, but this primer can help you get started with six steps to follow. They involve looking outside and inside your organization, thinking about how you will deal with threats and opportunities as they present themselves, building a good fit with strategy-supporting activities, aligning resources with goals, and organizing for execution. At the heart of these steps are Porter's classic five forces of competition: the threat of new entrants, the threat of substitute products or services, rivalry among existing competitors, the bargaining power of suppliers, and the bargaining power of suppliers.

STEP 1: LOOK OUTSIDE TO IDENTIFY THREATS AND OPPORTUNITIES. At the highest level, strategy is concerned with analyzing the outside environment and determining how the company's financial resources, people, and capacity should be allocated to create an exploitable advantage. There are always threats in the outside environment: new entrants, demographic changes, suppliers who might cut you off, substitute products that your customers could turn to, technological advances that could render your solution—or the customer's problem!—obsolete, and macroeconomic trends that may reduce the ability of your customers to pay. The business you have in mind may be threatened by a competitor that can produce the same quality goods at a much lower price—or a much better product at the same price. A strategy must be able to cope with these threats.

The external environment also harbors opportunities: a new-to-the-world technology, an unserved market, and so forth. So ask yourself these questions:

- What is the economic environment in which we must operate? How is it changing?

- What opportunities are there for profitable action?

- What are the risks associated with these opportunities?

STEP 2: LOOK INSIDE AT RESOURCES, CAPABILITIES, AND PRACTICES. Resources and internal capabilities can be a constraint on your choice of strategy, especially for a small startup with few employees and few fixed assets. And rightly so. A strategy to exploit an unserved market in the electronics industry, for example, might not be feasible if your firm lacks the necessary financial capital and the human know-how to exploit it. A strategy can succeed only if it has the backing of the right set of people and other resources. So ask yourself these questions:

- What are our competencies as an organization? How do these give us an advantage over our competitors?

- Which resources support or constrain our actions?

STEP 3: CONSIDER STRATEGIES FOR ADDRESSING THREATS AND OPPORTUNITIES. Clayton Christensen has recommended that strategists first prioritize the threats and opportunities they find (he calls them "driving forces" of competition) and then discuss each in broad strokes. If you follow this advice and develop strategies to deal with them, be sure to do the following:

- Create many alternatives. There is seldom only one way to do things. Sometimes, the best parts of two strategies can be combined to make a stronger third strategy.

- Check all facts, and question all assumptions.

- Some information is bound to be missing. To better assess a particular strategy, determine what information you need. Then get the information.

- Vet the leading strategy choices among the wisest heads you know. Doing so will help you avoid groupthink within your team.

STEP 4: BUILD A GOOD FIT AMONG STRATEGY-SUPPORTING ACTIVITIES. Porter has explained that strategy is more than just a blueprint for winning customers; it is also about combining activities into a chain whose links are mutually supporting and effective in locking out imitators. He uses Southwest Airlines to illustrate his notion of fit.

Southwest's strategy is based on rapid gate turnaround. Rapid turnaround allows the airline to make frequent departures and better utilize its expensive aircraft assets. These advantages, in turn, support the low-cost, high-convenience proposition it offers customers. Thus, each of these activities supports the others and the higher goal. That goal, Porter points out, is further supported by other critical activities, which include highly motivated and effective gate personnel and ground crews, a no-meals policy, and a practice of not making interline baggage transfers. Those activities make rapid turnarounds possible. "Southwest's strategy," writes Porter, "involves a whole system of activities, not a collection of parts. Its competitive advantage comes from the way its activities fit and reinforce one another."

STEP 5: CREATE ALIGNMENT. After you've developed a satisfactory strategy, your job is only half finished. The other half is to create alignment between the people and activities of the company and its strategy. Alignment is a condition in which every employee at every level (1) understands the strategy and (2) understands his or her role in making the strategy work. Make sure you have this powerful force working in your favor.

Alignment also involves other resources. Marketing must be focused on the right customers—the ones defined in the strategy. Compensation and bonuses must be aligned with behaviors and performance that advance the strategy. And physical assets must be deployed—aligned—with the highest goals of the organization.

STEP 6: BE PREPARED TO IMPLEMENT. A powerful strategy is impotent if your organization isn't prepared to implement it effectively. Unfortunately, some people get so carried away with the details of their strategy that they forget about the downstream activities required to make it work. One benefit of an entrepreneurial startup is that you're beginning with a clean slate. After you have a strategy, you have a free hand in organizing around it: hiring people with the necessary competencies, acquiring the right equipment, structuring these resources, and so forth. As UCLA's Alfred E. Osborne Jr. has put it, "I think of the 4 S's: structure follows strategy, and staffing follows structure, and you hold the strategy together with systems."

Strategy for platform businesses

Platform businesses enable exchanges between producers and consumers; web-based marketplaces like Uber, Alibaba, Etsy, and Airbnb are platforms that have recently stolen the startup spotlight because of their spectacular growth. The economics of these businesses can be very attractive: because they facilitate the exchange of goods and services rather than producing those goods and services themselves, they have low cost structures and high margins—eBay's gross margin is 70 percent, for example, and Etsy's is 60 percent.

With these kinds of businesses, different strategic forces come to play because much of the business's value comes from external sources. See the box "Network effects and strategy" for more on how—and why—you need

Network effects and strategy

In supply-side economies, firms achieve market power by controlling resources, ruthlessly increasing efficiency, and fending off challenges from any of [Porter's] five forces. The goal of strategy in this world is to build a moat around the business that protects it from competition and channels competition toward other firms.

The driving force behind the internet economy, conversely, is demand-side economies of scale, also known as network effects . . . In the internet economy, firms that achieve higher "volume" (that is, attract more platform participants) than do competitors offer a high average value per transaction. That's because the larger the network, the better the matches between supply and demand and the richer the data that can be used to find matches. Greater scale generates more value, which attracts more participants, which creates more value—another virtuous feedback loop that produces monopolies. Network effects gave us Alibaba, which accounts for over 75 percent of Chinese e-commerce transactions; Google, which accounts for 82 percent of mobile operating systems and 94 percent of mobile searches; and Facebook, the world's dominant social platform.

The five-forces model doesn't factor in network effects and the value they create. It regards external forces as depletive, or extracting value from a firm, and so argues for building barriers against them. In demand-side economies, however, external forces can be accretive—adding value to the platform business.

Source: Excerpted from Marshall W. Van Alstyne, Geoffrey G. Parker, and Sangeet Paul Choudary, "Pipelines, Platforms, and the New Rules of Strategy," *Harvard Business Review*, April 2016.

to consider your strategy differently if you're building a platform business or any other business that relies on the strength of the network it creates.

As you evaluate the importance of network effects to your business, also determine the right time to achieve that scale. If you are building a business that will depend on network effects, you might think you need to scale as soon as possible to capture as much of the market as possible. But Harvard Business School professor Andrei Hagiu argues otherwise. He maintains that many of the biggest platform businesses weren't first in their space: Vacation Rental by Owner (VRBO) existed before Airbnb, and Alibaba followed eBay in China. In fact, growing too early can mean that you won't have a chance to adequately test your offering and your business model before you're locked in. As a result, you might be giving up potential revenue, margin, or customers. Usually, LinkedIn founder Reid Hoffman observes, a company should scale when it has already gotten some data, understands the competition, and has ironed out the fit between product and market. The company is shifting from between ten and a hundred employees to a hundred or a thousand; from a hundred thousand or one million users to one or ten million; and to revenues of more than $10 million.

Be prepared for change

As we've seen, the initial strategies of startup companies often fail to hit the mark. Customers don't value the differentiation, or they don't respond to it as anticipated. Or the company chooses the wrong target customers. Companies fail because every startup business is an experiment to some degree. The outcome of this experiment can surprise and disappoint even the best planners. A classic example is a company called Webvan, whose founders and investors looked at the surge in online purchasing in the late 1990s and thought that a web-based grocery-delivery business was a perfect idea for affluent, web-savvy, time-starved households. But those customers balked at the higher price of buying their weekly groceries. To them, the extra convenience wasn't worth it. Webvan went bankrupt in 2001.

The entrepreneur's antidote to a disappointing strategy is a willingness both to recognize the bad news and to respond quickly with a revised

Cesar's strategy for the Electric Car Care Center

Strategy is about being different and choosing a different set of activities to deliver a unique mix of value to customers. Let's consider our hypothetical friend Cesar and the strategy of his auto repair and maintenance facility.

Cesar has clearly differentiated his business from current competitors. Every town and city has many automotive service businesses, but few places, if any, have a business that specializes in electric vehicles. Cesar can use that distinctiveness to gain customer attention and recognition. You can almost hear the advertising: "If your electric car needs maintenance or repair, bring it to the specialists at the Electric Car Care Center. They will do the job right."

Cesar must also deliver on that offer of greater know-how and high-quality work. To do that, he must acquire the right resources and align them in support of his distinctive offer. For example, he will have to acquire the tools and diagnostic equipment required by those vehicles. And he must hire or train mechanics who really know how to deal with

strategy, or a pivot. Recognition requires the ability to admit a mistake. Responding requires an energetic search for what went wrong and the flexibility to make adjustments and get back into the game.

Successful entrepreneurs are adept at both these capabilities. They are also masters of incrementalism—that is, if they find that something is working, they do more of it. If they achieve success in a small, niche market, they use what they have and what they have learned to enter another niche, altering the product or service as necessary.

Be prepared for competition

If your business model and initial strategy are successful, be prepared for company. Other entrepreneurs can introduce copycat businesses and try to the unique problems of electric cars. He has also outlined a marketing plan that involves sharing knowledge about electric car upkeep with potential customers through free seminars and social media. Consequently, some of his knowledgeable mechanics must also be able to teach what they know to others, either in front of a room or using the written word.

Finally, Cesar is also thinking ahead to future competition for his business. What happens when self-driving cars gain a foothold in the electric car market? Will Cesar's mechanics have the capabilities necessary to service those vehicles? He has a plan to get his team trained on the new cars once that training is available. He also sees many traditional services being disrupted by web-based platforms—what if someone starts a company that serves auto owners and cuts into his relationship with his customers? And what if car ownership declines in the face of the growth of ride-share services like Uber and Lyft? By identifying these competitive challenges early, Cesar can begin working on solutions before it's too late.

attain dominance in your market, getting to your target customers before you can reach them. Imagine what would happen to your company if a copycat business got $10 million from a venture capitalist firm while you were just starting to put together pitches for a second round of funding. The box "Cesar's strategy for the Electric Car Care Center" describes some ways that one entrepreneur considered competition in his strategy.

Large incumbents, on the other hand, may have more resources at their disposal to create an offering similar to yours. What would you do if Amazon or Facebook added your product idea as a feature? Incumbents can also dispatch your efforts in other ways. Venture capitalist Marc Andreessen gives the example of Silicon Valley: "It's World War III out here . . . Large tech companies will often move to take over startups with no intention of actually buying them, just to screw up their business for 18 months."

Indeed, Columbia Business School professor Rita Gunther McGrath argues that businesses shouldn't strive for the holy grail of sustainable competitive advantage, because there is no longer any such thing. Rather, she argues, businesses should build themselves to be nimble enough to build and exploit "transient" competitive advantages. Even if your initial strategy is successful and you can scale and exploit it well, you must plan ahead for the day when you'll need to abandon it for something else. In her formulation, stability isn't the goal; instead, it's about deliberate, continuous change.

If you want your venture to be competitive and profitable, you must have a powerful business model and a sound strategy. Although the market provides the ultimate test for these two important concepts, you should test and verify each of your assumptions before the business is launched. And remember that many minds are better than one. Explain your business model and strategy to as many trusted and experienced people as possible. They may spot defects or opportunities for improvement that you have missed.

Summing up

- A business model describes an enterprise's revenue sources, cost drivers, investment size, and success factors.

- Strategy differentiates the enterprise and gives it a competitive advantage.

- According to Michael Porter, strategic positions can be found in variety-based, need-based, or access-based positioning.

- The five steps of strategy formulation are (1) looking outside the enterprise for threats and opportunities; (2) looking inside at resources, capabilities, and practices; (3) considering strategies for addressing threats and opportunities; (4) building a good fit among strategy-

supporting activities; and (5) creating alignment between the organization's people and activities and its strategy.

■ A startup should be viewed as an experiment. If the experiment
fails to produce the desired result, be prepared to change—and to do
it quickly.

4.

Organizing Your Company

At the onset of your new venture, you will need to address the legal form your enterprise will adopt. Should it be a sole proprietorship, a partnership, a corporation, or a limited-liability company?

This decision is driven chiefly by your objectives and those of your investors. But taxation and legal liabilities also play a part. The trade-offs built into the law can make the choice difficult; to get the most favorable tax treatment, a business must often give up some protection from liability, some flexibility, or both. This chapter outlines the choices available to the new enterprise and summarizes the advantages and disadvantages of each.

Sole proprietorships

The oldest, simplest, and most common form of business entity is the sole proprietorship, a business owned by a single individual. For tax and legal liability purposes, the owner and the business are one and the same. The proprietorship is not taxed as a separate entity. Instead, the owner reports

A note about legalities

The information given in this chapter is based on US law but should not be considered legal advice. Always consult with an attorney on these matters. Similar structures for businesses exist outside the United States, and readers should consult their local legal and tax sources.

all income and deductible expenses for the business on Schedule C of the personal income tax return. The earnings of the business are taxed at the individual level, whether or not they are actually distributed in cash. In a sole proprietorship, there is no vehicle for sheltering income. And because the individual and the business are one and the same, legal claimants can pursue the personal property of the proprietor and not simply the assets used in the business (see the box "A note about legalities").

Advantages of a sole proprietorship

Perhaps the greatest advantage of this form of business is its simplicity and low cost (see the box "Tips for starting a sole proprietor business"). You are not required to file with the government, although some businesses, such as restaurants and child day-care centers, must be licensed by local health or regulatory authorities. Nor is any legal charter required. You can simply begin doing business.

The sole proprietorship form of business has other advantages:

- As owner or proprietor, you are in complete control of business decisions.

- The income generated through operations can be directed into your pocket or reinvested as you see fit.

- Profits flow directly to your personal tax return; they are not subject to a second level of taxation. In other words, profits from the business will not be taxed at the business level.

Tips for starting a sole proprietor business

You can start a sole proprietorship by simply doing it: you might offer your services as a consultant, buy and resell merchandise, write a subscription newsletter, and so forth. It's simple. Here are some useful tips:

- Keep your household and business finances separate. You can do that by setting up a separate bank account for your business; run all the business's checks and receipts through that account.

- Use QuickBooks or other accounting software to keep track of the many business expenses you'll encounter during the tax year. If you track them under the same categories used in the business expenses section of IRS form Schedule C, it will be simple to itemize these expenses and deduct them from taxable income. And scan, snap, or save every receipt—most small-business accounting software allows you to enter receipts straight into your files with your phone.

- If you run the business under a name other than your own—for example, Surfside Management Consulting—you may need to file a "fictitious name" or "doing business as" certificate in the city where the business is domiciled. Before you file, check that the name you want to use is not already taken by another business.

- Most US states prohibit the use of the words *Corporation, Corp., Incorporated, Inc.*—and even *Company* and *Co.*—after the business's name if it is not incorporated.

- You can dissolve the business as easily and informally as you began it.

These advantages account for the widespread adoption of the sole proprietorship in the United States. Any person who wants to set up shop and begin dealing with customers can get right to it, in most cases without the intervention of government bureaucrats or lawyers.

Disadvantages of a sole proprietorship

This legal form of organization, however, has disadvantages:

- The amount of capital available to the business is limited to your personal funds and whatever funds you can borrow. This disadvantage limits the potential size of the business, no matter how attractive or popular its product or service.

- Sole proprietors have unlimited liability for all debts and legal judgments incurred in the course of business. Thus, a product liability lawsuit by a customer will not be made against your business but rather against you.

- Your business may not attract high-caliber employees whose goals include a share of business ownership. Sharing the benefits of ownership, other than simple profit-sharing, would require a change in the legal form of the business.

- Some employee benefits, such as your life, disability, and medical insurance premiums, may not be deductible—or may be only partly deductible—from your taxable income.

- The entity has a limited life; it exists only as long as you are alive. Upon your death, the assets of the business go to your estate.

- As you will see later in this book, venture capitalists and other outside investors of equity capital will not participate in a sole proprietorship business.

General partnerships

A partnership is a business entity having two or more owners. In the United States, a partnership is treated as a proprietorship for tax and liability purposes. Earnings are distributed according to the partnership agreement and are treated as personal income for tax purposes. Thus, like the sole proprietorship, the partnership is simply a conduit for directing income to its partners, as in this example:

> *Matthew and Mathilde formed a partnership and started a restaurant called the Mat Café. By agreement, they split the profits of the business equally, the total of which amounted to $140,000 last year. Matthew, who had no other source of earnings last year, reported $70,000 in income on his personal tax return. Mathilde, who earned another $20,000 from a part-time job, had to report $90,000 on her personal income tax return ($70,000 in partnership income plus $20,000 from her other job).*

Partnerships have a unique liability situation. Each partner is jointly and severally liable. Thus, a damaged party can pursue a single partner or any number of partners—and that claim may or may not be proportional to the invested capital of the partners or the distribution of earnings. This means that if Matthew did something to damage a customer, that customer could sue both Matthew and Mathilde even though Mathilde played no part in the problem.

Organizing a partnership is not as effortless as with a sole proprietorship. You and your partner must determine, and should set down in writing, your agreement on a number of issues:

- The amount and nature of your respective capital contributions (e.g., one partner might contribute cash; another partner a patent; and a third, property and cash)

- How the business's profits and losses will be allocated

- Salaries and draws against profits

- Management responsibilities

- The consequences of the withdrawal, retirement, disability, or death of a partner

- The means of dissolution and liquidation of the partnership

Advantages of a partnership

Partnerships have many of the same advantages of the sole proprietorship, along with others:

- Except for the time and the legal cost of preparing a partnership agreement, it is easy to establish.

- Because there is more than one owner, the entity has more than one pool of capital to tap in financing the business and its operations.

- Profits from the business flow directly to the partners' personal tax returns; they are not subject to a second level of taxation.

- The entity can draw on the judgment and management of more than one person. In the best cases, the partners will have complementary skills.

Disadvantages of a partnership

As mentioned earlier, partners are jointly and severally liable for the actions of the other partners. Thus, one partner can put other partners at risk without their knowledge or consent. Other disadvantages include the following:

- Profits must be shared among the partners.

- With two or more partners being privy to decisions, decision making may be slower and more difficult than in a sole proprietorship. Disputes can tie the partnership in knots.

- As with a sole proprietorship, the cost of some employee benefits may not be deductible from income taxes.

- Depending on the partnership agreement, the partnership may have a limited life. Unless otherwise specified, it will end upon the withdrawal or death of any partner.

Limited partnerships

The type of partnership entity described thus far is legally referred to as a general partnership. It is what we normally think of when describing a partnership. There is another partnership form, however: the limited partnership. This hybrid form of organization has both limited and general partners. The general partner (there may be more than one) assumes management responsibility and unlimited liability for the business and must have at least a 1 percent interest in profits and losses. The limited partner or partners have no voice in management and are legally liable only for the amount of their capital contribution plus any other debt obligations specifically accepted.

The usual motive behind a limited partnership is to bring together individuals who have technical or management expertise (the general partners) and well-heeled investors who know little about the business—or who lack the time to participate—but who wish to participate in an opportunity for financial gain.

In a limited partnership, profits and losses can be allocated differently among the partners. That is, even if profits are allocated 20 percent to the general partner and 80 percent to the limited partners, the limited partners may get 99 percent of the losses. (Well-heeled limited partners often favor this arrangement when they can use the partnership's losses to offset taxable earnings from other sources.) Losses, however, are deductible only up to the amount of capital at risk. The distribution of profit is subject to all sorts of creative structuring, such as those observed in certain venture-capital and real estate partnerships. In some of those arrangements, the limited partners get 99 percent of the profits until they have gotten back an amount equal to their entire capital contributions, at which point the general partner begins to receive 30 percent and the limited partners' share drops to 70 percent.

C corporations

The C corporation is synonymous with the common notion of a corporation. When a business incorporates, it becomes a C corporation unless it makes a special election to become an S corporation, which is described later in this chapter. Although C corporations are vastly outnumbered by sole proprietorships in the United States, they account for over 60 percent of all US sales. Corporations dominate in this way because they constitute the vast majority of the nation's major companies.

In the United States, a corporation is an entity chartered by the state and treated as a person under the law. This means that it can sue and be sued, it can be fined and taxed by the state, and it can enter into contracts. The C corporation can have an infinite number of owners. Ownership is evidenced by shares of company stock. The entity is managed on behalf of shareholders—at least indirectly—by a board of directors.

The corporate form is appealing to entrepreneurs for several reasons. First, in contrast to the sole proprietorship, the C corporation's owners are personally protected from liability. To appreciate this protection, consider the case of the massive *Deepwater Horizon* oil spill in the Gulf of Mexico in 2010. Even if the damages against British Petroleum, Halliburton, and Transocean had exceeded the companies' net worth, the courts could not have pursued the companies' individual shareholders for further damages. An individual owner's liability is limited to the extent of his or her investment in the firm. This corporate shell, or veil, can be pierced only in the event of fraud. (Officers, however, can be held personally liable for their actions, such as the failure to withhold and pay corporate taxes.)

Another appealing feature is the corporation's ability to raise capital. Unlike the sole proprietorship and partnership, both of which rely on a single owner or a few partners for equity capital, a corporation can tap the capital of a vast number of investors: individuals as well as institutions, such as pension funds and mutual funds. Equity (or ownership) capital is contributed by shareholders when they purchase stock issued directly from the company. In return they receive a fractional ownership share in the assets and future fortunes of the company. A successful and growing company can often raise capital through successive public offerings of its stock. The corporation can also borrow money.

Advantages of a C corporation

The advantages of the C corporation, then, can be summarized as follows:

- Shareholders have limited liability for the corporation's debts and judgments against it.

- Corporations can raise funds through the sale of stock.

- Corporations can deduct the cost of certain benefits they provide to officers and employees.

- Theoretically, a corporation has an unlimited life span.

- Because a corporation can compensate employees with company shares, it is in a better position than proprietorships and partnerships to attract and retain talent.

- Ownership shares are transferable. Shareholders can sell some or all of their interests in the company (assuming that there's a market for them). They can also give their shares to family members or charities.

Disadvantages of a C corporation

The C corporation has several clear disadvantages. Perhaps the greatest is the problem of double taxation. The C corporation is taxed on its earnings (profits). Whatever is left over after taxes can be distributed to shareholders in the form of dividends or can be retained in the business to finance operations or growth. But consider what happens to after-tax dividends that are distributed to shareholders. These dividends must be reported by shareholders as taxable dividend income. Thus, earnings are taxed twice: once at the corporate level and again at the shareholder level.

To understand this double-taxation problem, consider this example:

> *Amalgamated Hat Rack earned $647,500 before taxes and paid a little more than 46 percent of this ($300,000) in state and federal corporate income taxes, leaving it with $347,500 in after-tax profit. If the company paid $10,000 of that in the form of a dividend to Angus McDuff, its founder and CEO, McDuff would be required to add that amount to his personal taxable income, which might be taxed by both the state and the federal government. Thus, the same income is taxed twice. (Note: There is a minor exception to this double-taxation issue for corporations that receive dividend income from other corporations.)*

Other disadvantages include the following:

- The process of incorporation is often costly. The corporation must create a set of rules for governing the entity, including stockholder meetings, board of directors meetings, the election of officers, and so forth.

- Corporations are monitored by federal, state, and some local agencies. Public corporations must publish their results quarterly.

Adopting the corporate form allows you to liquefy your personal equity in the company; paper wealth can be turned into real money. And it is a great way to raise the capital needed for growth. But every share sold dilutes your share of ownership and personal control.

S corporations

The S corporation is another creature of US tax law. It is a closely held corporation whose tax status is the same as the partnership's, but its participants enjoy the liability protections granted to corporate shareholders.

In other words, it is a conduit for passing profits and losses directly to the personal income tax returns of its shareholders, whose legal liabilities are limited to the amount of their capital contributions. In exchange for these favorable treatments, the law places several restrictions on the types of corporations that can elect S status. To qualify for S corporation status, an organization must meet the following requirements:

- Have only one class of stock, although differences in voting rights are allowed

- Be a domestic corporation, owned wholly by US citizens, and derive no more than 80 percent of its revenues from non-US sources

- Have thirty-five or fewer stockholders (husbands and wives count as one stockholder)

- Derive no more than 25 percent of revenues from passive sources, such as interest, dividends, rents, and royalties

- Have only individuals, estates, and certain trusts as shareholders (i.e., no corporations or partnerships)

The last provision excludes venture capitalists as potential shareholders because most venture-capitalist firms are partnerships.

Limited-liability companies

The limited-liability company (LLC) is a hybrid entity designed to afford the same benefits in terms of liability protections as those accorded to the S corporation, but with the tax flow-through benefits of a sole proprietorship or partnership. Although state laws differ somewhat, an LLC is like an S corporation but with none of the restrictions on the number or type of participants. Owners are neither proprietors, partners, nor shareholders; instead, they are called members.

The LLC is similar to a partnership in that the LLC's operating agreement (the equivalent of a partnership agreement) may distribute profits and losses in a variety of ways, not necessarily in proportion to capital contributions. Law firms are often organized as LLCs.

Aside from its taxation and limited-liabilities protections, the LLC is simple to operate. Like a sole proprietorship, for example, there is no statutory requirement to keep minutes, hold meetings, or make resolutions—requirements that often trip up corporation owners.

The disadvantages of a LLC include some of the same hassles associated with a partnership. The company will dissolve upon the death of the member (or one of the members), and the members must pay self-employment taxes.

Which form makes sense for you?

As you have no doubt gathered, tax implications are an important factor in the choice of a business entity. Indeed, the incentives of the US tax code give rise to certain tactics that can be risky. For example, the double taxation of a corporation's distributed earnings provides an incentive for owner-employees to pay all profits to themselves as compensation. Unlike dividends, compensation is deductible as an expense to the corporation and thus is not taxed twice. However, the Internal Revenue Service has certain rules on what is considered reasonable compensation; these rules are designed to discourage just such behavior.

Note too that the tax on individuals in so-called flow-through entities such as partnerships and LLCs is on the income earned and not on the actual cash distributed. The income of the partnership is taxed at the personal level of the partners, whether or not any cash is actually distributed. Thus, earnings retained in the business to finance growth or to create a monetary nest egg are taxed even though they are not distributed to the owners.

If your venture is projected to create large losses in the early years, then there may be some benefit to passing those losses through to investors, assuming that the investors are in a position to use them to offset other income and thus reduce their own taxes. This situation would favor the partnership or LLC. Similarly, if the business intends to generate substantial cash flow and return it to investors as the primary means of creating value for investors, then a partnership or LLC is still attractive. If, however, the business will require cash investment over the long term and if value is intended to be harvested through a sale or public offering, then a C corporation is the most attractive option.

Of course, a business may move through many forms in its lifetime. A sole proprietorship may become a partnership and finally a C corporation. A limited partnership may become an LLC and then a C corporation. Each transition, however, requires considerable legal work and imposes an administrative burden on the management and owners of the firm. The advantages of the right form of organization at each stage certainly may warrant these burdens. On the other hand, high-potential ventures on the fast track should avoid losing time and focus by jumping through these hoops. For them, the corporate form is almost always best. As corporations, they can use stock and options to lure an experienced management team and to conserve cash. They can even use stock in lieu of all-cash arrangements in paying for consulting services. Also, venture capitalists may not take these businesses seriously if they are not incorporated, because these investors will want a block of ownership.

Consequently, if you are an entrepreneur, consider the likely evolution of your business before selecting a particular form of organization, and consult with a qualified tax attorney or accountant before making this important choice.

Summing up

Table 4-1 summarizes the types of businesses discussed in this chapter.

TABLE 4-1

Forms of business

Form of business	Key benefits	Key disadvantages
Sole proprietorship	• Simple to organize and operate • One level of taxation	• Full liability of the owner • Cannot raise outside equity capital, thus limiting potential size of the business
General partnership	• Can bring in additional talent and personal capital • One level of taxation	• Full liability of partners • Capital limited to the pockets of the partners and their ability to borrow • Unless addressed through the partnership agreement, business dissolves with the death or withdrawal of any partner
Limited partnership	• Limited liability • One level of taxation	• Complex to set up
C corporation	• Theoretically capable of attracting equity capital through share ownership • Preferred form of venture capitalists • Able to deduct many benefit payments to employees • Shareholders enjoy limited liability	• Complex to set up and operate • Income subject to double taxation
S corporation	• Like a proprietorship and partnership, subject to only one level of taxation • Shareholders enjoy limited liability	• Complex to set up and operate • Limited in the number of shareholders • Venture capitalists cannot be shareholders
Limited-liability company (LLC)	• Simpler to set up and operate than a corporation • Limited liability for members • One level of taxation • Infinite number of possible members	• Cannot attract outside equity capital

5.

Writing Your Business Plan

A business plan is a document that explains a business opportunity, identifies the market to be served, and provides details about how the entrepreneurial organization plans to pursue it. To be effective, a good plan also describes the unique qualifications that you and your management team bring to the effort. It explains the resources you'll need and forecasts financial results over a reasonable time horizon.

For many years, anyone starting a business was encouraged to write a business plan, and most entrepreneurs took that advice. Those who didn't quickly learned that obtaining outside funding was almost impossible without a business plan. And of course, lenders and investors want to see a logical and coherent plan before putting their money at risk. Who wouldn't? But business plans are evolving, and today some observers argue that other tools work better for obtaining funding—and creating a roadmap for your business to follow.

In this chapter, we'll discuss the merits of a business plan and explain some of the alternatives before we describe the elements that go into a good plan and the stylistic best practices for creating them.

The benefits of a business plan

Ask most entrepreneurs why they need a good business plan, and they're likely to tell you, "You can't get funding without one." This observation is true, and it explains why many books, advisory services, websites, and even MBA courses have been developed to help people write bulletproof, knock-'em-dead business plans.

Any business that seeks outside funding from banks, angel investors, venture capitalists—even relatives—must have a solid business plan. Without it, creditors and investors won't take you seriously. They will conclude (perhaps correctly) that you haven't done the thinking necessary to successfully start and run a business, namely, identifying your customers and figuring out how you will deal profitably with them. The most tolerant funders will say, "Come back and see us when you've put together a complete business plan." The less tolerant will not give your business a second look.

But seeking funding is not the only reason to develop a solid plan. There are several other important ones:

- **A deep reality check and blueprint:** The act of writing a plan will force you and your team to think through all the key elements of your business. Even as your business evolves through experimentation, you need to consider and capture your assumptions about value proposition, competitive differentiation, staffing, partnerships, finances, and so forth.

- **Advice:** Exposing the details of your business idea to trusted and experienced outsiders who review your initial plan will help you identify missed opportunities, unsupportable assumptions, overly optimistic projections, and other weaknesses. By finding and fixing these problems on paper, you will improve your prospects with funders and reduce the chance of future operational failure.

- **Financial projections that can be used as an initial budget:** Actual results that fall short of planned results will prompt you to investigate and take corrective action.

Keep all these uses in mind as you build your plan.

How business plans are changing

Business plans—traditionally long, text-heavy, and numbers-heavy documents—originally developed from strategic planning in the US military during World War II. They became popular for would-be entrepreneurs in the 1980s, and by the turn of the millennium, there were hotly competitive business-plan contests at top business schools and the most sought-after VC firms. The appeal was partly the sense of opportunity and security that come from having a plan: if the plan predicts that your business will make a lot of money, who won't want to invest?

Today, there is a movement in the entrepreneurial community to rethink the role of the business plan. For one reason, the numbers in a business plan are not a strong predictor of success. "No business plan survives first contact with customers," warns serial entrepreneur and lean-startup expert Steve Blank. And indeed, no matter how well crafted, a business plan is full of untested assumptions, at least some of them probably inaccurate. Between the entrepreneur's deliberate padding and honest enthusiasm, the numbers—especially the detailed month-by-month projections over years into the future—are rarely realistic. Even as early as 1997, Harvard Business School professor William Sahlman was writing that the best business plans focus not on those numbers but rather on the people and the business model behind them. Those more knowable factors go into determining how a company will achieve its success. To Blank, building a business plan is still a valuable exercise in thinking through how your business might work, but you shouldn't mistake it for fact. And serial entrepreneurs

Evan Baehr and Evan Loomis suggest that there are better tools (the business-model canvas, for example) to help you do this thinking.

Other experts argue against the traditional business plan because a long, dry document is no longer the only way (or the best way) to grab the attention of potential investors. In the tech sector in particular, entrepreneurs are opting for shorter, less formal, more narrative, and highly visual ways of seeking funding. They use newer formats such as pitch decks and demos. These documents often overtly reflect the spirit of experimentation and acknowledge that the future of a startup cannot be predicted accurately. You will need to determine the right approach for the type of business you are building.

Whatever the length and style of the document that you create—we'll call it a business plan in this chapter—you'll want to think through several core elements, including descriptions of the opportunity, the solution, the market, the model, and the team involved. This chapter will describe those key elements, but there are other resources available for building and refining your plan. You'll find some in the "Further Reading" section of this book, but business plan coaching and mentoring are also available.

Key elements

Many VC firms review more than a thousand business plans every year—and fund only a few. This means that they have little time to figure out what you're trying to say. Nor do they have time to deal with people who haven't given them the information they need. The same is true of banks and angel investors. Assuming that you have a worthy idea, you will improve the odds of success if you can grab the reader's attention and keep it. To do this, you must address the reader's concerns in a well-organized way, whatever the format of your plan.

And remember that the numbers, while important to think through, are likely to be inaccurate. That's why you must show your work: the plan must demonstrates your professionalism, expertise, and trustworthiness, and not just your optimism.

FIGURE 5-1

Prototype business plan format

Lo-Sugar Foods Company

Contents

Appendix

Figure 5-1 contains a prototype format for a company we will call Lo-Sugar Foods Company, a new manufacturer of unsweetened packaged breakfast and snack foods. It aims to capitalize on the popularity of low-sugar diets in North America and Europe. The company's research estimates that 4.5 million Americans and 1.2 million Europeans are now following low-sugar diets, which US government studies have confirmed to be effective in weight reduction and weight control and in improving overall health. They see an opportunity to continue growing their business and developing new products.

There is nothing sacred about the format shown in the figure. In fact, you would be wise to tailor your plan's format to the likely interests of your readers, just as you would customize your résumé when you're looking for a job. Thus, you should follow the first rule of every form of writing: know your audience. The goal is always to give readers the information they need to make a decision.

Let's consider each major section of this document in more detail.

Contents and executive summary

The contents section (or table of contents) makes it easy for readers to see at a glance what the plan has to offer and how to navigate it.

The contents should be followed by an executive summary. In terms of capturing the attention of potential financial backers, the executive summary is the most important part of the entire document, so take the time to get it right. Financial backers and those who might give you advice may never make it further than this—after all, they probably have an enormous pile of other proposals vying for their attention. Assume you have just a minute or two—if that—to convince them to keep reading.

In a traditional business plan, the executive summary is a short section of two to three pages. It isn't a preface or an introduction; instead, it is a snapshot of the entire plan, something that explains your business to an intelligent reader in only a few minutes. Newer approaches include even shorter elevator pitches—a hundred words or even just a sentence—and are often more story-based to speak to the reader's emotions. In a pitch deck, you'll want an overview slide that announces what your company is and what problem it solves in a big-picture way. Some entrepreneurs create a separate two-minute video elevator pitch and post it on a private You-Tube channel to make their pitch more easily sharable. Whatever form you choose, you want the pitch to be something memorable that the reader can easily recount to others as well.

The opportunity

There is no point in starting or expanding a business unless you have identified a lucrative opportunity. Use the opportunity section of the business plan to describe this prospect. First, outline the problem, its scope, and the market trends that may affect how your market experiences this problem in the years ahead, and then introduce the solution you are proposing. You need to help readers see and appreciate the business opportunity you have identified. So describe the opportunity in clear and compelling terms.

For the Lo-Sugar Foods Company, for example, you would use this section to describe the latest figures about rampant obesity in the United States and signs of the same in Western Europe—and how obesity is affecting people's health, their quality of life, and the costs of care for individuals, companies, and governments. You would point to research you've found estimating that twenty-nine million Americans and eight million

Europeans are now following low-sugar diets, and you would cite independent scientific studies that confirm the effectiveness of low-sugar diets. You could also provide an overview of consumer spending on health foods and weight-control foods.

Also use the opportunity section of your business plan to highlight the economics underlying the problem and the factors that will drive your solution's success, such as market penetration and product innovation. But don't get carried away. Keep it brief, focused, and upbeat.

This is also a suitable place to cite the magnitude of the funding you are seeking and to explain how it will be used in pursuing the opportunity. For example, the Lo-Sugar plan might include something like this:

> *Lo-Sugar is seeking $2.75 million in funding to pursue this opportunity. The bulk of those funds will be used to exploit the company's current success and the growing interest of another company (a national vendor of high-protein/low-carbohydrate foods) in Lo-Sugar's existing products.*

Although it is important to document the opportunity with objective data, don't turn this section into a boring data dump. Don't bury your compelling story under a mountain of facts. Instead, summarize the data, and explain its implications for investors. Put any additional detail into an appendix.

The company and its offering and strategy

Use this section of your business plan to expand on your proposed solution to the problem you have identified: the product or service itself as well as your company and how it is organized. Include any data you have on your solution's traction in the market thus far. Here is an example:

> *Lo-Sugar is a Colorado-based corporation founded in 2018 with the goal of serving individuals following a low-sugar diet. Its experienced management team has developed and test-marketed several products with low natural and added sugars, primarily breakfast and snack foods. These products are not merely low in*

*sugar; tests have confirmed that they are also tasty and satisfy-
ing—qualities that differentiate them from other similar offerings.
The products are as follows:*

- *Mellow Mornings, a whole wheat and barley breakfast cereal
  with 90 percent less sugar than leading conventional breakfast
  cereals. Mellow Morning meets the specifications of the leading
  low-sugar advocates.*

- *Crackle Brackle, a crisped, steel-cut oatmeal product for breakfast and for baking. Like Mellow Morning, Crackle Brackle
  meets the specifications of leading low-sugar diets.*

- *Yesgurt, the company's dairy offering. It too meets low-sugar
  diet requirements while being flavorful and smooth.*

  *Each of these products was well received in market tests [here
  the business plan would refer the reader to the plan's appendix for
  details] and is currently being sold through two regional health
  food stores: Nutrimarket Stores and Vitamins & Veggies. Other
  products are in development.*

Goals

Investors will want to know how you plan to grow, so include a section on
your goals for the company. If there is a chance that the company will become a tempting acquisition target for a larger, less innovative competitor,
mention this possibility. Here is an example:

Lo-Sugar has three goals:

1. *To broaden its product line.*

2. *To expand market penetration through stores and through a
   private labeling agreement with one of the major diet companies
   (currently in negotiations).*

3. *To expand the business to where it either becomes a dominant
   player in the healthy-food niche or is acquired by one of the*

> *giants in the packaged-food industry. In this industry, small*
> *companies with one or two successful products are often bought*
> *out at premium prices.*

If your company's products are not yet market-ready, you should describe your plans for product rollouts. Include snapshots of any viable prototypes you've created, as well as an artist's rendering of the final physical product. If your products are market-ready, include high-quality photos.

Business model and strategy

In a separate section, discuss the company's business model and strategy. A business model is about how you plan to make money; strategy is about differentiation and competitive advantage.

What are your costs? Where will your revenue come from?

Explain what is different about your company's approach to the marketplace and how that difference will give the company a sustainable competitive advantage. Differentiation may reside in the product or service—for example, a technically superior way of servicing electric cars to provide greater value to customers. On the other hand, differentiation may come from your approach to customers, as in Uber's model of a platform that connects drivers and passengers, bypassing traditional taxicabs. (The box "Intellectual property" discusses the importance of protecting your innovative ideas.)

What makes your product or service, or means of delivery, different—and more desirable—in the eyes of customers? How will that difference translate into a competitive advantage that will produce profits and growing equity value? Investors want clear answers to these questions. Spell them out here.

Also describe your competitors. In addition to explaining why customers will choose your product or service instead, show that you clearly understand how your industry operates. Also consider how your competitors may react to your success—what happens if they copy your best-selling product? How will you maintain your customers' loyalty?

Intellectual property

Is your competitive advantage based on a proprietary technology or process? Is the technology or process patented or patentable? Does the company own patents, copyrights, or valuable trademarks? If it does, when will they expire?

Many businesses are formed around one or another piece of intellectual property. Some of these key assets affect competitive advantage over time. Readers of your plan will want to know what steps you've taken to protect that property and to keep technical and market know-how within the organization, where it will produce revenues and profits for investors. This might mean legal protections like patents—or other strategic forms of defense like first-mover advantage (being first to scale in a market) or creating a business model that is difficult to replicate.

Ownership

The company section of a business plan is also a fitting location for ownership information:

- Who are the current owners, and what percentages do they control?

- How is ownership evidenced—for example, in terms of common and preferred stock?

- Have you issued any options, warrants, or convertible bonds that could expand ownership?

- Which owners are involved in the day-to-day workings of the business?

The team

A description of your team is one of the most important parts of your plan. Investors are keen to know about the people behind the business—the individuals they see as its core assets. "Without the right team," Sahlman writes of business plans, "none of the other parts really matter."

Without giving lengthy biographies of each team member, highlight the experiences or qualifications the key team members bring to the enterprise. Why are they (and you) the right individuals to accomplish the mission? (See the box "Questions about your team every business plan should answer.")

Beyond its current members, how do you anticipate the team will need to grow? What capabilities will you need to achieve your strategy?

Here's how Lo-Sugar's business plan describes its people:

> *Our leadership team is made up of Joanne Galloway, Philip Lindstrom, Gunther Schwartz, and Carlos Talavera. Together, they bring exceptional technical expertise and business experience to our company.*
>
> * *Joanne Galloway has fifteen years of product and general management experience with packaged-food companies, most recently with Gigantic Foods Corporation.*
>
> * *Philip Lindstrom has a PhD in nutrition. He joined the company in 2016 after working for ten years in product development for Behemoth Foods.*
>
> * *Gunther Schwartz, the team's manufacturing expert, has been in the processed-foods business for twelve years with both Behemoth Foods and Food Science Laboratories, a food-research consulting organization. Among Mr. Schwartz's accomplishments is the extrusion process used to manufacture Snackarinos and Caloritos, two highly successful packaged-snack brands owned by Behemoth Foods.*
>
> * *Carlos Talavera left his position as vice president of marketing at Healthtone, a leading packaged-foods company, to join Galloway and Lindstrom in founding Lo-Sugar.*
>
> *[Here, the business plan mentions that complete résumés can be found in the business plan's appendix.]*

Questions about your team every business plan should answer

- Where are the founders and other key team members from?
- Where did they go to school?
- Where have they worked—and for whom? What are their current roles?
- What have they accomplished—professionally and personally— in the past?
- What is their reputation within the business community?
- What aspects of their experience are directly relevant to the opportunity they are pursuing?
- What skills, abilities, and knowledge do they have?
- How realistic are they about the venture's chances for success and the tribulations it will face?
- Who else needs to be on the team?
- Are they prepared to recruit high-quality people?
- How will they respond to adversity?
- Do they have the mettle to make the inevitable hard choices?
- How committed are they to this venture?
- What are their motivations?

Source: Adapted from William A. Sahlman, "How to Write a Great Business Plan," *Harvard Business Review*, July–August 1997.

A table indicating your key team members' names, titles, and salaries is also useful, as in table 5-1. Most plans use an org chart to indicate the reporting relationships between employees if the connections aren't straightforward.

TABLE 5-1

Lo-Sugar key team members

Team member	Position	Salary
Joanne Galloway	CEO	$100,000
Philip Lindstrom	VP Product Development	95,000
Gunther Schwartz	VP Manufacturing	95,000
Carlos Talavera	VP Sales & Marketing	95,000
Diane Johnson	Financial consultant	Day rate
Mikhail Wolfe	Administrative assistant	50,000

Assuming that your company is a corporation, the team section of the plan is also an appropriate place to identify the board of directors (see the box "The board of directors"). You should indicate the names of board members, their positions on the board, their professional backgrounds, and their history of involvement with the company.

Marketing plan

If the team section of your business plan gets the most attention from readers, the marketing plan runs a close second. Investors know that marketing is the activity most associated with success or failure. All ventures need an attractive product or service, but a company will fail if its potential customers never hear of it. A sound and realistic marketing plan is the best assurance that your company will have a solid connection with its customers. Be clear about all aspects of marketing, including the following:

- Who your customers or your primary market is—the type of customer you have to reach to capture your full market potential

- Market size, namely, the number of potential customers and your projected potential sales revenues

- The requirements of various customer segments—for example, the importance of purchase convenience, rapid delivery, product customization, and so on

- Ways to effectively access each segment through, for example, distributors, e-commerce, and a captive sales force

- Appropriate sales and promotion approaches—social media campaigns, a creative content marketing strategy, a freemium model, direct email

- An analysis of how your customer makes purchase decisions

- Customer price sensitivity

- Acquisition cost per customer, and the cost of retaining customers

- The strengths and weaknesses of competitors and how they are likely to react when the company enters the market

To make your plan credible, you should support these issues with solid market intelligence. Summarize the supporting intelligence here, and refer readers to whatever market research you've provided in the business plan's appendix.

Operating plan

Whether you're in the business of manufacturing or distributing physical products or running a website, an app, or a platform business, you face

---

The board of directors

Every corporation must, by law, have a board of directors. But it's not just an empty legal requirement—a good board can be an invaluable sounding board for ideas and a source of sage advice.

Put some of your best efforts into recruiting board members. You want people who have abundant business experience and, if technology is essential to the business, considerable scientific or engineering know-how. Board members should also be respected in the broader business community. Their capabilities and integrity will speak volumes to whoever reads your business plan, financiers in particular.

a host of operational issues. What supplier relationships do you have or envision? How much inventory will be required? Which day-to-day operating tasks will be handled internally, and which will be outsourced? An operating plan considers the many details of converting inputs to outputs that customers value.

Financial plan

If a company is already operating, it will have (or should have) a set of financial statements: a balance sheet, an income statement, and a cash-flow statement. In a nutshell, the balance sheet describes what the company owns—its assets—and how those assets have been financed (through liabilities and the funds of the current owners) as of a particular date.

The income statement reveals the company's revenues, what it spent to gain those revenues, and the interest and taxes it paid over a specified period. Finally, the cash-flow statement tells readers the sources and uses of cash during the same period. Together, these three financial statements reveal much to the trained eye of potential investors. (Note: If you are not familiar with these statements, see appendix A for an explanation of the basics.)

Generally it's best to place the full financial statements in the appendix to your business plan. Use this space for key data from those statements—data that will give readers the big picture of your business and its intended future. Key among this data are your sales and expense projections, described earlier in this book as a pro forma income statement. For a company such as Lo-Sugar, lenders and investors will be interested in a breakout of key items in the statement, such as the anticipated revenues from various channels of distribution, as shown in table 5-2. Here we see anticipated sales and sales growth by channel and the percentage of sales represented by each. Consider doing the same for key categories of operating expenses, such as marketing costs (see table 5-3).

Naturally, sales projections and other items in these pro forma statements are based on assumptions. Experienced investors are keenly aware of these limitations and will want to know what those assumptions are and why you made them. Make that part of your discussion.

TABLE 5-2

Forecasted revenues by distribution channel (percentage of sales)

Distribution channel	2018	2019	2020
Health food stores	$112,000 (100%)	$160,000 (80%)	$200,000 (38%)
Supermarkets	0	40,000 (20%)	80,000 (15%)
Private-label business	0	0	240,000 (46%)
Total sales	$112,000 (100%)	200,000 (100%)	520,000 (99%)

TABLE 5-3

Marketing expense	2018	2019	2020
Sales commissions	$11,000 (10%)	$20,000 (9%)	$52,000 (9%)
Research	70,000 (63%)	80,000 (36%)	85,000 (15%)
Promotion	20,000 (18%)	32,000 (15%)	50,000 (9%)
Total expense	$101,000 (91%)	132,000 (60%)	187,000 (33%)

Style

Every business plan is a combination of style and substance. Not being wordsmiths, most entrepreneurs concentrate on the substance and short-change the style. That's unfortunate, because inattention to style makes a plan dull and difficult to read.

Some successful entrepreneurs work with a writer who has experience in business plan writing. Others act as their own wordsmiths and observe the rules of good writing: use words sparingly, keep sentences simple, make the most of design elements, and use graphics judiciously.

Use words sparingly

In the business world, shorter is always better if it communicates the re-quired information. So heed rule 17 in William Strunk and E. B. White's timeless *Elements of Style*, and omit needless words:

> *Vigorous writing is concise. A sentence should contain no unnec-essary words; a paragraph no unnecessary sentences; for the same*

reason that a drawing should have no unnecessary lines and a machine no unnecessary parts. This requires not that the writer make all his sentences short, or that he avoid all detail and treat his subjects only in outline, but that every word tells.

This quote from Strunk and White is itself a perfect model of their rule. They use no unnecessary words; every word makes a contribution. Economy of words has two big benefits for the business plan writer: your key messages will stand out, and conciseness saves your reader's valuable time in a world that pulls our attention in every direction and in which our attention spans get shorter and shorter.

This is even more true if you are writing your plan in a pitch deck format. See the box "Pitch deck style" for more on how to tailor your deck's style to your audience.

Use simple sentences

The sentence, the basic unit of written expression, usually makes a statement. The statement can be simple or complex. Consider the following two sentences:

1. On the one hand, we witness rising levels of obesity among children and adults, both in North America and in Western Europe, which in turn have increased the popularity of low-sugar diets, which in turn have created a business opportunity for Lo-Sugar Company and other makers of low-sugar foods.

2. The growing popularity of low-sugar diets has created a business opportunity for makers of low-sugar foods.

The second sentence, unlike the first, is spare and to the point. It's more likely to register with readers. It does not contain all the information found in the first. If that information is important, it should be provided in a separate sentence.

Packing more information into each sentence is not necessarily bad; nor does it necessarily violate rules of grammar. However, complex

Pitch deck style

In their book *Get Backed,* Evan Baehr and Evan Loomis describe the writing style and design of two kinds of pitch decks: presentation decks and reading decks.

WRITING STYLE FOR PRESENTATION DECKS

A deck used as a visual aid during a presentation should have very few words—no more than one sentence per slide. Nor do presentation decks need to have complete sentences. Often, one word or a short phrase is enough to introduce the idea that you will carry forward. If you have already completed your reading deck, try deleting every word in it except for the headers, and see if the words give enough context to still convey what the slide is about.

WRITING STYLE FOR READING DECKS

With decks you plan to send to others to read, the slides have to do a lot of work to communicate everything you would have said in person. The printed words have to catch their attention quickly, clearly communicate the basic point you want to put forth, back that point up with evidence, and then move on. Watch out for sentences that sound impressive but mean nothing. "We plan to pursue an effective marketing strategy" is a waste of time to read. If you create a slide for your marketing strategy, put the words "Marketing Strategy" in the corner, and then write out your strategy in a sentence of fifteen or fewer words. If your strategy has multiple phases, create headings that describe each phase, and then add short, straightforward explanations after those headings. Reading decks should also be "scanning" decks. If the reader only has fifteen seconds to look through the whole thing, he or she should still be able to get a pretty good idea of what it is about.

Source: Adapted from Evan Baehr and Evan Loomis, *Get Backed: Craft Your Story, Build the Perfect Pitch Deck, Launch the Venture of Your Dreams* (Boston: Harvard Business Review Press, 2015), 66.

sentences make the reader work harder and may create confusion. As a writer, your challenge is to know when a sentence has reached its optimal carrying capacity.

Use design elements to lighten the reader's load

Readers of your business plan are busy people who have learned to skim; they drill down only to relevant details. You can facilitate their skimming through the use of design elements. These elements include headings, subheads, lists, and graphics. Even white space can be used as a design element. All are useful in long documents. Used judiciously, design elements have a few benefits:

- They make your written documents more inviting to the reader.

- They improve reader comprehension.

- They help speed the reader through your material.

Use headings and subheads

Headings and subheads signal that a new or related topic is about to begin. They give your work greater eye appeal and "skimmability." You can also use headings and subheads to impart key ideas. For example, our heading "Use headings and subheads" is also a key idea. A time-constrained reader can gather the key points of any section in your business plan by simply reading these headings and subheads.

Break up long blocks of text

Long, uninterrupted blocks of text are off-putting to readers and are difficult to skim. Headings and subheads can help you break those blocks into identifiable small bites. So can short paragraphs. Some experts recommend that paragraphs average no more than two hundred words.

Lists are another effective way to break up long, intimidating blocks of text and to increase the impact. You can use lists to summarize key points or to get your ideas across quickly. If you are describing something in which sequence is important, use a numbered list, as in the following example:

Our study of the market for low-sugar foods uncovered four steps that those wishing to lose weight typically follow:

1. *Eat less.*

2. *Exercise more.*

3. *Try specific (and often short-lived) diet programs like Atkins or Weight Watchers.*

4. *Home in on a specific diet, such as a low-sugar diet, to adopt for the long term.*

Notice how the list breaks up the page and gets conclusions across in a way that they cannot be missed.

A bulleted list can also break up a long paragraph, and it need not be limited to a sequence. For example, you might use a bulleted list when you:

- Need to organize a list of items

- Need to list parts of a whole

- Want to call out three key ideas

But don't translate all your ideas into long, complex bullets, either. Such lists just become additional big blocks of text.

Let graphics tell part of the story

Business plans inevitably contain lots of numerical data. When it comes to transmitting data quickly, simple charts are hard to beat—especially if you are presenting your business plan in the form of a pitch deck. Readers can see at a glance what they would otherwise have to extract from many lines of text and numbers. Which of the following two examples would make a more memorable, sharable impression?

Text-only example:

Our survey found that 2 percent of the people who come downtown in a typical day do so by bicycle. Some 9 percent arrive by public transportation. Thirty-five percent respond that they walk to the downtown, while the largest single group—54 percent—arrive by car.

Text and graphics example (figure 5-2):

According to our survey, people arrive downtown by various means, mostly by car.

To create effective visuals, says Scott Berinato, Harvard Business Review editor and author of *Good Charts*, you should first consider the point you want the chart to make before you click "insert chart" in Excel or Google Sheets. Experiment with different formats by first sketching by hand to see which of these formats makes your point most clearly—a pie chart, a bar chart, a tree map? What data do you really need to include?

Keep the text in the graphic minimal, and don't try to cram in too much information—each chart should convey a single message. You want readers to get your point at a glance. For example, in figure 5-3 the first chart is accurate and attractive, but the point is unclear. If you're trying to show that growth in national health spending is falling, don't get distracted by other data that you have, like gross domestic product, or in detailed data labels. The second chart is much more effective at getting the message across.

FIGURE 5-2

How people get downtown

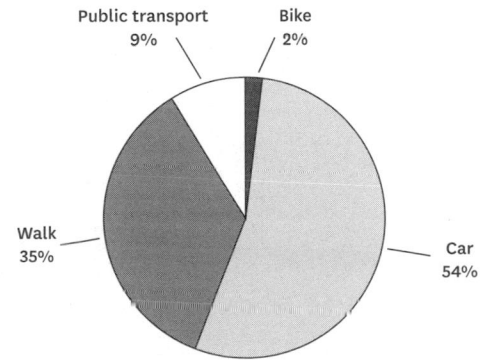

FIGURE 5-3

Persuasive charts

The chart on the right makes a much clearer, easier-to-digest point.

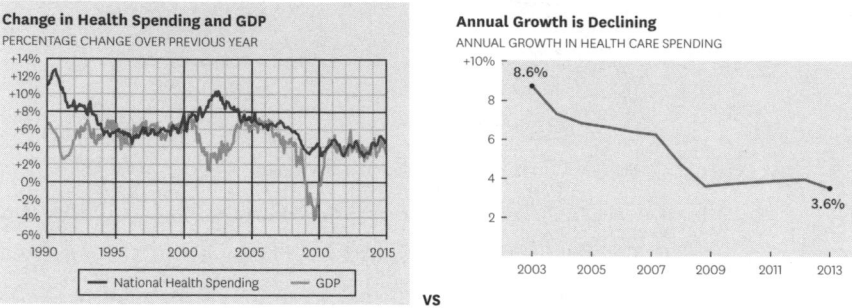

Source: Scott Berinato, "Visualizations That Really Work," *Harvard Business Review,* June 2016.

Similarly, don't get carried away with design elements. Microsoft Word and PowerPoint give you an arsenal of design features: boldface, italics, fonts, color palettes, 3-D effects, clip art, animations, and so forth. Used judiciously, these add to the appearance and readability of your text. Overuse them, however, and you will create the opposite effect—they'll be a distraction *and* they'll make your work appear amateurish. So keep it simple.

Consider your reader

As you develop your business plan, always keep the interests of your readers in mind. Put yourself in their place. Your audience is looking for convincing evidence that you have found a real business opportunity—one with substantial growth possibilities. Considering the risks they will be taking with their money, they want to see major upside potential.

Your readers will also be looking for clear indications that you have done your homework—that you understand the market, have targeted the right customers, and have developed a sound strategy for profitably transacting business with them. Prospective investors want assurance that you and the management team have the knowledge, experience, and drive to turn an opportunity into a profitable business. And what is important to potential lenders and investors should be just as important to you. So as you write your plan, stop periodically and ask yourself, Is this a real opportunity? Do I understand the market and the customers I hope to attract? Can we really make this thing work?

Finally, tell your readers how they will get their money out of the company. Investors want an exit strategy: a buyout by management, an acquisition by another company, an IPO of shares, and so on. Even if you plan to be in the business for the long haul, your investors want liquidity at some point—and the sooner the better.

Summing up

- When creating a business plan, choose a format that makes sense for your audience, your business, and the industry.

- Whatever format you choose, your business plan should tell readers in a persuasive way everything they need to know to make a decision.

- Obtaining outside funding is only one reason to write a business plan. Perhaps just as important, the act of writing a plan will force you to think through all the key elements of the business.

- The executive summary should, in compelling terms, explain the opportunity, why it is timely, and how your company plans to pursue it. The summary should also describe your expected results and provide a thumbnail sketch of the company and the management team.

- Among other things, the business plan should state the company's goals and explain how investors will eventually cash out.

- Pay attention to style. Use as few words as necessary to get your points across. Avoid long, complex sentences whenever possible.

- Make your document easy to skim by using simple data visualizations, headings, subheads, white space, and numbered and bulleted lists to break up blocks of text.

PART THREE

Financing Your Business

6.

Startup-Stage Financing

Money greases the wheels of enterprise. Without it, even the best-conceived business plan would remain nothing more than a document.

Financing is an essential ingredient of enterprise at every size—from the corner bookstore to Amazon. It is also needed at every stage of business development: at the launch and again when the startup forges through various levels of growth. Even a mature business with annual sales in billions of dollars needs continued financing to stay on the cutting edge of its field.

This chapter describes the typical phases of the business life cycle, from startup to maturity. It then focuses on the first phase, describing the financing requirements that early-stage businesses typically encounter and providing an overview of the sources you can turn to in securing funding.

Types of business and their life cycles

Of course, not every business is the same, and businesses' life cycles and financing needs vary accordingly. Harvard Business School's Karen Gordon

Mills (former administrator of the SBA) and Fundera Inc.'s Brayden Mc-Carthy have conducted research on the state of small business and financing; unless otherwise noted, the numbers in this section describing the distribution and types of US businesses come from their working paper on this topic.

The majority—roughly 70 percent—of small-employer businesses in the United States are what Mills and McCarty call Main Street firms: the dry cleaners, mechanics, medical clinics, and similar companies that play an important role in local communities. Often, these companies aim to serve the personal or family income needs of the owner, and once these businesses are established, they are more focused on sustaining this income than they are interested in growing it.

This type of business has a startup phase, followed perhaps by a period of gradual growth, followed by a no-growth or slow-growth phase of maturity. The owner requires startup financing to purchase or lease equipment, rent a workplace, establish an inventory and fixtures, and provide working capital. In some cases, the entrepreneur is simply purchasing an existing business from someone else. (This approach to entrepreneurship is described in the *HBR Guide to Buying a Small Business.*)

Roughly 17 percent of small multi-employee businesses in the United States are supply-chain firms. These niche enterprises serve a focused need in a particular industry, geographical area, or area of an existing supply chain. Supply-chain firms are particularly important to the economy: they provide job and wage growth, innovation, and important support for larger firms. Some 37 percent of US employment can be attributed to these firms, and 80 percent of US patents in 2013. After the startup phase, these businesses continue to focus on growth.

Just 3 percent of small multi-employee firms in the United States qualify as high-growth. These companies are most likely to be found in high-tech sectors and have a disproportionate contribution to job creation and to the US economy generally. The little company started by Steve Jobs and Steve Wozniak in Jobs's garage is one of these high-growth companies; its Apple II launched the era of the personal computer and propelled the little company to big-company status, where it holds court as the firm with the highest market capitalization today. Facebook, Amazon, Airbnb, and Uber also began small but grew very rapidly from their inception.

For these companies, too (and for everything in between), there is a startup phase, a period of growth, and a mature phase. What varies is the scale of the growth and the length of the growth period. Rapidly growing companies typically require more successive phases of financing at ever-higher levels.

Remarkably few entrepreneurial companies make it through all three phases. Many enterprises fail within a few years. Still others succeed and are acquired by larger corporations before they reach their full potential.

Startup-phase financing

For the startup phase (the earliest phase of the business life cycle), the initial financing typically comes from personal sources:

- Personal savings

- A second mortgage on the founder's home

- Credit card lines of credit

Many people refer to these sources as bootstrap financing because all the sources rely on the entrepreneur's own resources, and there is no big money involved.

In this stage, you might also begin to seek some early outside, or seed, investment:

- Loans from friends and relatives

- Bank debt from small banks and online lenders (particularly important to Main Street firms)

- Short-term trade credit from suppliers

- Crowdfunding

- Equity investment from an accelerator program

If the founder and the management team have strong reputations in the business or scientific community, they may attract capital from angel investors, private equity, or even a VC firm or hedge fund. This is especially true if the founding team has enjoyed past entrepreneurial success. Financiers love people with a demonstrated Midas touch, and they pursue such people actively. In these cases, the company may attract investors long before it has a marketable product or service and certainly before it enters the growth phase. This early-stage equity investment has become increasingly common in the past few years as access to financing has decentralized. Venture capital used to be an exclusive club of formal firms, but now angels, accelerators, and crowdsourcing offer a broader array of options even for early-stage entrepreneurs looking for equity capital.

But selling equity has its downsides—you are selling away pieces of ownership of your venture. You're giving up some control and some potential profits. But if you have to generate funds quickly, equity capital may be worth the trade-offs.

And early-stage equity investment is still rare. According to the Kauffman Foundation, 40 percent of initial startup capital, even for fast-growing companies, is instead debt that originates from banks, with an almost equal amount of owner equity. Figure 6-1 shows the different sources of financing for *Inc.* magazine's five thousand fastest-growing companies in America in 2014.

To better understand this phase of financing, consider the case of a fictitious company that we read about earlier.

When Angus McDuff started a woodworking business, he was well prepared for self-employment. He had been a supervisor at a small shop that made wooden lamps, and he knew all about shaping and fitting lumber into commercial products. He knew the material suppliers on a first-name basis, and he was often in contact with wholesale and retail distributors of his company's finished products. He had also gotten to know many of the lamp shop's end customers over the years.

McDuff used the final year of his employment productively. In his spare time, he designed a small line of wooden hat racks, used his experience in the lamp business to calculate his production costs, and learned

FIGURE 6-1

Sources of funding for *Inc.* magazine's five thousand fastest-growing US companies in 2014

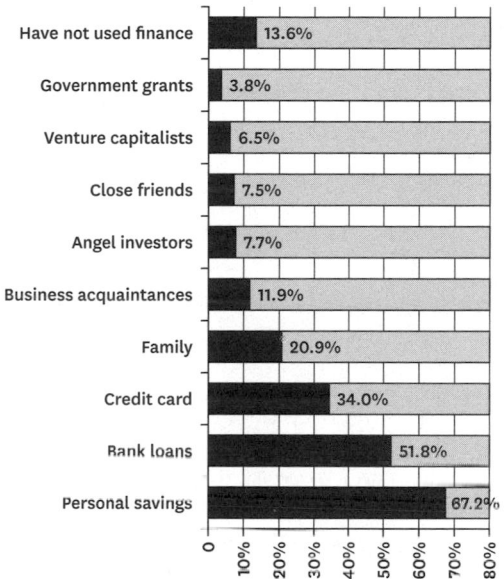

Source: "How Entrepreneurs Access Capital and Get Funded," *Entrepreneurship Policy Digest*, Kauffman Foundation, June 2, 2015.

a great deal about the channels of distribution through which he'd sell his new products.

Starting the venture, however, required more than knowledge: he also needed financial and production assets. McDuff calculated that he would need enough cash—say, $8,000—to tide him over during a three-month startup period in which his costs were likely to outstrip his revenues. He'd also need an inventory of lumber, hardware fixtures, and other materials, which would cost him roughly $7,500. Those items of material inventory would be transformed into finished-goods inventory over time.

He would also have to pay for an annual property and liability insurance policy and the first three months of rent on a small workshop. He calculated that he'd need $6,500 for these assets (table 6-1).

TABLE 6-1

Current asset requirements

Cash	$8,000
Inventory	
Lumber	4,000
Hardware	2,500
Other	1,000
Total inventory	7,500
Prepaid expenses	
Insurance (1 year)	1,500
Rent (3 months)	5,000
Total prepaid expenses	6,500
Total current assets	22,000

McDuff's business, which he decided to call Amalgamated Hat Rack Company, also needed some fixed assets: a wood lathe, a few power and hand tools, workbenches for the shop, and a panel truck for picking up materials and making customer deliveries. Fortunately, McDuff's employer offered to sell him an old panel truck and many of the required tools, two used wood lathes, and several surplus workbenches for a total price of $10,000.

With these purchases, McDuff completed the fixed-asset section of his balance sheet (table 6-2). When the fixed assets were added to his current asset requirements, he figured that he'd need assets totaling $32,000 to launch his venture.

So how was he going to finance these startup costs? Fortunately, McDuff and his wife, Alice, had $25,000 available in a savings account. Alice's uncle offered to contribute $5,000 in the form of a zero-interest loan. "You can pay me back at a thousand per year," he told them. "And good luck with the business."

Angus also knew that a number of his customers from the lamp business wore hats and were enthusiastic about his work, so he launched an Indiegogo crowdfunding page with pictures of several hat racks he had made and posted it to his Facebook page. As news of his new business

TABLE 6-2

Fixed asset requirements

Used panel truck	$7,500
Lathes	900
Other tools	800
Shop fixtures	800
Total fixed assets	10,000
Total current assets (from table 6-1)	22,000
Total current and fixed assets	32,000

spread, he raised another $2,000—and, as a bonus, he started getting feedback on the kinds of hat racks people really wanted.

This gave him $32,000. He was finally ready to step away from his role at the lamp company and begin making hat racks full-time.

And that's how Amalgamated was initially financed. You've already seen the asset side of the balance sheet. Table 6-3 is the liabilities *and* owners' equity side, which spells out how the company's assets were financed.

Many, if not most, small businesses are initially financed in a manner similar to the Amalgamated case—mostly with the owner operator's personal savings and with contributions from friends and family members. Some entrepreneurs also resort to using their credit card or home lines of credit for startup capital, as expensive as this practice is.

Once your bootstrapped company has begun to show some signs of success, there are also some limited external sources of capital available to startup-stage ventures—often called the seed stage. Let's look at some of these sources more closely.

Trade credit

Many small-business owners obtain thirty- to sixty-day trade credit from their suppliers as one component of their startup (and ongoing) financing. For example, a shoe-store owner may be able to obtain $3,000 worth of shoes from a wholesaler, with payment due in sixty days. By having picked

TABLE 6-3

Liabilities and owners' equity

Current liabilities	
Current portion of five-year loan	$1,000
Long-term liabilities	
Balance of five-year loan	4,000
Total liabilities	5,000
Original owners' equity	25,000
Crowdfunding proceeds	2,000
Total owners' equity	27,000
Total liabilities and owners' equity	32,000

inventory wisely, the owner may be able to sell all or most of the shoes during that sixty-day period and use the proceeds to pay the wholesaler's bill in full when it comes due. In effect, the supplier will have financed the store's inventory without charge—a better deal for the owner than using a bank line of credit or another device that involves interest charges.

Commercial bank loans

Some startups may find limited financing from commercial banks, which are covered in detail in the next chapter. Entrepreneurial debt funding from banks has been tight since the 2008 recession, despite attempts by lawmakers to lower the risk for banks. Because of these limitations, other options—be they crowdfunding, angel syndication, or online lending—are increasingly important options for early-stage startup needs.

Crowdfunding

If your business idea truly has a broad consumer reach—or deep reach into a narrow market—it can generate early capital using crowdfunding sources like Kickstarter or Indiegogo. In 2015 alone, over $2 billion of funding was generated through crowdfunding in the United States alone. With many types of crowdfunding, people give money in exchange for rewards, which are often early sales of your product. By offering such rewards, you also get feedback on a product, validate market interest, and test messaging and pricing.

Crowdfunding may allow you to bypass traditional funding completely. The Wharton School's Ethan Mollick describes how a hot technology of the moment—virtual reality—was largely ignored by venture capitalists and investors after the cringe-worthy hype of the 1990s. But then, in 2012, a member of a virtual-reality fan message board asked the group for help raising funds, refining the technology, and designing the business plan around a product called Oculus Rift. His Kickstarter campaign raised nearly $2.5 million, and the product was purchased by Facebook for $2 billion less than two years later.

Crowdfunding can also level the playing field between men and women. Traditional fund-raising often relies on established networks and unwritten rules, so there is a bias toward funding white men—in fact, less than 8 percent of venture-capital-backed companies have female cofounders. But crowdfunding tends to favor women; Mollick's research shows that women are 13 percent more likely to succeed in raising money on Kickstarter than men.

In equity crowdfunding, people buy actual ownership of your business. These buyers no longer need to be accredited. Thanks to the Jumpstart Our Business Startups (JOBS) Act of March 2015, the Securities and Exchange Commission (SEC) now allows almost anyone to be an equity investor, with certain restrictions. But equity crowdfunding also raises some problems, says entrepreneurship professor Dan Isenberg. Equity is sufficiently complex, he explains, that successes from typical crowdfunding can't be extrapolated to equity fund-raising, and, furthermore, the due diligence required for equity investments renders the system too high-cost to be effective. Still, with other options for small-business funding hard to come by, an increasing number of businesses are choosing this option.

Accelerators

Accelerator programs such as Y Combinator at TechStars typically offer fixed-term, cohort-based support for new companies through financing,

immersive education, and customized mentorship. These highly competitive programs aim to accelerate the company's experiments and hypothesis
testing so that they can become a profitable business more quickly. Accelerator graduates Airbnb and Dropbox exemplify the success of this path.

The process often includes honing a pitch or demo, with the program
culminating in a "demo day" in which participants showcase their offerings. Table 6-4 demonstrates how accelerators differ from other sources of
funding and support for early-stage businesses.

While accelerators are appealing, they have some downsides. Ian
Hathaway, a fellow at the Brookings Institution, warns that not all accelerators are made alike: his research subjects at top programs did raise venture capital, gain customer traction, and exit by acquisition faster than
participants at other programs. But subjects at other programs generally
did not see such a strong impact on their companies' performance. And

TABLE 6-4

The four institutions that support startups

	Incubators	Angel investors	Accelerators	Hybrid
Duration	1 to 5 years	Ongoing	3 to 6 months	3 months to 2 years
Cohorts	No	No	Yes	No
Business model	Rent; nonprofit	Investment	Investment; can also be nonprofit	Investment; can also be nonprofit
Selection	Noncompetitive	Competitive, ongoing	Competitive, cyclical	Competitive, ongoing
Venture stage	Early or late	Early	Early	Early
Education	Ad hoc, human resources, legal	None	Seminars	Various incubator and accelerator practices
Mentorship	Minimal, tactical	As needed by investor	Intense, by self and others	Staff expert support, some mentoring
Venture location	On-site	Off-site	On-site	On-site

Source: Susan Cohen, "What Do Accelerators Do? Insights from Incubators and Angels," *Innovations* 8, no. 3–4 (2013): 20. Adaptations by Ian Hathaway.

as with other forms of equity investment, you're giving away part of your company in return for the funding when you use an accelerator.

Indeed, most businesses never grow large and won't be a good fit for accelerators or equity funding; Angus McDuff's hat rack company may be one of these companies. It may expand over the years to the point of generating $10 million to $20 million in annual revenue, but that's the limit. In the next chapter, we'll describe funding options if your business does face the prospect of a substantial growth phase.

Summing up

- Startup-phase financing is initially bootstrapped from personal savings, credit cards, and other personal sources of income, followed by friends and family and, in some cases, by small bank loans.

- Trade credit from suppliers is another low-cost source of financing.

- Other early sources of financing include online banks, accelerators, and crowdfunding.

7.

Growth-Stage Financing

During the growth stage, your business expands its sales and develops a growing base of customers. As a result, you'll need more capital—for expanding your operation, hiring and training new employees, and even acquiring other small businesses. Your company may already be generating some positive cash flows that can help finance these initiatives, but you'll probably need more cash if your growth is strong or if your strategy is to build brand visibility. Having now proven your business's credibility, though, you can generally tap external capital more easily than you could in the startup phase. For slow- to moderate-growth firms, much of that capital comes from bank debt. If your business is likely to grow large quickly, on the other hand, you will need to obtain equity capital, a topic covered in chapter 8.

Debt

When your company is growing, you often obtain your debt capital from local banks. Banks are often reluctant to offer long-term loans to small firms. Bankers are justifiably nervous about making long-term or un-secured loans to startup businesses, because the failure rate is high. They are more eager to extend short-term demand loans, seasonal lines of credit, and single-purpose loans for machinery and equipment. Small businesses tend to be more successful getting loans from small community banks rather than from larger banks, and they report more satisfaction working with these local lenders as well. Even then, small businesses typically take out fairly small bank loans: 54 percent of small firms hold less than $100,000 in debt.

Most local banks will extend loans to a startup only if they are comfortable with the situation and the qualifications of the borrower. What makes bank lenders comfortable? Bankers ask three questions before they lend money, and they rarely part with their capital if they cannot obtain satisfactory answers to all three:

1. Will the borrower be able to pay me back?

2. Is the borrower's character such that he or she will pay me back?

3. If the borrower fails to repay me, what marketable assets can I get my hands on?

In seeking an answer to the first question, a banker will evaluate the entrepreneur's skills and the business plan:

- Does the applicant understand the market and have a feasible plan for satisfying it?

- Does the entrepreneur have the experience or knowledge—or both—required to operate this type of business?

- Is the business plan realistic, complete, and based on reasonable assumptions?

- Are the plan's revenue and cost projections realistic and conservative? Because loan repayments will be made from cash flow, a lender will be particularly interested in projected cash flow.

If the business is already operating, the banker will look to the prospective borrower's current ratio to get a sense of his or her ability to repay the loan. The current ratio is represented by this simple formula:

Current Ratio = Current Assets ÷ Current Liabilities

Because current assets (cash, securities, accounts receivable, inventory) can be turned readily into cash, this ratio imparts a sense of a company's ability to pay its bills (current liabilities) as they come due. The size of the current ratio that a healthy company needs to maintain depends on the relationship between inflows of cash and demands for cash payments. A company that has a continuous and reliable inflow of cash or other liquid assets, such as a public utility or a taxi company, may be able to meet currently maturing obligations easily despite a small current ratio—say, 1.10 (which means that the company has $1.10 in current assets for every $1.00 of current liabilities). On the other hand, a manufacturing firm with a long product-development and manufacturing cycle may need to maintain a larger current ratio.

To confirm the absolute liquidity of an organization, a bank credit analyst can modify the current ratio by eliminating from current assets all the assets that cannot be liquidated on very short notice. Typically then, this ratio, called the acid-test ratio, consists of the ratio of so-called quick assets (cash, marketable securities, and accounts receivable) to current liabilities. Inventory is left out of the calculation.

Acid-Test Ratio = Quick Assets ÷ Current Liabilities

Paradoxically, a company can have loads of choice assets—office buildings, fleets of delivery trucks, and warehouses brimming with finished-goods inventory—and still risk insolvency if its ratio of current (or quick) assets is insufficient to meet bills as they come due. Creditors don't take payment in used delivery trucks; they want cash. Lenders generally answer the second question—"Is the borrower's character such that he or she will pay me back?"—by examining your credit history. Whether it's a car loan, a home mortgage, or a business loan, a banker will want to see evidence that you pay your bills on schedule.

The third question—"What assets can I get my hands on?"—is about collateral. Collateral is an asset pledged to the lender until such time as the loan is satisfied. In an automobile loan, for example, the lender retains title to the vehicle and makes sure that the buyer has made a sufficiently large down payment so that the lender can repossess the car, sell it, and fully reimburse itself from the proceeds if the borrower fails to make timely loan payments.

Business loans are similar. The lender wants to see assets that can, if your business fails, be sold to satisfy the loan. Those assets might be current assets such as cash, inventory, and accounts receivable; they might also include fixed assets such as vehicles, buildings, and equipment. Loans backed by the SBA offer these kinds of guarantees in the business owners' stead. For more on these US government–backed loans, see the box "SBA loans."

Debt is one of the lowest-cost sources of external capital because interest charges (in the US tax system) are deductible from taxable income. This deductibility, of course, doesn't do a company much good if it has no taxable income to report yet.

Online lenders

Over the past decade, a growing number of online lenders such as Kabbage, OnDeck, and Funding Circle have begun to compete for local banks' share of the small business and entrepreneurial lending market both in the US and throughout the world, most markedly in China. By 2015, some 20 percent of small-employer firms in the US reported applying for funding from an online lender. Though most were approved for at least some credit, they reported lower satisfaction than those who had worked with a small bank or credit union. Other new and growing forms of financing come from peer-to-peer lending networks such as Lending Club and Prosper.

SBA loans

The SBA manages three loan programs intended to help small businesses owned by US citizens obtain financing. The administration itself does not grant loans; rather, it sets guidelines for loans, and its partners (lenders, community development organizations, and microlending institutions) make the loans. What makes these deals palatable to financial institutions is that the SBA guarantees repayment up to certain levels, eliminating some of the lender's risk. Certain legislation passed in the wake of the 2008 recession to stimulate small-business development made these loans even more attractive to both lenders and borrowers.

Information about the SBA loan program can be found at www.sba .gov, along with abundant information about starting and managing a small business.

Source: Karen Gordon Mills and Brayden McCarthy, "The State of Small Business Lending: Innovation and Technology and the Implications for Regulation," working paper, Harvard Business School, Boston, 2016.

The right amount of debt

Carefully consider how much bank debt your company can handle. The degree to which the activities of a company are supported by liabilities and long-term debt as opposed to owners' capital contributions is called leverage. A firm that has a high proportion of debt relative to owner contributions is said to be highly leveraged. For owners, the advantage of having high debt is that returns on their actual investments can be disproportionately higher when the company makes a profit. On the other hand, high leverage is a negative when cash flows fall, because the interest on debt is a contractual obligation that must be paid in bad times as well as good. A company can be forced into bankruptcy by the crush of interest payments due on its outstanding debt.

The debt ratio is widely used to assess the degree of leverage used by companies and its attendant risks. It is calculated in different ways, two of which are illustrated here. The simplest is this:

$$\text{Debt Ratio} = \text{Total Debt} \div \text{Total Assets}$$

Alternatively, you can calculate the debt-to-equity ratio by dividing the total liabilities by the amount of shareholders' equity:

$$\text{Debt-to-Equity Ratio} = \text{Total Liabilities} \div \text{Owners' Equity}$$

In general, as either of these ratios increases, the returns to owners are higher, but so too are the risks. Creditors understand this relationship extremely well and often include specific limits on the debt levels beyond which borrowers may not go without having their loans called in.

Creditors also use the times-interest-earned ratio to estimate how safe it is to lend money to individual businesses. The formula for this ratio is as follows:

$$\text{Times-Interest-Earned Ratio} = \text{Earnings Before Interest and Taxes} \div \text{Interest Expense}$$

The number of times that interest payments are covered by pretax earnings, or EBIT (earnings before interest and taxes), indicates the degree to which income could fall without causing insolvency. In many cases, EBIT is not so much a test of solvency as it is a test of staying power under adversity. For example, if EBIT were to be cut in half because of a recession or another cause, would the company still have sufficient earnings to meet its interest obligations?

Equity and beyond

The counterweight to heavy debt is owners' equity. Equity capital is obtained through the sale of shares to investors, including the entrepreneur.

The typical entrepreneurial enterprise in the growth phase is neither large enough nor proven enough to become a public company—that is, to launch an initial public offering (IPO) of shares. As a result, it cannot tap broader equity markets. If the company is in a hot growth industry, or if it is close to producing a breakthrough with some game-changing product, it may gain the attention of a VC firm or an angel investor. If this private investor likes the looks of the business, it may make a sizable capital contribution. These sources of equity are covered in chapter 8. But it is relatively unusual for an early-phase company to generate this kind of capital.

Most companies never get beyond this early phase of growth. They either fail or are acquired. But those that succeed have access to a broader spectrum of financing opportunities—in particular, the public stock market. The prospect of even greater growth is a powerful lure to equity investors, who hope to buy shares while shares are still cheap and the company is unrecognized.

Local banks are also important sources of external financing as growth continues. The business now has a confidence-inspiring record of producing revenues and paying its bills. Its current and times-interest-earned ratios are favorable. And it has assets that it can pledge as collateral for asset-based loans or leases. The company may also have grown so much that it has outgrown the lending capacity of its local bank, in which case the company can move upstream to a large money-center bank.

The major milestone in the growth phase for those few enterprises that show exceptional promise is the IPO. These offerings are managed by one or more investment banking firms selected by the issuing company. The investment bankers help the issuing company navigate through the strict regulatory requirements of issuing shares to the public. More important, the investment bank and its syndicate of broker-dealers (stockbrokers) provide direct access to millions of potential investors: individual investors, mutual funds, pension funds, and private money managers. Subsequent chapters will provide you with more information on investment bankers. Table 7-1 summarizes the pros and cons of various forms of capital sources during the growth phase. We'll cover angels and VCs in more detail in chapter 8 and IPOs in chapter 9.

TABLE 7-1

Sources of capital for growth-stage financing

Internal cash flow from operations	• Cost-free if shareholders aren't anxious for dividends.
	• May not be enough to finance substantial growth in the productive base of the business.
Debt capital	• Costly, but interest payments are deductible from taxable income (if there is any income).
	• Interest rate is a function of prevailing rates, the term of the loan, and the creditworthiness of the borrower.
	• Debt increases the riskiness of the enterprise.
Venture capital	• The most expensive capital available, since the VC will take a significant share of ownership—and of future prospects for the company.
	• The entrepreneur must share power with the VC.
	• Unlike any other form of capital, this one comes with business advice that may be valuable.
Initial public offering	• Perhaps the only way to round up a large bundle of money. But like venture capital, the IPO dilutes the ownership interests of the entrepreneur and earlier investors. Also, the duties of being a public company are often onerous.

Maturity-phase financing

Companies cannot continue growing forever. Eventually, growth tapers off for one or more reasons:

- Success and profitability draw competitors into the market.

- Demand for the product or service is largely satisfied (market saturation).

- There is a shift in the technology used in the company's products— or the technology used by your customers.

- As the organization grows larger, it loses ambition, agility, or the ability to innovate.

Whatever the cause, few companies sustain high growth rates for more than a decade. This does not mean that growth necessarily stops and that continued financing is not needed. Even saturated markets for mature products, such as automobiles, continue to expand incrementally as the population increases and as people in developing countries become more affluent and demand them. For a $1 billion enterprise, even a 3 percent growth in revenues may require additional financing. Then, too, mature companies are often involved in mergers, acquisitions, restructuring, or other activities, all of which have important financing implications.

Assuming that the mature company is creditworthy, it has many options for obtaining additional external funds. For short-term needs, it can issue commercial paper (explained later in the chapter), tap its bank line of credit, or negotiate a term loan with a bank or other financial institutions, such as insurance companies and pension funds. The mature company can use its existing assets and cash flow as collateral to lower the cost of loans. Alternatively, the company can obtain significant funds through sale-and-leaseback arrangements.

The healthy, mature company also enjoys access to public capital markets for debt (bonds) and equity capital (stock). Here, timing is all-important. The company naturally wants to sell its bonds when interest rates are low and sell its shares when share prices are high.

Financing growth at eBay

To better appreciate the sequence of financing experienced by growing entrepreneurial enterprises, consider eBay, perhaps the most successful company of the dot-com age. It exploded from a home-based hobby business to a sizable corporation in only a few years. The company's early history (1995 through 2000) illustrates the role played by various forms of financing.

eBay was started in 1995 by Pierre Omidyar, a young man with experience in software development and online commerce. Omidyar set up his business on a free website provided by his internet service. His only business assets then were a filing cabinet, an old school desk, and a laptop. When Omidyar's hobby business grew quickly, he had to buy his own server, hire someone to handle billings and the checks that came in the mail, and eventually move the operation from his apartment to a small office. Omidyar and his business partner, Jeff Skoll, soon began paying themselves annual salaries of $25,000.

This early period of growth was essentially self-financed: the cash coming in the mail from transaction fees was sufficient to cover the business's expenses and investments. But a period of hypergrowth was right around the corner. By the end of December 2000, this little online company had grown from serving a handful of auction devotees to dealing with the transactions of twenty-two million registered users. By then, it offered more than eight thousand product categories; on any given day, the company listed more than six million items for sale in an auction-style format and another eight million items in a fixed-price format.

An infrastructure of office space, customer support, proprietary software, information systems, and equipment was required to host a business with this volume and keep it churning. eBay developed systems to operate its auction service and to process transactions, including billing and collections. Those systems had to be continually improved and expanded as the pace of transactions on the site increased.

To keep the wheels of growth turning, the company spent liberally on new site features and categories. eBay reported $4.6 million in product-development expenses in 1998, $24.8 million in 1999, and $55.9 million in 2000. Even larger sums were spent on marketing, brand development, and acquisitions aimed at broadening the company's services and extending its reach to other parts of the world.

Before long, eBay had expanded its balance-sheet assets dramatically. Here are a few highlights (rounded to millions) from the company's annual report to the SEC for the fiscal year ending December 31, 2000:

Cash and cash equivalents: $202 million

Short-term investments: $354 million

Long-term investments: $218 million

Total assets: $1,182 million

With total assets of nearly $1.2 billion, eBay was light-years away from Omidyar's apartment operation. Where did the money come from to finance those assets? eBay's remarkable growth was principally financed in two ways: first, by cash flows from operations (self-financing) and second, by loans and the sale of ownership shares (external financing). Let's examine these sources individually, because they are important to growing companies.

eBay's cash flows from operations

In the early days, cash flow from operations was an important source of growth financing. The company's cash-flow statement—which totals the cash flow entering and leaving the enterprise through operations, investments, and financing activities—documents the effect of internally generated financing. (If you are unfamiliar with the cash-flow statement, see appendix A.) Table 7-2 contains the highlights of eBay's cash-flow statement for 1998 through 2000.

The first row, net cash provided by operating activities, shows that the company ran some portion of its operations and paid people's salaries, taxes, and other bills (operating activities) from operating cash flow. What's more, the level of positive cash flow from operations grew substantially from year to year, helping to fund growth. Thus, an important portion of

TABLE 7-2

eBay's cash flow, 1998 through 2000 (in thousands of dollars)

	2000	1999	1998
Net cash provided by operating activities	$100,148	$62,852	$6,041
Net cash used in investing activities	(206,054)	(603,363)	(53,024)
Net cash provided by financing activities	85,978	725,027	72,159
Net increase (decrease) in cash and cash equivalents	(19,928)	184,516	25,176
Cash and cash equivalents at end of year (after accounting for beginning balance)	201,873	221,801	37,285

Source: eBay 10-K report, 2000.

eBay's asset growth was financed internally, from its successful and profitable operations. Instead of returning even a cent of that cash to shareholders in the form of dividends, the company plowed everything back into the business. This practice is typical of fast-growing companies.

eBay's external financing

Internally generated cash was sufficient to finance operations in the early days, but not nearly sufficient to fund eBay's meteoric growth. Large as they were, eBay's operating cash flows paled in comparison with the cash outflows caused by investments during the same period. In the best of those years (2000), cash flow from operations covered slightly less than half of the investment outflow. To make up the difference, the company resorted to external financing (depicted in the line labeled "Net cash provided by financing activities" in table 7-2).

eBay's financial statements, which are too voluminous to show here, indicate that almost all its external financing took the form of stockholders' capital; that is, the company and its subsidiaries raised cash by selling shares (almost all common shares) to investors. The first of these sales was a $5 million private placement with Benchmark Capital, a Silicon Valley VC firm. In return for its cash, Benchmark was given a 22 percent equity interest in eBay.

The next big capital-raising event in eBay's history was its 1998 IPO. An IPO is a major milestone in a corporation's life cycle in that the offering marks the company's transition from a private to a public enterprise. As you'll see in a later chapter, this new status opens up much larger opportunities to raise equity capital. The universe of potential capital contributors expands from the small and clubby circle of private investors to a much broader group of individual investors, mutual funds, and pension funds.

An IPO also enables the existing investors, including the venture capitalists and shareholding employees, to cash in some or all of their shares—turning paper certificates into real money. eBay's Omidyar, for example, held more than forty-four million shares of his company's common stock before its IPO. In the wake of the offering and the stock price run-up in the months that followed, Omidyar became a billionaire four times over. The value of Benchmark's shares rose to the point that it could claim a 49,000 percent return on its investment—one for the record books!

eBay's financial managers and investment bankers used the company's high stock price and public appetite for shares to float yet another common stock issue in 1999. This one netted the company more than $700 million, most of which was used in the company's campaign of expansion.

Other forms of external financing

Thus far in this chapter, we've described supplier trade credit, bank loans, and common stock issues as important forms of external financing. Today's mature corporations also use a few other important forms of financing:

- **Commercial paper:** Large corporations with high credit ratings often use the sale of commercial paper to finance their short-term requirements. They use it as a lower-cost alternative to short-term bank borrowing. Commercial paper is a short-term debt security, generally reaching maturity in 2 to 270 days. Most paper is sold at a discount from its face value and is redeemable at face value on maturity. The difference between the discounted sale price and the face value represents interest to the purchaser of the paper. Investors having temporary cash surpluses are the usual purchasers of commercial paper; for them it is a reasonably safe way to obtain a return on their idle cash.

- **Bonds:** A bond is also a debt security (an IOU), usually issued with a fixed interest rate and a stated maturity date. The bond issuer has a contractual obligation to make periodic interest payments and to redeem the bond at its face value on maturity. Bonds may have short-, intermediate-, or long-term maturities (e.g., from one to thirty years). Generally, they pay a fixed interest rate on a semi-annual basis.

- **Preferred stock:** This type of equity security is similar to a bond in that it pays a stated dividend to the shareholder each year, and after the shares begin trading in the secondary market, then the share prices, like bonds, fluctuate with changes in market interest rates and the creditworthiness of the issuer. Also like bonds, preferred stock is used by some corporations as an external form of equity financing.

Matching assets and financing

One of the principles of financing—whether the funding is to start a company, maintain its operations, or advance its growth—is to make a proper match between the assets and their associated forms of financing. The general principle is to finance current (short-term) assets with short-term financing, and long-term assets with long-term or permanent financing.

The use of supplier trade credit for financing inventory, as described in chapter 6, is an example of matching short-term assets with short-term financing. The shoe-store owner matched sixty-day financing against an asset expected to be sold within that period. Similarly, companies finance their infrastructure of office space, systems, and equipment with either long-term debt or capital supplied by shareholders—more permanent forms of financing.

Countless enterprises follow this principle. When states and municipalities build bridges, hockey stadiums, water treatment plants, and so forth, they typically finance them with twenty- to thirty-year bonds— financing vehicles whose maturities roughly match the productive life of the assets.

To understand why this principle is important, consider first what might happen if you tried to finance the purchase of your new home (a long-term asset) with an 8 percent, nonamortizing $200,000 loan that came due in only three years. Under the terms of the loan, you'd pay $16,000 in annual interest and then would be obligated to repay the $200,000 at the end of the third year. This would be feasible if you could negotiate another loan at the end of three years to replace the one that's due and if interest rates were still affordable. But that's two ifs. Money might become so tight that you could not locate a new lender when you needed one, or the lender you found might want 10 or 12 percent. In either case, foreclosure would be likely. You couldn't operate with such a situation, and neither can a business enterprise.

The opposite mismatch situation—borrowing long to finance a short-term asset—is just as bad. Some people take out second mortgages on their homes to finance a dream vacation. Such are the temptations of home equity loans. The vacation will soon be over, but the payments will go on and on. In business, we expect that the assets we acquire with borrowed money will produce incremental revenues (or cost savings) at rates and over periods more than sufficient to pay their financing costs. The same can be said for owners' capital.

Summing up

- Growth-phase entrepreneurs look to internally generated cash flow, asset-based loans, and external equity capital for financing.

- Bankers look to a borrower's ability to repay, character, and collateral before making a loan.

- The current ratio, the acid-test ratio, and the times-interest-earned ratio give lenders insights into the ability of a prospective borrower to repay a loan.

- Debt is generally the lowest-cost form of capital because interest payments are tax deductible; however, carrying debt makes an enterprise riskier.

- A public issuing of shares (initial public offering, or IPO) is a major milestone for the few entrepreneurial firms that reach it. An IPO provides a major infusion of cash to fuel growth.

- Maturity-phase financing for creditworthy companies may include bank loans and the sale of commercial paper, bonds, and stock.

- It's best to finance short-term assets with short-term financing, and long-term assets with long-term debt or shareholders' contribution.

8.

Angel Investment and Venture Capital

Many businesses never get to the point of needing or wanting outside equity capital. The founders can use internally generated cash and loans to expand the enterprise to a size that, to them, is manageable and satisfactory. Best of all, this route avoids selling a share of ownership to outsiders.

Other businesses, however, have broader opportunities for growth. To realize this growth, these firms must at some point seek equity capital from outside investors to finance that growth. Debt financing and internally generated cash are rarely feasible solutions.

Equity capital provides rights of ownership; it gives its contributor an ownership interest in the assets of your enterprise and a share of its future fortunes. In most cases, it also gives the contributor a voice in how your business should be run. Make no mistake, by accepting equity funding, you are ceding some measure of the control of your business.

For these growth-potential firms, a new vocabulary has emerged from Silicon Valley. Your startup phase of fund-raising is called the seed stage. As you're gearing up to release your first product, you may need to raise more funds, often from angel investors—this is your Series A round of funding. Finally, if your company keeps growing, you'll need yet more funds—your Series B. For this round, you'll probably turn to venture capital.

This chapter describes in more detail these two most immediate sources of equity capital that come from people outside the business after friends and relatives have been considered: angel investors and venture capitalists. It explains how you can connect with them and discusses the pros and cons of taking their money.

Angel investors

The attention paid to venture-capital firms (VCs) might lead you to believe that these firms provide most of the equity funding used by entrepreneurial companies during their developmental stages—that is, before these companies issue their first shares to the public. A few firms having huge growth potential do connect with VCs almost immediately—long before they have marketable products or services. But many small and midsize ventures never show up on the radar of VCs. And only a small percentage of high-potential businesses obtain VC funding—fewer than 1 percent of US companies have raised capital from VCs. Instead, many, if not most, middle- and high-potential ventures obtain equity capital from angel investors. These high-net-worth individuals fund more than sixteen times as many companies as VCs do, and the share of companies that VCs fund is shrinking. Angel deals represent less in dollars than VC deals do— approximately $24.1 billion and $48.3 billion, respectively, in 2014—but angels dwarf VCs in the number of deals per year—73,400 versus 4,356.

Who are these angels? These high-net-worth individuals are usually successful businesspeople or professionals who provide early-stage capital to startup businesses in the form of either debt, equity capital, or both. They provide financing for the following types of startup and early-stage firms:

- Those that are too small to get the attention of VCs

- Firms often too limited in their revenue potential at maturity to interest VCs

- Firms considered too risky for bank loans and for most VC appetites

Thus, business angels fill a huge financing void and are a good fit for a first stage of serious equity—your Series A round of funding. Companies that began with angel investments include Google, Amazon, Starbucks, and PayPal.

Angels are often self-made millionaires and are accustomed to taking calculated risks with their own money—risks that have the potential of producing exceptional returns. Many enjoy the game of finding and exploiting commercial opportunities. And they don't live only in Silicon Valley. Nor do they look only for tech companies. Consider this example.

> *Jack, a sixty-two-year-old Minneapolis businessman, owns a profitable short-haul trucking and truck maintenance company with $43 million in annual revenues. He built the business from the ground up. He also owns minority interests in two other successful businesses in the area and is an active member of their boards.*
>
> *Financially secure and confident of his business acumen, Jack enjoys learning about investment opportunities in the Minneapolis area and taking active investment positions in the ones that he likes and understands. Occasionally, Jack has joined forces with two close friends—both wealthy businesspeople—in these investments. One is a longtime friend and an accountant, the owner of a local CPA firm. The other, a former employee, owns and manages several apartment buildings in the city. "Three minds are better than one," he says.*

Jack is one of an estimated three hundred thousand business angels in the United States. According to research by the University of New Hampshire's Center for Venture Research, angels invested nearly $25 billion in over seventy-one thousand ventures in 2015. Angel investing is also growing outside the United States: in Europe, the total market doubled between 2011 and 2016, and in Canada, it tripled.

Assuming that you have a solid business plan and the know-how to launch and operate a successful company, people like Jack represent your best opportunity to secure substantial outside capital. And money is not the only thing they have to offer. These successful businesspeople can offer advice and feedback when you need it. They also have valuable local networks that can be helpful to you. Whether you need to find a good attorney, accounting services, a banker, a supplier, a key employee, or office space, your angel can usually put you in touch with reliable people.

Connecting with angels

Angels aren't always easy to spot. Unlike VC firms, angels do not advertise themselves, and they tend to keep their investment activities to themselves and their circle of trusted associates.

One way to connect with angel investors is to join the online platform AngelList; startups now raise more than $10 million a month through the platform. Like other social networks, it allows you to post a profile—in this case, outlining your company's merits—and then connect with other influencers.

Serial entrepreneurs Evan Baehr and Evan Loomis suggest posting your profile only when you've raised at least a third or even a half of the total amount you are looking for from quality investors. When a potential investor sees this funding and recognizes that those other investors have done their due diligence, the angel will be more quickly interested in your firm.

If your business is local or regional, you'll want to find a local angel. The Angel Capital Association website also provides a directory of angel groups and platforms by region. Another way to reach local angels is to find a way into their network—through your lawyer, your accountant, or other entrepreneurs of your acquaintance. Talk with patent attorneys, and share your business plan. Ask successful entrepreneurs in your area, "Whom should I approach about private financing?" If the person they suggest cannot help you, ask that person the same question: "Do you know anyone who might want to invest in my company?" Follow every lead until you connect with the right person. Doing these things may get the word out to the right people in the local angel network.

Angel groups and networks

Business angels traditionally have operated individually or in small, informal, and collegial groups that are now giving way to more-formal organizations and networks both in the United States and in Europe. These groups are making angel investing more professional, more formal, and—for the angels—more efficient. They have more depth and breadth in their expertise and more investing power than solo angels have. In some ways, they are becoming more like VC firms, with professional screeners doing some of the legwork and initial analysis. On the upside, these organizations make the chore of finding and contacting a potential financier less time-consuming and less hit-or-miss for entrepreneurs. On the downside, angel groups are more bureaucratic and make decisions less quickly.

Getting angel funding

Even as angel-deal totals are rising, the number of angel deals slightly decreased in 2015–2016. The Center for Venture Research suggests that the increasing selectivity of angels has caused the decrease. So once you have connected with an angel, how do you persuade them to fund your venture?

- Target angels in professions related to your enterprise. For example, if yours is an information systems startup, hunt for people whose wealth was made in that industry. For example, one of the founders of Sun Microsystems saw a prelaunch demonstration of Google's search engine and gave that company's grad student entrepreneurs a check for $100,000. As a seasoned veteran of the tech industry, he could appreciate the technology's potential. If you hope to build a business around a new medical device, get the word out to local physicians.

- Have your act together: either a working prototype, a well-managed and lean operation, or, at a minimum, a rock-solid business plan.

- Be ready with a well-rehearsed, right-to-the-point verbal presentation. You should be prepared to explain clearly and specifically how the angel's money will be used to fuel profitable growth.

- Have a credible exit plan for your investors. Angels want to eventually convert their paper ownership interests into real money.

- Focus on your team. Shai Bernstein (assistant professor of finance at Stanford's Graduate School of Business), Arthur Korteweg (University of Southern California's Marshall School of Business), and Kevin Laws (chief operating officer of AngelList) have studied angel investors' motivation. They found that what matters most for these investors is the people. More important than your firm's initial traction and its initial investors are the profiles of the founders: where they went to school, their previous work experience at prestigious firms, and so forth. The researchers hypothesize that investors want to know about the founders because of credibility: if a graduate of Harvard Business School is choosing to devote their career to this venture—rather than any number of other attractive opportunities—then there must be something to it. Other research has also shown that potential angels heavily consider the founders in their decisions. In particular, the investors look at the founders' coachability and weigh their trustworthiness and character over their competence.

Venture capital

As a high-risk investor, a VC or a VC firm seeks an equity position in a startup or an early-growth company with high potential. In return for capital, the VC typically takes a significant percentage of ownership of the business and a position on its board. VCs take part in the strategic management of their fledgling companies and often help connect them with suppliers and potential business allies through their networks. In many cases, VCs also help recruit the technical and managerial personnel these companies need to succeed. They also provide useful advice. (For information on a related form of funding, see the box "Corporate venture capital.") Venture capital is your Series B funding.

Angels and VCs can provide the capital that growth businesses need to scale to their full potential. For any company that looks forward to an IPO, having a VC on its side is almost essential. A good VC firm has the sophistication, connections, and experience to get an IPO off the ground and on terms that maximize shareholder value.

Generally, VCs seek out small firms that have the potential to return ten times the investors' risk capital within five to ten years. Most aim to harvest their investments during the IPO or follow-up issues of company share and then to move on to the next opportunity.

Whereas business angels generally stay in the shadows of new business financing, VCs have a far more visible presence. What is hot with VCs

Corporate venture capital

Aside from VC firms, another source of venture capital exists: large organizations. Some firms traditionally have approached investment in new businesses as a strategic move. By considering such an investment, they get information about what's new in the industry and a first look at a company they might want to acquire. This approach is growing: from 2011 to 2015, the number of corporate VCs in the United States increased from 1,068 to 1,501, with the amount these firms invested quintupling to $75 billion. These firms, however, are increasingly looking for financial performance as well as a strategic investment.

Source: Excerpted from "Corporate VCs Are Moving the Goalposts," *Harvard Business Review,* November 2016.

changes with the times; the majority of enterprises that attract VCs today are in industries connected to the tech world: software, hardware, biotech, medical devices, and media and entertainment.

The businesses that most attract VCs tend to be risky ones with proven management and substantial growth potential. For these financiers, a first-rate person with a good idea is far more attractive than a good idea with second-rate management. Many of the companies VCs focus on haven't yet developed a marketable product or service. And because investments in these companies lack immediate liquidity, the VCs anticipate that their funds will be tied up for several years. In the investor's mind, high risk and illiquidity are offset by high potential payoffs. For example, Arthur Rock's $1.5 million investment in fledgling Apple Computer was risky, but it was valued at $100 million three years later, when the company went public. Such lucrative payoffs are what VCs live for. Consequently, if your venture lacks the potential to take them to the moon, your search for VC financing will probably be fruitless.

And for all the heat and light that VC funding gets, venture funding is actually a rarity for startups. Fewer than 1 percent of US companies have raised money from VCs historically, and the number of VCs and dollars invested by them is trending downward. Instead, companies are turning to the growing list of alternatives such as angels, crowdfunding, and their own customers. (See the box "An alternative to venture capital" for a brief example.) A fast-growing business with huge growth potential can hardly avoid using outside equity capital, but others can avoid it—or can delay its necessity while they build real value for themselves. Here are a few tips for doing so:

- Rely as heavily as possible on bootstrap financing. This type of financing doesn't force you to give up ownership.

- Manage growth at a pace you can handle with existing financing.

- Be tightfisted with the money you have. Keep expenses low, and find every opportunity for doing more with less.

An alternative to venture capital

Take Claus Moseholm, cofounder of GoViral, a Danish company created in 2005 to harness the then-emerging power of the internet to deliver advertisers' video content in viral fashion. Funding his company's steady growth with the proceeds of one successful viral video campaign after another, Moseholm and his partners built GoViral into Europe's leading platform to host and distribute such content. In 2011, GoViral was sold for $97 million, having never taken a single krone or dollar of investment capital. The business had been funded and grown entirely by its customers' cash.

Source: Excerpted from John Mullins, "VC Funding Can Be Bad for Your Start-Up," HBR.org, August 4, 2014.

- Outsource nonessential functions whenever possible. Farming out will allow you to do more with less capital. The modern economy is flush with contractors for every part of a business.

The venture-capital process

If venture capital is a realistic prospect for you, you'll want to know where the money comes from, how the capital flow to high-potential firms is managed, and how returns are distributed. Scholar-practitioners William Bygrave and Jeffry Timmons show how the funds flow in figure 8-1. The VC firm shown here is a limited partnership in which passive limited partners contribute most of the capital. These partners may be wealthy individuals, pension funds, university endowments, or corporations. For them, risky venture financing constitutes a small part of their overall portfolios.

The VC firm acts as the (active) general partner, employing a cadre of bright new MBAs, securities lawyers, and experienced deal makers to identify, screen, and invest in high-potential firms identified in figure 8-1

FIGURE 8-1

The flow of venture capital

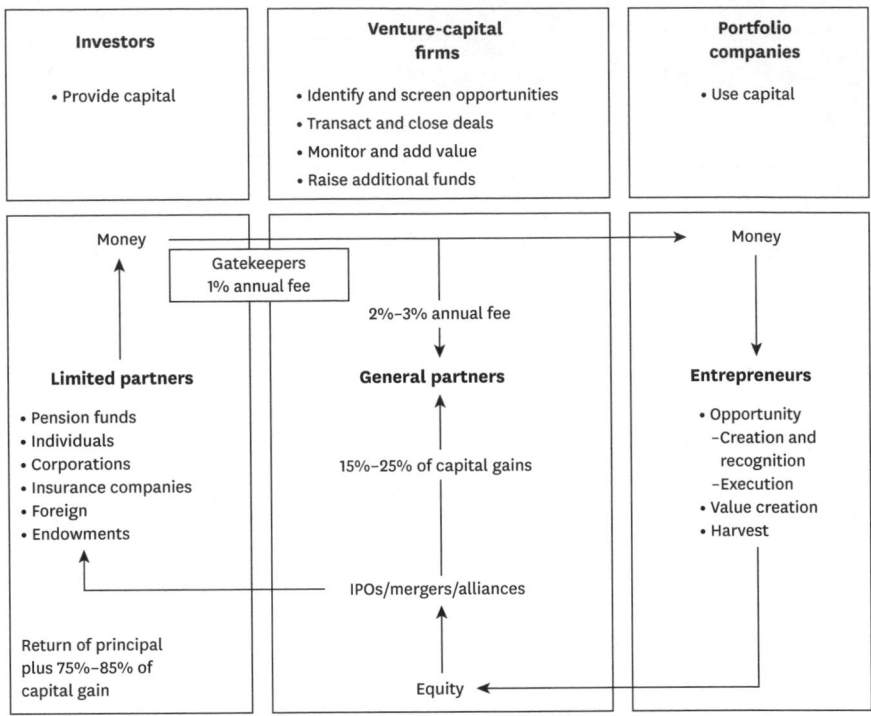

Source: William D. Bygrave and Jeffry A. Timmons, *Venture Capital at the Crossroads* (Boston: Harvard Businees School Press, 1992), 11. Reproduced with permission.

as portfolio companies. The wise VC firm will diversify its bets among many deals, knowing that some will fail and others will only break even, but maybe one in fifteen will be the bonanza that makes them rich. As a practical approach to diversification, VC firms form small syndicates in which the lead investor conducts the due diligence and takes a seat on the entrepreneurial company's board. Other members of the syndicate contribute smaller amounts to the total financing and generally take a passive approach to the investment.

The VC's capital contribution often takes the form of convertible preferred stock. This stock has voting rights—something that gives the VC a measure of control over the enterprise and its officers. The terms of the deal also give preferred shareholders the right to convert their securities to common shares at their discretion. Conversion will be stipulated at 1:1 or some other ratio. As preferred shareholders, they are entitled to cumulative dividends that must be paid before any dividends can be paid to common shareholders.

VCs love this type of arrangement because preferred shareholders stand ahead of common shareholders in the event of liquidation. This status reduces some of their risk. Meanwhile, the conversion feature allows them to participate in the upside potential of the company. In effect, convertible preferred shareholder status gives VCs the best of both worlds: some protection in case the business fails and the right to enjoy whatever success the company produces. (A common alternative to convertible preferred shares is convertible debt with warrants.)

After an investment is made, the VC does three things:

1. Monitors the progress of its portfolio companies

2. Uses its network of contacts to help portfolio companies strengthen their technical and management teams

3. Shapes company plans and strategies through its influence on their boards

The end of the VC process comes when the VC harvests part or all of its investment, usually when its portfolio companies go public or are purchased by other corporations. Typically, harvest comes after four or five years. The investors and the VC firms share in harvested profits according to the terms of their partnership.

Connecting with venture capitalists

If your enterprise meets a VC firm's criteria, the firm might find you before you find it. Competitive VCs go hunting for promising deals. They keep in touch with connections in high-tech spawning beds such as MIT's research labs, Stanford University, and startup accelerators and incubators, and they work entrepreneurial networks in Silicon Valley, North Carolina's

Research Triangle, San Diego's biotech community, and so forth. But if you need venture capital, you cannot wait for VCs to find you. And you cannot wait until you really need a cash infusion; you should line up venture money six or eight months before it is actually needed.

To connect with a VC, you could search for firms that are a good match for your enterprise (or use a directory like *Pratt's Guide*—see the box "VC locators"). Then you could email your executive summary, your YouTube pitch link, or a brief pitch deck of your business plan to each firm that specializes in your industry (some have specific application instructions on their websites). Don't bother sending the entire plan; investors don't have time to read it. If the VC is intrigued by your executive summary, he or she will ask for a more thorough plan. The limited time a prospect has to spend on your plan underscores the importance of crafting a clear, compelling, and creative pitch.

Unfortunately, sending out blind emails is about as effective as sending out blind résumés when you're hunting for a job. To the VC, you are only one of thousands of faceless supplicants. To change this perception and improve your odds, you need to find a way to personally meet the VC or have your case recommended by someone the VC respects. Here are a few techniques to make such contacts:

- Go through a highly regarded accelerator program. Accelerators are an indirect way to get the attention of VCs; research has shown that companies that graduate from top accelerator programs are able to raise VC funding more quickly. (That wasn't true of companies coming out of accelerator programs across the board, however, so be selective.)

- Attend entrepreneurial forums. Cities with many high-tech start-ups periodically hold events that bring entrepreneurs and financiers together. Typically, each of many VC firms has a separate table, and each eager entrepreneur is given a five- to ten-minute opportunity to visit the table and make the pitch. Attend these forums whenever possible. But be totally prepared. Have a brief but compelling elevator speech about the opportunity you've identified and how your team intends to exploit it.

- Be ready with a presentation that you can customize for the length of your meeting and the audience. Whenever you do make contact with a VC, ask for an opportunity to come to the office to make your pitch. Your presentation should be brief, well organized, compelling, and well rehearsed. Deliver the highlights, and be prepared to supply the details if asked.

- Have well-connected people on your team. The VC may not know you or your company, but if the financier knows and respects someone on your team or your board of directors, you may get a face-to-face meeting. Keep this in mind as you form your management team and select advisers and board members. Use an attorney who is highly respected by local VCs. All other things being equal, select board members who have personal connections to financiers.

VC locators

Pratt's Guide to Private Equity & Venture Capital Sources, edited by Stanley E. Pratt and available at online and specialist bookstores and in an entirely digital online version, is a comprehensive list of VC sources. It is organized in a way that you can quickly locate VCs having the desired characteristics and interests. This $1,000 book is updated periodically.

The website VCgate offers an extensive directory of VC, private-equity, merchant banking, and other investment firms from around the world. The VCgate database, which purports to include some thirty-eight hundred listings from the United States, Canada, Europe, and Asia, makes searching quick and efficient. Finally, *Forbes* ranks the world's individual VCs annually on its Midas List, available on its website.

Making a presentation

Assuming that you contact an angel or a VC and have been invited to make a presentation about your company, how can you make it as successful as possible?

Babson College professor and researcher Lakshmi Balachandra says to remember that your audience will have read your materials before deciding to call you in. You're there in main not to present your idea as if it's the first time your audience is hearing it, but rather to answer their questions, to assuage any concerns they might have, and to let them get to know you better. Here are three broad tips that come from her research:

- **Maintain a calm demeanor.** While expressing your passion for the business helps with some less formal funding sources, research from Balachandra and others suggests that professional funders equate equanimity with leadership strength.

- **Build trust.** Your audience is looking to learn about your character even more than they want to assess your competence. Skills are teachable or hirable, but your personality will change very little. Prospective financiers want to work with someone who isn't going to make a risky proposition even more volatile through dishonesty or other bad behavior. Balachandra's research shows that entrepreneurs who projected trustworthiness increased their odds of being funded by 10 percent.

- **Listen actively, and express openness to new ideas.** Early-stage investors in particular are going to be interested in molding you and giving you advice that they hope will help their investment pan out. They're looking for someone who is open to outside coaching and who won't let their ego get in the way.

Overall, preparation is key. Rehearse your presentation until you have it down cold. You must convey the impression that you are in control of the facts and that you have great confidence in the company and its future.

After you have made the presentation, expect some pointed questions from your audience. Anticipate key questions, and have rock-solid answers for each one.

The downsides of taking venture capital

Because outside capital carries a heavy cost, you are well advised to find a way to self-fund. London Business School professor John Mullins describes some of the downsides of taking venture capital:

- **Distraction from your day job:** Getting a business off the ground is hard enough without having to seek funding—another full-time job.

- **Onerous terms:** VCs are wary of risk and will require terms that protect them and are hard on you. Be particularly careful as the concise language of their term sheet gets turned into the details of the legal agreement: those details may be more unfavorable than you expected.

- **Burdensome advice:** You'll be required to take the advice of your funder—whether or not you agree. Mullins also sees a lack of evidence pointing to the efficacy of that advice.

- **Dilution of ownership and returns:** When you raise equity capital, you're giving away ownership of part of your company. Venture capital specifically can be the most expensive form of capital you can use.

Consider, for example, eBay, which in 1997 took $6.7 million from Benchmark Capital in return for 22 percent of company ownership. Whereas a commercial bank might have made $2 million in interest from a loan of that size over three years, eBay's VCs chalked more than $2 billion in the same period. Certainly, Benchmark did help the young company recruit an effective and experienced CEO and other members of the management team, but a good executive recruiter would have done the same for less than $200,000. The VC also played a major role in arranging for the company's successful IPO, but was that work worth $2 billion, when investment banking advice can be obtained on a consulting basis for a reasonable fee? The lesson: venture capital can be enormously costly to you, especially if your business succeeds. The box "How much of your company should the VC firm get?" helps you avoid such disproportionate sharing of your hard-earned profits.

There is also the matter of control and possible conflicts of interest. VCs with a major stake in your business can make your life miserable if you

How much of your company should the VC firm get?

If a VC firm likes your company and your prospects, it might agree to making a cash infusion via convertible preferred stock or some type of convertible debt, as described earlier. But because the VC can convert to common shares as its option, it is really taking a share of ownership. The question is, What share of total ownership should the VC receive in return for its money? Should $5 million entitle the VC to a 20 percent share of ownership? Or 40 percent? Or 51 percent?

This critical issue for you as an entrepreneur hinges on the estimated value of the firm. If the VC says, "We've estimated the value of your company at $6 million," ask for a detailed explanation of how that figure was determined. Valuation is part science and part art. And because the VC firm is much more experienced in both, it has a negotiating advantage over you. To level the playing field, bring in professional assistance to develop your own assessments of *enterprise value*. This is the best way to be sure that you're dividing the ownership equitably.

The methodologies used in business valuation can be very complex—too complex to cover in this chapter. Nevertheless, you owe it to yourself to be acquainted with them. (For an overview of the methods typically used, see appendix C of this book.)

cannot work together harmoniously. The VC firm may even have enough control to fire you. Also, the VC might plan to quickly flip the company through an IPO or to sell the business to a big corporation, cash in its investment, and move on, whereas you may wish to remain private for a while longer and build the enterprise in line with a long-term vision. For these reasons many entrepreneurs look on VCs as a necessary evil or, in the worst cases, as "venture vultures."

The more solid your business is when you negotiate with outside investors, the better deal you will make for yourself. Instead of giving away the company—and control—you'll keep more of it for yourself. A viable business that isn't desperate for money can obtain much better terms.

Summing up

- The most likely source of outside venture funding comes from so-called angel investors.

- Angels are high-net-worth individuals who provide early-stage capital to startup businesses.

- Networking is often the best way to connect with angels.

- Venture capital comes from an individual or a firm that seeks large capital gains through early-stage equity or equity-linked financing of high-potential entrepreneurial enterprises.

- Entrepreneurs should not waste their time pursuing venture capital unless they have all the characteristics VCs look for.

- Most venture capital takes the form of convertible preferred stock or something similar, such as convertible debt with warrants.

- Venture capital is nice to have, but it is costly both in economic terms and in loss of control of the enterprise.

- When giving a pitch presentation to an angel investor or a VC, choose calm over passion, and build your audience's trust in your character and coachability.

9.

Going Public

Growing firms with exceptional revenue potential have another option to achieve a significant cash infusion: they can seek financing through an IPO. This process presents ownership shares to the world of individual investors and institutional investors such as pension funds and mutual funds and results in a significant exchange of paper ownership shares for the hard cash the company needs for stability and expansion.

An IPO marks a major milestone in the life of a company. It signals that your enterprise has earned the confidence of people outside its inner circle of participants—it has "made it." Going public also makes your company accountable to a much broader universe of stakeholders, analysts, and regulators.

Perhaps fewer than 5 percent of readers will have any direct use for the information contained in this chapter, because only a tiny fraction of startup companies ever go public. The requirements are high—the conventional rule of thumb is that a company needs around $100 million in annualized revenue as well as several consecutive profitable quarters. Few entrepreneurial companies ever reach this bar and get to the point where an IPO is either necessary or feasible. Nevertheless, the rewards of this form of financing make IPOs intensely interesting to company founders, key employees, and early-stage contributors of capital.

This chapter examines the pros and cons of becoming a public company and explores what it takes to be a candidate for this form of financing. You'll get an overview of the IPO process itself, from planning to the actual deal, including the role of investment bankers. We'll also touch on the post-deal environment.

Note that this chapter is written from the perspective of US companies and US securities laws and procedures. Readers outside the United States should consult their own securities laws and procedures.

Weighing the decision to go public

You've probably read many accounts of founders and key employees of entrepreneurial companies who had quite ordinary financial circumstances the day before their firms went public. By the end of the next day, those same individuals were millionaires.

Founder Pierre Omidyar, for example, owned the equivalent of forty-four million common shares on the eve of eBay's IPO in 1998—pieces of paper for which there was no market. He was living in a rented house and driving an old Jetta. The next day, those shares began trading on NASDAQ and began a long upward ascent. Before long, Omidyar's paper shares had a market value north of $4 billion. Other employees and early-stage investors shared in the wealth. But the process wasn't without its challenges, and any company contemplating an IPO should understand both the promise and the negative implications.

Pros

Gaining personal wealth (and liquidity of that wealth) is one of the benefits of going public, but it is not the only advantage. At the same time, the cash that flows onto the company's balance sheet from the IPO has these positive effects:

- Costly interest-bearing debt can be paid off.

- The company has the financial capacity to develop new products and the marketing capabilities to sell them.

- An improved debt-to-equity ratio enables the company to obtain debt financing on better terms than otherwise would have been possible, if the company needs this financing.

- The company can use cash and its own marketable share to finance strategic acquisitions.

- The financial stability of the enterprise is improved, enabling it to attract talent, suppliers, and joint-venture partners.

- Becoming a public company opens the door to future rounds of financing through stock and bond sales.

Note: An IPO does not give absolute liquidity to company insiders. US securities regulations place certain restrictions on the sale of insider-owned shares.

Cons

The proceeds from an IPO provide important benefits for owners and investors, but as many CEOs and chief financial officers (CFOs) will attest, public company status is a mixed blessing. Here are the most important drawbacks of becoming a public corporation:

- **The IPO expense:** Just getting the IPO through SEC registration and off the ground generates major legal, accounting, printing, and advisory expenses. Then there are SEC and state securities filing fees and payments to the exchange that lists the stock. A company should expect to pay $2 million in out-of-pocket expenses when preparing for an IPO; the amount can soar to $100 million for larger deals. These expenses cover legal fees, a commission to the underwriter, and any improvement of internal business processes to meet regulatory requirements as a public company going forward.

- **Management time and attention:** The preparation that goes into an IPO absorbs an enormous amount of top management time and attention over several months. So too does the road show, which takes the CEO and CFO on a time-consuming and costly jaunt to investor meetings around the country. Even after the deal, these two officers must devote part of their time to handling inquiries from investors and security analysts. The company may have to create a position for an investor relations manager to deal with these new stakeholders.

- **Public scrutiny:** The company is now an open book. Its financial results and the compensation of key executives are available to anyone who is interested. The company's 10-K filing will contain information that competitors are bound to find valuable: the names of key suppliers, product-development plans, overall strategy, and so forth.

- **Loss of control:** When an enterprise sells shares to the public, the founder and key managers usually lose a major portion of their ownership. Outsiders—mostly institutional investors—now own blocks of your company's stocks. And there may be thousands of small owners with fewer than one thousand shares.

- **Pressure for short-term gain:** Although most CEOs deny it, the expectations of analysts and investors for predictable year-to-year earnings gains can put decision makers in a difficult position. They may be reluctant to take steps to ensure long-term benefits if doing so will jeopardize short-term results.

The making of an IPO candidate

Do the benefits of being a public company outweigh the drawbacks? Sometimes they do, and sometimes they don't. Even if they do, your enterprise may not be a candidate for an IPO. In fact, an IPO is a pipe dream for all but a small percentage of corporations. This section recounts some of the factors you need to consider before counting your enterprise as an IPO candidate.

Through most of the post–World War II era, US companies didn't go public until they had established a solid record of sales and earnings. After all, investors in an IPO are asked to buy shares of a money-making machine; they want evidence that the machine actually works.

The conservative practice of requiring a record of sales and earnings is occasionally set aside when a company owns proprietary technology and has a tested management team. In these cases, investors are willing to gamble that the company's potential will produce profitable results. During rare periods—the dot-com boom of the middle to late 1990s being one—companies with nothing more than a clever idea were able to sell initial public shares. Many of these companies failed to demonstrate their worth in the years that followed, and the effects of that experience still affect the IPO process today.

Thus, the ability to launch a public offering is partly a function of investor moods and expectations, combined with the ability to meet regulatory requirements. Typically, however, entrepreneurial firms need these characteristics to be viable IPO candidates:

- A reasonable deal size. Given the cost of launching an IPO, there's little point in seeking less than $10 million. And if you're raising that much money, you must have a solid plan for using it.

- Evidence of growth. The firm should have growing sales, with evidence that earnings will follow. Investors expect rising stock prices from double-digit growth in sales and from a higher rate of earnings growth. If the earnings record isn't yet there, all signs should point to substantial profitability in the years ahead. This growth should support a price-earnings multiple (also called the P/E ratio) higher than the historical S&P 500 or the Russell 2000.

- Outstanding products or services that are difficult to copy.

- A credible CEO who can communicate the enterprise's vision to cautious outsiders.

- At least three years of audited financial statements (if you don't have them now, you can create them through a "look-back," provided you have solid enough records).

- High-quality employees.

- A logical strategy for growth and a predictable revenue stream.

In a study of successful IPOs, Ernst & Young found another trait that few would consider a condition of making the transition from private to public company. It found that successful companies began acting like public companies long before they did the deal: "[These companies] made improvements in their employee incentive programs . . . in strategic planning, internal controls, financial accounting and reporting, executive compensation, and investor relations policies." Investors in these firms were buying ownership in a firm that already had the hallmarks of professional management.

Preparing for an IPO

One of the big questions for a growing company is *when* to file for an IPO. Too soon, and you may not make the most of your company's potential; too late, and you may miss a bullish investment market. The box "When to go public" presents the story one successful CEO told about deciding when to do it and how the company made the most of its preparation period.

The IPO process in a nutshell

Now that you understand the pros and cons of going public and whether your firm is a candidate, let's take a look at the process itself. That process has several steps; some must be conducted sequentially, whereas others can be handled in parallel. Very briefly, these steps are as follows:

When to go public

By Scott Dietzen, CEO of Pure Storage

The Pure Storage IPO, in October 2015, was the culmination of a long process. The company [a vendor of data storage solutions] was six years old and had completed six rounds of private funding. Pure Storage had nearly twelve hundred employees, and its annualized revenue was nearly $500 million. We'd waited longer and grown larger than many startups do before going public. We could have done it a year or so earlier, and there were risks in waiting: by the time we finally listed on the New York Stock Exchange, the IPO market had cooled—in fact, some companies pulled their offerings in the face of market weakness.

But in retrospect, the timing worked out, and we wouldn't have changed it if we could have.

For a young growth company, figuring out when to go public is complex—and the conventional wisdom (along with some steps in the process) has changed significantly in recent years. Companies often face pressure from multiple stakeholders—employees, customers, investors—who want liquidity sooner rather than later. At the same time, some startups are coming to realize that staying private longer may have significant advantages (see figure 9-1).

Here's how we approached the choice.

BETTER TO WAIT

In theory, we could have gone public in 2013. We were certainly big enough—by that point we had tens of millions of dollars in revenue. But we saw reasons to wait.

One was that Sarbanes-Oxley [act by US Congress in 2002] has made it more expensive to be a public company. And although other companies were interested in acquiring us, we wanted Pure to be a long-term

(continued)

FIGURE 9-1

Waiting game

Over the past decade, venture-capital-backed companies have tended to stay private longer. The higher regulatory requirements imposed by Sarbanes-Oxley are responsible in part for this trend.

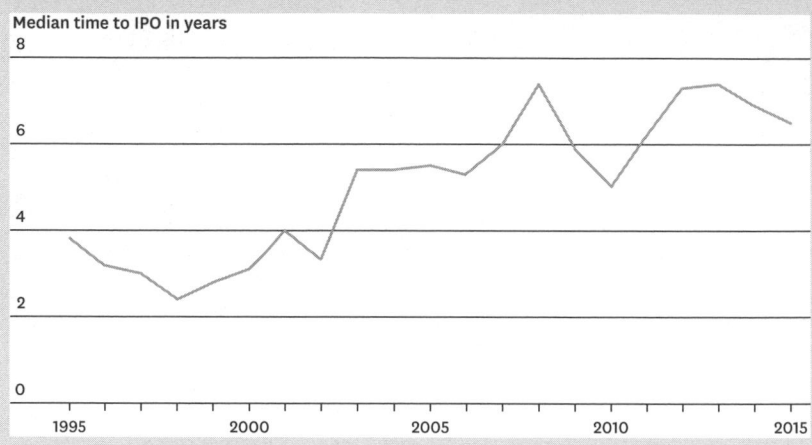

Source: "Pure Storage's CEO on Choosing the Right Time for an IPO," *NVCA Yearbook*, June 2016.

play; as a small public company, we would find it harder to fend off M&A [mergers and acquisitions] interest than if we stayed private and maintained control. But the biggest reason stemmed from the precedents set by Google and Facebook, which both stayed private much longer than venture-backed companies have historically. (Google was nearly six years old at its IPO, and Facebook was eight, whereas Netscape went public sixteen months after its founding.) The delay worked out extremely well for both companies, and it drove a change in the conventional wisdom. Companies used to do an IPO as soon as they possibly could; now many choose to wait.

A couple of things were driving us to go public, however. For one, our customers encouraged us; many of them prefer to do business with a publicly traded company. They want to be able to see your financials and to understand how your business is doing. They know that public companies are subjected to a higher level of scrutiny. It gives them a sense of security and trust.

The other thing was valuation. Private companies' valuations have skyrocketed in recent years—and that has created complications when coupled with a wary public market. No one wants to go public at a valuation below the last private round. As we approached our financing, we tried to create win-win situations; I believe that the job of the CEO is not to aim for the highest possible valuation every time you seek financing but instead to craft a fair deal with investors who will be good advisers. Going public would let us avoid another private round, one at a valuation we couldn't match with our IPO.

PREPARATION AND LUCK

After I arrived at Pure, we did two more venture rounds and then two rounds of private funding led by Fidelity and T. Rowe Price, mutual fund companies that ordinarily invest in public companies. This form of financing is relatively new and is the result of Facebook and other companies' delaying their IPOs. Mutual fund portfolio managers missed some of the growth of such companies because they couldn't invest before the IPO, so they've started making private placements. That's advantageous for everyone. The funds get in on a period of higher growth, and they also get intelligence on what's happening in an industry. We were able to build a relationship with important public-market investors; not only were they great sources of advice in the time leading up to our IPO, but we expected that they would remain big investors afterward. This new source of investment allows companies like ours to stay private longer.

We also took steps to give our employees flexibility with their Pure shares. It can be easier to retain employees when a company is private, because they're waiting for the liquidity that comes with the IPO—they don't want to leave before they can cash in stock options. At the same time, that may create pressure to do an IPO early. To avoid that pressure,

(continued)

we gave employees selective liquidity when we did our financing rounds. They could liquidate a certain percentage of their vested shares while providing a source of supply for institutional investors. More companies are allowing their workers to diversify their portfolios in this way, especially as they stay private longer.

We had to get ready to go public. The first step was to expand the board. We had strong directors, including our VCs, but we needed to add people with operating experience at large companies. In particular, we wanted someone with finance experience at a publicly traded company to chair our audit committee; we brought in Mark Garrett, the CFO at Adobe Systems, to fill the role. We needed a relationship with an investment bank, and we were fortunate to be working with Allen & Company, which handled our fifth and sixth private rounds. We created a two-class structure for our stock, to help the founders and the management team maintain control if a hostile buyer tried to acquire us. Finally, we needed the right chief financial officer. In 2014 we hired Tim Riitters, a former Google finance exec, who helped us put in new systems to give us the better visibility into our financial performance that we'd need to operate in the public markets.

By early 2015, it was clear that we had all the pieces in place. During our last private round, in 2014, the business had been valued at more than $3 billion. I couldn't see any advantage to doing another private round, so we began planning for the IPO. But a key consideration is that once you start the process, you can become vulnerable. When you file an S-1 form with the SEC disclosing your IPO plans, you enter a "quiet period," with strict limits on what you may say publicly. If you're in a

1. **Select an underwriter.** The underwriter—the investment banker you choose—will handle the details in collaboration with the management team (see the section "The role of the investment bank," below). In larger deals, there will be one lead underwriter and one or several comanagers.

competitive space, as we are, you run the risk that competitors will spread "fear, uncertainty, and doubt" at a time when you can't easily respond. Our business is a frontal assault on established storage companies such as EMC and HP (now Hewlett Packard Enterprise). But as it turned out, our timing was fortunate: in the months surrounding our IPO, Dell agreed to buy EMC, and HP announced its plan to split into two companies, which meant that key competitors were distracted by internal events.

Every CEO worries about the economic climate. While we waited to go public, we definitely saw a deterioration in market receptivity to IPOs. You just try to keep the ball rolling, complete all the steps to be ready, and hit while the IPO window is open. Not every company gets it right: at least five that had planned to do an IPO around the time we did ended up delaying or pulling out.

We went public at a share price of $17 and an overall valuation of just over $3 billion. Since then our stock price has fluctuated—a reflection of the turbulent market rather than any negative surprises at Pure. We're still reporting losses, but we've been able to make the case to investors that when you look at our growth rate, improving margins, and increasing operating efficiency, you see that this is a very healthy business. Pure is one of the fastest-growing enterprise technology companies the world has ever seen. We have to invest to maintain that—which is one reason that doing our IPO when we did made sense.

Source: Reprinted from Scott Dietzen, "Pure Storage's CEO on Choosing the Right Time for an IPO," *Harvard Business Review*, June 2016.

2. **Prepare the registration statement for filing with the SEC.**
   The registration statement, a document required by federal law, forces the applicant company to disclose past business results, information about the company, and the intended use of the proceeds of the IPO.

3. **Conduct due diligence.** In the case of IPOs, *due diligence* is the investigation of facts and statements of risk contained in the registration statement; it aims to ensure that this material is accurate and that other relevant facts have not been omitted. Is the company using an unorthodox accounting convention? Is it involved in any current lawsuits? Has it been granted patents, or are patents pending? Due diligence is the responsibility of those who prepare and sign the registration statement.

4. **Print and distribute the prospectus.** The preliminary *prospectus* (also called a red herring) is part of the registration statement. It contains information about the company and the intended use of the issue proceeds, and it is sent to prospective investors to generate interest in the deal.

5. **Prepare and conduct a road show.** At a series of meetings, usually held in major cities around the country, potential investors can grill the CEO or CFO (or both) about the company and the intended offering of securities.

6. **Agree on a final price and the number of shares to be sold.** This step is one of the most important steps in the IPO process. What is a fractional share of ownership in a company actually worth? Important as this question may be, the answer is based as much on art as on science. A price range will be indicated in the prospectus sent to investors—for example, $15 to $20 per share. As the big moment approaches, however, the underwriter will look at demand for the shares, the price that comparable companies managed to get in recent IPOs (if comparables can be found), and the projected earnings of the company itself. The underwriter will also suggest a price that will give investors in the newly issued shares a better-than-even chance of making money on their transactions—that is, a price slightly lower than the price at which the shares are likely to trade in the days immediately after the offering. If the issuing company does not like the price, it can put the brakes on the offering.

7. **Commence trading.** After the price has been established and the final regulatory loose ends have been tied up, shares can begin trading on the exchange chosen.

8. **Close the purchase and sale of the shares.** In this final act of the IPO process, stock certificates are delivered to the shareholders, and the underwriter delivers the proceeds (less fees and expenses) to the issuing company. The company now has its money.

This process generally takes four to five months. If all has gone well, the entrepreneurial firm ends up with a substantial amount of cash in its war chest and is prepared to begin the second stage of its life—that of a publicly traded corporation. The underwriter will try to support that second stage by providing ongoing research to investors on the newly public company. This research keeps the company in the public eye and, if the news continues to be good, it supports the share price.

Certainly there is much, much more to the IPO process than described here. For example, there are restrictions on company-generated publicity before, during, and immediately after the filing period and on so-called lockup agreements, or the sale of shares by insiders. The rules regarding the issuing of securities in the United States are, indeed, many and arcane—and that is why professional help is essential.

For a first-person overview of the IPO process—and the excitement it generates—see the box "IPO day."

The role of the investment bank

Going public is a specialized activity, one that requires unique skills and capabilities that no entrepreneurial company has (or should have) on its payroll. Instead, you'll get these skills and capabilities through an investment bank. (See more on why you need an investment banker in the box "The need for an investment banker.")

An investment bank is not like the more familiar commercial bank. It is not in the business of taking deposits and making loans. Instead, it acts

IPO day

By Annie Bourne, Managing Director of Ivy Road, LLC

I had a front-row seat to one of the most successful IPOs of the dot-com boom. In July 1999, I left a law firm for a business development role at a startup with a strange name—Akamai Technologies. On day one, because we did not yet have a general counsel, the company told me—the only ex-lawyer then on staff—to manage the IPO. Because of the phenomenal technology, timing, and team, the Akamai IPO became one of the most successful IPOs of that era.

So what actually happens inside a company on IPO day? Here's what happened in my experience (which, granted, was over a decade ago). Several of the company leaders reappear, having spent the prior two weeks flying around Europe and the US on private jets, spinning the company's prospects to potential investors. Before that, there's a lot of government-regulated preparation. Bankers and lawyers write a document that describes the business and the risks of investing in it to potential investors. They build a financial model of existing and expected revenues. They file it with regulators, wait for comments and respond to them. Then the company leaders start the roadshow, which hopefully creates enough excitement about the company among large investors that the bankers can line up buyers—if you're lucky, stacks of buyers—for a chunk of the "book" of available shares. Then, in a seemingly unscientific frenzy in a paneled room on Wall Street, the bankers decide what price to place on the opening shares, and when to start selling them.

For the employees, the actual day of "going public" is very strange. At Akamai, in the early afternoon, we left our desks and met in a conference room to watch. There was not much to see. A large TV monitor sat above eye level on a tall rack. Plates of cheese cubes and crackers covered a table. We squeezed in, shoulder to shoulder, heads tilted up to the screen. Most of our faces were unfamiliar to one another; the company had hired a lot of top people leading up to the IPO with the lure of pre-IPO options.

The screen flickered. Then green numbers appeared. We cheered! AKAM stock was then available for purchase on the NASDAQ. Just like that. We watched the green numbers change—just simple rows of green numbers. Someone explained that the numbers represented the "bid" and the "ask"—what someone would pay for a share, and the price at which someone else would sell it. The bankers priced the shares at $26. They opened for trading at $114.50, and buyers chased it higher and higher until it settled down and finally closed at $145.19 at the end of the trading day.

As those green numbers changed on the screen, we cheered more and ate cheese, while some colleagues had just become immeasurably wealthy—at least on paper. By law, vested employees were "locked up" and could not trade their vested shares until several months later. (Several months later, the boom would bust and much of that paper wealth would flutter away, but no one wanted to see that coming.) Akamai was so young, and the boom so frothy, that most employees had not yet vested any shares.

Our cofounder [and chief technology officer], Danny Lewin, had suddenly turned from a struggling graduate student to a staggeringly wealthy man. His share of the company was worth over a billion dollars at the end of the day. It would have turned anyone's head. But at 29, somehow Danny knew that the IPO—this moment of triumph—could also destroy his company. This was because, ironically, the collective efforts of his employees had created value that had made many of them independently wealthy. They did not need to be there anymore, even if the company still needed them.

That day, Danny did something remarkable. In the midst of the IPO celebration, Danny invited everyone to a conference room to discuss his

(continued)

grand vision of the company's future. While green numbers still rose on the monitor, the party room emptied. The conference room filled. Danny, another young redhead who wore faded jeans and white T-shirts, covered whiteboards with his vision. He spun us all up on the immense and powerfully exciting challenges ahead. The same big idea that made investors buy the company would make employees stay to build it.

Source: Annie Bourne, "To Be a Fly on the Wall at Facebook on IPO Day," HBR.org, May 17, 2012.

as an agent and a deal maker for business entities seeking capital. In return for a fee of 6 to 10 percent of the offering price, the investment banker does the following:

1. **Helps the issuing corporation get its regulatory act together:** Specifically, it helps the corporation over the stringent regulatory hurdles that go hand in hand with issuing securities. These hurdles include the development of a prospectus. In its preliminary form, the prospectus provides full disclosure to potential investors about the company, its business, its finances, and the way it intends to use the proceeds of its securities issuance. As mentioned above, the preliminary prospectus is called a red herring.

2. **Sets the price of the securities being offered:** When shares are being offered to the public for the first time, no one knows for certain how they should be priced. Those shares haven't been traded back and forth by willing buyers and sellers, so there is no certainty as to the market-clearing price. The capital-seeking corporation naturally wants its shares priced as high as the market will bear; doing so maximizes the cash going into its coffers. But investors expect a new issue to be priced at a bargain relative to seasoned securities. The investment banker has expertise in this difficult pricing area and mediates between these disparate interests.

3. **Arranges for the distribution of shares:** The issuing corporation may have the shares, but the investment banker has access to potential purchasers. By putting a syndicate of distributing broker-dealers together, the investment banker can "move the merchandise" into the portfolios of pension funds, mutual funds, and individual investors. The investment bank usually takes the shares off the hands of the issuing corporation at a given price, marks them up to some predetermined profitable level, and uses its own distribution channels and those of its syndicate partners to sell them to the investing public. In this sense, the investment banker underwrites the risk of selling hundreds of thousands of shares.

To choose an investment banker, you'll probably have three to five candidates make presentations to you and your leadership team. You should look for a good fit with your industry. They should also have the sales and distribution capabilities you need and should be able to provide good analyst coverage for you once you go public. You'll also be interested in their take on the current market and what they think your valuation should be—and confirmation that they agree that you are ready to go public.

The need for an investment banker

Whatever route you take to secure outside capital, be it an IPO or an alternative, make sure to get the advice of an experienced investment banker. Commercial banks and securities broker-dealers have special departments that do this work. Their services are expensive, but they have the technical expertise and the investor contacts you need to make a favorable deal. For more information on this subject, see the sources listed in "Further Reading" at the end of this book.

Alternatives to an IPO

An IPO can be just the thing a growing company needs to expand to its potential. But very few companies have the size or growth potential for this type of financing. Some enterprises are in industries so out of favor with the investing public that the deal would have few takers. Still other companies deliberately forgo IPOs to avoid the problems associated with going public. Are these companies cut off from substantial equity capital? Are their current owners unable to harvest their investments? The answer is no. There are alternatives to an IPO: sale of a large block of equity via a private placement, and sale of the company itself. We'll consider the first of these alternatives in this chapter and examine company sales in a later chapter.

Private placement refers to the sale of company stock to one or a few private investors instead of to the public. In many cases, these private investors are sophisticated financial institutions such as insurance companies, pension funds, and endowment funds that seek a higher return than could be obtained from public investing. A key benefit of private placement is that these deals are exempt from SEC registration requirements (although some states do have requirements). Thus, the entrepreneurial firm can obtain a sizable piece of capital without the time and expense of a public offering. Nor will its management and business results be subject to the public scrutiny that follows an IPO.

Private placement financing can take several forms: senior or subordinated debt, asset-backed debt, and equity. Because these are private deals, the company and the investor may be able to work out arrangements that suit both parties. For example, if the company prefers debt but the investor insists on an opportunity to share in the firm's upside potential, an investment banker might design a debt instrument with a below-market interest rate (good for the company) but with warrants attached (good for the investor).

A *warrant* is a security that gives the holder the right to purchase common shares of the warrant-issuing company at a stated price for a stated period. The stated price is generally set higher than the current valuation of the shares.

Summing up

- An IPO is a pipe dream for all but a few corporations.

- An IPO brings much-needed cash to a growing company and, for its owners, an opportunity to liquidate and diversify their wealth.

- The downside of an IPO is its expense, absorption of management time, dilution of ownership, ongoing public scrutiny, and pressure to produce short-term gains.

- Consider the right time to go public, weighing current market conditions as well as your interest in keeping control of the company.

- Don't consider an IPO unless your corporation has these qualities: a CEO who knows how to communicate, a deal size of $10 million or more, a record of double-digit growth in revenues and earnings (or earnings clearly ready to follow), outstanding and difficult-to-copy products or services, quality employees, and a logical strategy for growth.

- From the perspective of a cash-hungry US corporation, there are eight steps to an IPO: selecting an underwriter, preparing and filing a registration statement with the SEC, conducting due diligence, distributing a preliminary prospectus (a red herring), mounting a road show by top management, determining the share price and number of shares in the issue, beginning trading, and closing the purchase and sale of shares.

- An investment bank provides two important necessities: the technical knowledge for getting the deal through the registration process and the sales network needed to distribute the company's shares to the investing public.

- A private placement is often a good alternative to an IPO.

PART FOUR

Scaling Up

10.

Sustaining Entrepreneurial Growth

If your company has large growth potential and your goal (and that of your investors!) is to achieve that growth, you'll work together toward increasing your revenue and market share and, ultimately, your profits. You may even pursue a grander vision: to change how people work and live.

Sometimes, scale can make or break a startup, especially if it is a platform business or a web-based marketplace. Reid Hoffman, cofounder of PayPal and LinkedIn, argues that in these types of business, fast scaling is necessary for a couple of reasons. First, it creates value for users. For example, LinkedIn offers a deep user base of professionals, eBay connects both buyers and sellers, and Amazon succeeds with its low margins and high volumes. Companies also need to scale quickly to reach customers faster than their competitors do, for first-mover advantage—the ability to connect with customers and secure their loyalty in a certain segment before anyone else does. Hoffman calls growth at the aggressive rate that these businesses require blitzscaling.

Growth, however, is a mixed blessing—especially rapid growth. As you've seen earlier, infusions of external capital are usually required if the business is to keep pace with a growing demand for its product or service. And every dollar of outside capital has a negative effect. Debt capital raises fixed expenses, making the enterprise more risky. Outside equity capital dilutes the founders' ownership—and control.

Finding more capital is only one of the challenges created by growth. You'll also run into larger challenges in marketing, strategy, human resources, and—perhaps most of all—the transition from entrepreneurial to professional management. In this chapter, we'll address the changes your business needs to make as it grows, and in chapter 11, we'll discuss the accompanying changes in leadership and management.

The impact of growth

Hewlett-Packard Corporation (HP) traces its origin to a small garage in Palo Alto, California. There in 1938, Bill Hewlett and David Packard developed an audio oscillator. Walt Disney Studios ordered eight units to use in producing sound effects for one of its films, *Fantasia*, and the two young engineers formalized their partnership the next year. The enterprise listed two employees that year—Bill and Dave—and reported $5,369 in revenues.

Within a year, HP had more than doubled its revenues, hired another employee, and moved into a larger rented workshop. The war years brought military orders for signal-generating equipment—so many orders that the company had to build a new facility and hire more people to handle all the work. By 1943, the height of the war years, HP had 111 people on its payroll and nearly $1 million in revenues.

Founders Hewlett and Packard learned a thing or two about running a business during those early years and about managing their own transitions from technical whiz kids to leaders and managers. Packard's wartime experience as an army officer no doubt helped. The two men learned rule number one: that management is about getting results through people.

Their own skills were insufficient; Hewlett and Packard had to marshal the talents and energy of many employees.

Innovations in electronics and a surging postwar economy created new challenges for the company founders. They had to identify new market opportunities in the peacetime economy and develop strategies for satisfying them. Equally important, Hewlett and Packard had to develop a style of management and a company culture that would attract talented people and encourage them to contribute to the fullest. That style and culture, later dubbed the HP Way, evolved gradually during the late 1940s and early 1950s.

By contemporary standards, the growth of HP from a two-man partnership to a globe-spanning enterprise with almost ninety thousand employees serving nearly a billion customers seems rather slow. Nineteen years crept by before the company reached the milestone of one thousand employees. How the company should grow and how big it should become were matters of intense internal debate in those days, according to the company's own chroniclers. Even more remarkably, HP did not become a public company until 1957, nearly two decades after Bill and Dave went to work in their Palo Alto garage. That deliberate pace stands in sharp contrast to the record of more recent wunderkind startups. Amazon's revenue was $5.1 million in 1996 and $1.64 billion three years later. Airbnb was founded in August 2008. By 2010, forty-seven thousand people stayed with Airbnb hosts in the summer alone, and by 2015, that number was 17 million. Uber, founded in 2009, has reportedly gone from $688 million in ride-share bookings in 2013 to a reported $10.84 billion two years later.

Your venture may never achieve either this kind of explosive growth or even the slow build to the scale of Hewlett-Packard. But simply breaking out of the startup phase and experiencing moderate growth will expose you to some of the same perilous transitions and challenges those companies and their founders experienced. Expanded adoption and sales trigger requirements for growth in all the activities that support it: customer service, marketing, transaction accounting, and after-sales service, as well as materials purchasing, inventory management, manufacturing, and logistics for physical product. Growing sales oblige you to study new channels of distribution, the feasibility of extending product lines, and possible entry into new markets. New customers create a demand for customer service and for strategies to retain their patronage.

Growing sales must also be supported by growing employee head count—developers, security engineers, marketers, operations, sales, sales support, customer service, and so forth. You must have the human resources staff to recruit staff, comply with labor laws, and manage employee benefits, all on a larger scale. And don't forget about finance. Without a knowledgeable CFO and accounting staff to keep payments, collections, and spending on an even keel, the enterprise could easily capsize and sink. More than a few promising ventures have failed because they did not manage their way through their initial success.

If you've broken out of the startup phase and are experiencing revenue growth, ask yourself three questions:

- Is our strategy sustainable?

- Do we have unique advantages that would let us expand into other markets?

- Is scaling up the business a practical possibility?

Ideally, you will have given these questions much thought in planning your business. Even so, you need to revisit them and recalibrate where necessary. Let's consider each issue in some detail.

Growth strategy

By definition, strategy is what differentiates a business in a way that confers a competitive advantage. Robust revenue growth is evidence that your strategy is working. The question is, How much longer will it continue working? Perhaps your strategy is based on a new and superior product or technology or on your ability to deliver an ordinary product at a lower price or in a manner that is extremely convenient for customers. But what happens if your competitors improve their offerings, the technology matures, new technology arises, or the context changes in some other way?

Few strategies are sustainable over the long term. Eventually, some change will undermine the competitive advantage: new regulation, deregulation, the introduction of a new and superior technology, or a new process for making a product faster, cheaper, or better. In other cases, an entrepreneurial firm (such as yours) creates a new market; if that new market is profitable and expanding, other entrepreneurs will recognize its potential and enter with products or services of their own.

The market for home video is a good example. Blockbuster, founded in 1985, was by 1993 the market leader in home movie and game rentals, with its brick-and-mortar stores almost ubiquitous in towns across America. But when Netflix introduced its mail-service video program in 1999, with no late fees and a much greater variety of videos available, it began making incursions into Blockbuster's business. Additional competition from Redbox and on-demand cable channels further challenged the brick-and-mortar behemoth. Despite several attempts at its own online business, Blockbuster began closing stores in 2006 and ceased operations in 2013.

Could this happen to your business?

To sustain growth, keep looking several steps ahead. Recognize patterns in your industry to anticipate solutions offered by your competitors. Find ways to bar the door to *new* competitors. Netflix did this by using its DVD business as a way to introduce customers to the new technology of streaming video. People who were already Netflix customers found it easy to switch their video-watching habits from DVDs to movies streamed directly and immediately to devices in their homes. By then building its own original-content division, Netflix controlled both the content and a distribution mechanism to customers. The strategy, which became a virtuous circle that competitors had a hard time breaking into, has placed Netflix as a leader in its industry.

It's unlikely that Netflix's strategy would be appropriate for your business, but there are other ways to be the vendor of choice or to discourage rivals from entering your market. Here are a few:

- **Exploit the learning curve.** If you are the first in the market, continual improvement in product design and manufacturing efficiency will allow you to offer your item for less and yet maintain the same profitability. Late-to-market competitors that fail to catch you on the learning curve will be doomed to slim profits or none at all.

- **Don't price for maximum profits.** Competitors are drawn to markets with high profit margins. If you are first in your market, you can make the market unappealing to rivals if you and your investors are willing to price low and accept a modest profit margin. Faced with modest profits, would-be competitors are likely to stay away.

- **Continually refresh your offer to customers.** Think of all the ways you can make your product more appealing: by adding new features or color choices, lowering the price, making it more convenient to purchase, eliminating quality problems, or providing amazing customer service. And think more broadly: how can you reinvent your product to solve an as-yet unmet customer need?

- **Be constantly vigilant about competition.** As you grow, who is going to notice you and try to stop you? How can you change course or refine your strategy to avoid or beat a competitor's challenge?

Such initiatives can create barriers to competition or make you the vendor of choice in a crowded field. Together, they will help you sustain growth.

Expanding into new markets

Does your venture have unique advantages that would help you move successfully into other markets? For example, there may be geographic regions where you currently have no distribution. Assuming that customer needs in those unserved regions are the same as, or similar to, those you are currently satisfying, geographic expansion is the answer—either through your own sales and marketing efforts or indirectly through distributors or a sales representation arrangement.

Other untapped markets may be found within your current geographic range. Here a few ideas for doing so:

- Find new uses for the same product. A classic example: almost every household has a small box of baking soda (sodium bicarbonate) in the kitchen. Most families will not use more than one box per year for cooking. One of the leading suppliers aimed to increase other kinds of consumption of the product. Its advertising campaign encouraged people to put an open box of its baking soda in the refrigerator to absorb food odors. And, of course, it recommended changing that box every month. Mixing baking soda in the cat's litter box was yet another sales-generating idea. This campaign greatly increased sales to existing customers and created many new ones.

- Find ways to alter or customize your product to the needs of other niches. For example, the Swiss manufacturer of Swatch watches learned to develop dozens of unique watches—for men, women, teenagers, sports fans, and other groups—using the very same internal timepiece elements. The only thing that changed was the exterior case design. But that single change enabled the watchmaker to exploit different market niches at very low cost.

What plan does your enterprise have for recharging the growth engine? A steady stream of new products can help, but new-product development is risky and expensive. As these examples indicate, sustained sales growth does not always require invention.

Scaling up your organization

Sales growth challenges the entrepreneurial firm's capacity to keep pace. A service venture that bases its production on employee output must keep hiring qualified people if it hopes to grow. Consider a management consulting firm. Its production is handled through professional employees. Thus, to fuel its growth engine, the firm must hire individuals who can sell and deliver consulting services. Only people with unique skills and experience are capable of providing these services, and some training may also be required. But capable personnel may be in short supply and expensive. The management team would have to ask itself, "Can we scale up our human assets fast enough to satisfy demand and our own expectations of growth?" The same question applies to other service firms.

Product-based businesses must also scale up to meet the demands of growth. For these companies, scaling up ordinarily involves substantial commitments of capital made well in advance of actual sales. For example, a manufacturer must usually plan and begin construction of production facilities a year or more before the first widget comes off the line. Doing so requires both capital and a strong conviction that customer demand will actually be there a year or more in the future.

LinkedIn's Reid Hoffman describes how this kind of rapid growth places demands on the kinds of guidelines businesses typically maintain:

> In hiring, for instance, you may need to get as many warm bodies through the door as possible, as quickly as you can—while hiring quality employees and maintaining company culture. How do you do that? Different companies use different hacks. As part of blitz-scaling at Uber, managers would ask a newly hired engineer, "Who are the three best engineers you've worked with in your previous job?" And then we'd send those engineers offer letters. No interview. No reference checking. Just an offer letter. They've had to scale their engineering fast, and that's a key technique that they've deployed.

This kind of creative thinking—and risk taking—allowed Uber to grow more rapidly than if they had stuck to predetermined processes.

For manufacturing firms, one antidote—at least in the short run—is to outsource (for caveats about this approach, see the box "Tips on outsourcing"). There are usually plenty of competent manufacturers willing to sell unused capacity. This is exactly what Jim Koch, founder of Boston Beer Company, did when he began his venture to brew and distribute Samuel Adams Boston Lager and its various specialty beers. Koch, a sixth-generation brewer, left his management consulting job to start the company. And like most smart entrepreneurs, he started small. He set up an R&D facility inside an abandoned Boston brewery, where he developed his initial recipes. The actual brewing and bottling—capital-intensive activities—were done on a contract basis under the supervision of Koch's brewmaster at a high-quality Pennsylvania brewery. Thus, the entrepreneur maintained control of the features that made his product distinctive; the contract brewery contributed what Koch lacked and scaled his output to customer demand. As Boston Beer Company's sales grew and distribution expanded around the United States, the company employed similar brewery outsourcing arrangements to scale up quickly and without major capital outlays.

Tips on outsourcing

Outsourcing can help you scale up rapidly without creating fixed assets that you cannot afford—or assets that would drag you down if demand were to falter. And it frees up managerial time and attention for the things that really differentiate your company. But observe these two cautions in outsourcing activities to others:

- Avoid outsourcing any activities that connect you directly with customers—such as sales, customer service, market research, and product or service development. These interfaces provide communication links between you and your constituency, enhancing your ability to learn about them and their ability to learn about you. If you outsource these links, your customers will become your outsourcing partner's customers.

- Avoid depending too much on any single outsource partner. Think what would happen if a manufacturing, assembly, or distribution partner were to fail or otherwise stop doing business with you. Hedge your bets by diversifying your outsource relationships.

As your business scales up, it also needs to change. You may need to modify your strategy, reshape your offering, shift your structure, or reconsider how you hire.

Summing up

- Growth forces companies through transitions.

- Continued growth is usually a function of a sustainable strategy, the ability to expand into other markets, and mechanisms for scaling up the volume of output.

- Companies have several mechanisms for sustaining growth. They include (1) exploiting the learning curve to maintain a cost advantage, (2) not pricing for maximum profit (high profits attract competitors), and (3) continually refreshing the offer to customers.

- To scale up, businesses often have to change their guidelines around processes like hiring to make themselves more nimble.

- Companies can often scale up to meet rising demand by outsourcing peripheral tasks to suppliers. However, outsourcing core tasks—particularly those that put the outsource partner in direct contact with customers—can have very bad consequences.

11.

Leadership for a Growing Business

Although sales may seem to be the greatest growth challenge for a growing venture, organizational issues often eclipse it. You and your startup team must periodically reinvent your organization to cope with changing circumstances. As Amar Bhidé of the Fletcher School at Tufts University puts it, "To attain sustainability, the capabilities of the firm (as opposed to those of the entrepreneur) have to be somehow broadened and deepened. More qualified personnel have to be added, the specialization of functions increased, decision making decentralized, systems to cope with a larger and more complex organization instituted, and the employees oriented towards a common long-term purpose." To accomplish all these worthy goals, you and the other founders must usually reinvent yourselves; that is, you must change your mode of working from doing things yourselves to doing things through other people. Many find this reinvention difficult. They fail to change, becoming liabilities to the very companies that they founded.

You and your core team contribute important assets to the company: a common vision, technical skills, management skills, and personal energy and time. Growth puts a strain on each of these contributions:

- Your vision must be instilled in newly hired employees.

- The technical skills that made your startup successful become relatively less important as the need for operational and management skills increases.

- Your founding team's management skills may not be up to the challenge of a larger organization.

- Your personal energy and time are finite, but the need for energy and time to direct and control the expanding enterprise keeps growing.

The right leadership approach for your size

To remain relevant and effective, you and the rest of the leadership team must find new ways to operate. Harvard Business School professor Michael J. Roberts has described the four possible approaches to leading a startup faced with rapid growth:

- Managing content

- Managing behaviors

- Managing results

- Managing context

Roberts describes each of these approaches in more detail. Let's examine them as well.

Managing content

The most direct approach to getting things done is to do them yourself or to directly supervise those who do. Whether it's hiring a new employee, working out the design of a new product, or moving goods through production and into the stockroom, the content manager is intimately involved. In a startup organization, the CEO and leadership team often follow this approach. And why not? The scope of activity is small, and employees are few.

Managing content gives you substantial control. And control appeals to many entrepreneurs, who are often motivated to start their own companies out of an innate need or desire to control their own work and future. But as operations expand, the entrepreneur's time and energy cannot keep pace. Also, his or her ability to make good decisions may falter with the arrival of new challenges that require special skills or experience. Failing to recognize when managing content is no longer appropriate can cause the business to fail.

Managing behaviors

In this approach, according to Roberts, you specify how people should behave; you identify the behaviors that lead to success and codify them through policies, rules, and procedures that employees are told to follow. Unlike the content-oriented manager, the behavior-mode founder of, say, a medical diagnostic laboratory doesn't supervise the day-to-day work of test-lab workers. Instead, the founder trains them to run specific tests and then audits their compliance with that training.

This approach makes better use of your time and effort, enabling you to maintain control over a growing enterprise. Instead of trying to manage everything, you rely on policies, rules, procedures, job design, and behavior-auditing systems to do the heavy lifting.

This approach is most useful when employees are inexperienced or need clear direction. For example, the manager of a newly trained group of salespeople might tell them, "I want each of you to talk with twenty prospective clients every day. Do that, and you should get one new account per day, or five every week. After six months, you'll have a solid base of commission business." If employees agree to this work strategy, the manager can then use his or her time to monitor compliance with the twenty-contact rule, helping where needed.

Managing results

Unfortunately, the manage-behavior approach assumes that you'll get the results you want if people behave in the manner you've prescribed. This doesn't always happen. In the salesperson example just given, maybe talking to the required number of prospects doesn't actually yield a new account every day.

Worse, the approach assumes that your prescription is the only way to reach that goal of five accounts per week. But that's not always the case. In many scientific and engineering endeavors, for example, employees must solve complex problems for which there are no clear guidelines. In these cases, leaders must look to their talented and creative employees to find optimal solutions. A leader using a results approach says, for example, "We need to design a military vehicle that is fuel-efficient (twenty-five miles per gallon on paved roads), that is capable of driving over rough terrain, and that can protect the driver and five passengers from small-arms fire." The leader tells the employees what the result should look like and gives them the responsibility for producing it. Returning to our salesperson example, you might simply tell each employee that the annual goal is to produce a minimum of 150,000 euros in commission revenue.

Results-focused management saves time for time-strapped entrepreneurs. Instead of specifying what people in different jobs should do and how to do it, they can concentrate on providing the resources, the training, and the motivation that people need to produce results.

Managing context

Leaders who take a more context-based approach also focus on results, but they seek it more broadly by shaping the culture, values, and structure of the organization. Generally speaking, they aim to create an environment that will naturally attract and retain highly competent employees and allow them to do their best work. According to Roberts, these managers select employees, develop them, and rely on general communication to shape the context of the work. Upper management spends little or no time telling people what to do or how to do it. In our salesperson example, a leader might give the sales team freedom not only to determine the best way to win new accounts but also to set their own goals. The salespeople might consequently create goals like winning back lapsed accounts or measuring the profitability of certain kinds of accounts to make better decisions about which leads to pursue in the long term.

Is there a best way to manage a startup? Certainly not. But there may be a best mode for a particular company at a particular point in its development. For example, McDonald's owes much of its success to its highly controlled, behavior-mode style of management, which relies on procedures and job design to prepare and serve its products with high efficiency. It would never tell its crews, "Figure out the best way to handle all those customers who are lined up for our food." It has spent years developing an efficient operational blueprint. Yet the rigid, by-the-book rules that work for McDonald's would be disastrous for a creative design company such as IDEO.

So be alert to your current needs, and understand how they are changing. As Roberts warns, the transitions between these approaches need extra attention; as the volume and scope of work grows, the manager has less time for hands-on involvement. While young, small, simple enterprises tend to depend on a content management style, with leadership closer to the front lines, larger and larger organizations call for the other leadership styles in turn.

Which management method are you using today? Is it appropriate for your current state of development and growth? Table 11-1 is Roberts's assessment of when the different approaches are most appropriate, along with the assumptions, behaviors, and tools associated with each.

Although the four leadership approaches discussed in this section may help you think about how best to manage in different circumstances, no law of nature dictates that an executive can use only one mode at any given time. You may find reasons to use more than one mode, depending on the

TABLE 11-1

Four leadership approaches

	Leader's focus			
	Content	**Behavior**	**Results**	**Context**
Situation	Young, small, simple enterprise	Somewhat larger, more involved enterprise	Large, complex organization	Very large, very complex, mature organization
Driving assumptions	Insufficient knowledge, experience to plan Subordinates not capable of independent action or decisions	Too little time to do everything Subordinates can act independently but in accordance with managerial prescription	Too little time Subordinates can achieve better outcomes with their own means	Too little time and knowledge Right people in the right environment with the right mission will succeed
Behavior	On the front lines Barking orders Pitching in to help out	Developing process and procedure Observing	Attending meetings, reviews Studying plans, papers, reports Writing memos	Lots of time on key hires and promotion Tone-setting events
Key skills, tools	Action Decisions	Policies Procedures Behavior audit	Plans Budgets Organizing structure and systems	Communication Leadership by example

Source: Michael J. Roberts, "Managing Transitions in the Growing Enterprise," in *The Entrepreneurial Venture*, 2nd ed., eds William A. Sahlman, Howard H. Stevenson, Michael J. Roberts, and Amar Bhidé (Boston: Harvard Business School Press, 1999), 390.

circumstances. Perhaps a hands-on approach to helping a newly appointed manager succeed is compatible with a results-oriented mode of dealing with the overall operation.

Is it time to change the guard?

Many entrepreneurs have demonstrated a capacity not only to launch a successful venture but also to actively guide it successfully through years of growth. Examples include Larry Page and Sergey Brin at Google, Bill Gates at Microsoft, Herb Kelleher at Southwest Airlines, Scott Cook at Intuit, and Richard Branson at Virgin Group. Each leader successfully adapted his management mode to the needs of the business as it grew and changed. Not all entrepreneurs have this adaptive capacity; they either cannot change the behaviors that served them well in a small, entrepreneurial setting—and habits of behavior are very difficult to change—or they actively resist changes that would dilute their control.

In either case, the inability of the founder-leader to adapt as the enterprise becomes larger and more complex can have these damaging consequences:

- Employee initiative is smothered by the founder's insistence on controlling all activities and making all important decisions. The best employees eventually leave in frustration.

- The organization misses opportunities because it can operate only at the pace of the overworked founder.

- The scope of the enterprise is limited to the knowledge and vision of the founder.

Getting help

Reflect on your own management capabilities and your ability and willingness to change as your business expands. Is your business at a transition point, where your style of leading and management must change? Can you adapt? Are you willing to adapt?

If you are willing to adapt but have difficulty in doing so, find people who can and will give you objective criticism on your leadership style. You'll want people who are not afraid to tell you if your grip on the business is too tight (or too loose) and where you need help. They can also tell you when it's time for you to go—that is, when it's time to bring in professional management. Feedback of this type will help you adjust to the demands of the business and will support the collaboration that every enterprise needs to succeed.

Those whom you ask for this kind of feedback could include other members of the management team and members of your board. Other practical possibilities include the following parties:

Your funders

Entrepreneurs Evan Baehr and Evan Loomis write, "If you want advice for your startup, ask for money. If you want money, ask for advice. To succeed, you will need both." Many of the sources of funding discussed earlier in this book come with experienced entrepreneurial professionals who can give you guidance. For example, serial entrepreneur-turned-venture-capitalist Marc Andreessen believes that the skills that make a good CEO can be taught (whereas those that make a good innovator are more innate), so he sees part of his VC firm's role as specializing in that training. But the author of *The Gig Economy*, Diane Mulcahy, warns that VCs differ widely on how much they actually coach their CEOs. As you're looking into funding, get the names of the CEOs of other companies that the VC is funding. Ask these executives how effective the VC firm's mentoring is.

Talk with the CEOs of the VC firm's other portfolio companies. Ask if the VC partner is accessible, how much they add to boardroom discussion, and whether the CEO has received constructive help in dealing with company problems.

An advisory board

As your business scales, an advisory board can not only act as a sounding board for new ideas, but also provide skills, mentorship, and a broader network. But it can be hard to determine whom to invite onto your board if you don't know yet what kind of expertise you are missing. See the box "How to build a board" for more on how to overcome these challenges and get your board up and running.

An executive coach

Executive coaches provide a one-on-one, customized approach to altering behavior, with the goal of improving on-the-job performance. In general, these professionals follow one of two approaches. The traditional approach, which we will call *diagnosis and development*, has strong roots in psychology and is deeper in its method, but it takes longer to deliver. The other, called the *prescriptive approach*, has more in common with the everyday coaching that managers give to their subordinates. It is faster and more direct. Each approach has its advantages. Executive coaching is expensive, but it may be worth it to you and your company.

Stepping aside

If you cannot or will not adapt to the changing requirements of your company, it may be time to change your role or step aside. There is certainly no shame in either of these options. eBay's Pierre Omidyar, for example, confined himself to the chairman's job, handing the management of the company over to Meg Whitman as CEO; in fact, Omidyar had brought on a VC firm in part to better recruit management expertise to the company. Some people are simply not suited to be leaders of large organizations. Either they lack managerial and interpersonal skills, or the job of business leadership is incompatible with their temperaments or deep-seated life goals. Consider this fictional example:

> Esther is a molecular biologist. She has spent her professional life in university settings, both teaching and conducting funded research. In 2018, she developed a molecule that had potential therapeutic value for use in chickens and turkeys. Under the terms of her employment, she was free to exploit the commercial possibilities of her discovery in return for a 25 percent share claimed by her university. Thanks to her reputation, Esther received seed financing from both the university and a VC firm.
>
> Esther was content in her role as CEO of the business in the early-development stage. The bulk of her time continued to be spent in the lab, where she felt most at home. But as her discovery entered the testing phase and the company hired a product manager and an administrative assistant, she began to feel out of her element. Approval and commercialization of the product made her life less fulfilling. She found that she was wearing her executive hat much more and her lab coat much less. Nor did she like dealing with the VCs who now owned part of her company and the MBAs they virtually forced her to hire. One night, she told her husband,

How to build a board

Look outside your existing network of contacts. As you sit down to think about whom to invite onto your advisory board, remember first that this should not be a group of your friends and fans. You're looking to drive new business opportunities and new ways of thinking with diverse experience, expertise, viewpoints, and skill sets. Work to find people outside your inner circle—people who have built successful businesses and can pass that knowledge on to you. Think about who would be a constructively critical audience and who can provide access to other valuable contacts, from potential customers, suppliers, and strategic partners to financiers, publicists, and other professional service vendors.

Recruit a well-known community member or an industry influencer as your first board member. There is a reason that film producers begin their projects by lining up the most bankable talent they can. The talent's involvement helps attract others who want to work with the celebrity or who simply see a star's commitment as reassurance that the project will take off. In the same way, entrepreneurs should work first to recruit the people who will attract others and who will give an advisory board strong credibility from the start.

Invest the time in developing relationships with your board members. Since most members are not compensated, their reward is the satisfaction of sharing their knowledge and experience and helping you succeed. So make them feel appreciated! (Meanwhile, if a prospective board member does insist on being compensated, determine how uniquely valuable they are. If there's a possibility of a long-term business relationship, you might want to offer that person some kind of remuneration.)

Establish goals and expectations for the board up front, including how often it meets and where. Usually, in-person meetings once every three to six months will suffice, but you may want to reserve the right to consult with individual members on an ad hoc basis if a particular issue comes up. When the board does meet, make sure you have an agenda with specific goals. Your board members are busy professionals, so don't waste their time. Perform a yearly assessment of how the board is working. If you can afford it, invite them to an off-site at a comfortable locale at your expense to have them discuss the board's progress.

Have a framework for changing the board members. Because you are a high-growth entrepreneur, your business will evolve, and you will probably need advisers who bring different skills to the table at different phases of growth. Most members will not have the time to serve on your board for more than two or three years, anyway. And others may not be as helpful as you had hoped. So, make it clear up front that they serve as needed and spell out term limits.

Be clear on the role of your advisory board. Finally, if you're thinking of setting up an advisory board, be very clear on what it is and what it's not. The board is not a formal board of directors, which has well-defined duties, including a fiduciary responsibility. An advisory board holds no legal or financial responsibility for the decisions you make. Instead, it is a group of volunteers with knowledge and skills that you, the business owner, lack, and whose purpose is to help you make your company a success. An advisory board can assist you, challenge you, guide you, and open your eyes to new opportunities.

Source: Adapted from Kerrie MacPherson, "Who Advises the Entrepreneur?" HBR.org, October 22, 2016.

"Now that we've demonstrated the therapeutic value of ChickenFix, everything seems anticlimactic."

Clearly, Esther's heart isn't in her executive role. Her life is dedicated to science and discovery and not to getting regulatory approval, working out manufacturing and distribution arrangements, and building a larger enterprise.

In Esther's situation and that of many others, the best thing a business can do is to bring in professional management, with the founder staying on as chair of the board (the box "Do you need professional management?" can help you decide whether this step is appropriate). This solution also works when the founders are simply incapable of handling the kind of work entailed in business building: negotiating with suppliers, sales, setting up procedures and control systems, dealing with people problems, scrambling for money, and delegating tasks. Unfortunately, many businesses do not recognize the need for professional management soon enough to avoid a crisis.

According to transition experts Eric Flamholtz and Yvonne Randle, founder-entrepreneurs often find it very difficult to let go. Some try to

Do you need professional management?

Does this scenario sound familiar? If so, you should consider professional management for your business.

- Every decision must be made at the top.

- Policies for handling routine functions are almost nonexistent.

- The firm's human resources are not being developed.

- You make decisions, but no one follows through with action.

- Accounting functions are haphazard and amateurish.

- You're having trouble recruiting competent people.

- People are spending a lot of their time putting out fires.

change their behavior as a way of avoiding this step back, but they often fail. Others, the authors write, "merely give the illusion of turning the organization over to professional managers." Flamholtz and Randle cite the case of one founder who hired two experienced managers, made a big deal about how he was turning over the reins, but then continued to control everything himself.

As Flamholtz and Randle explain in *Growing Pains*, their insightful book on the challenges of entrepreneurial growth, "developing certain systems and processes are essential if a firm is to continue to grow successfully and profitably during its life cycle." Professional managers know how to develop those systems and processes, and your company will need them at some point if it continues to grow.

From the perspective of your firm today, how does professional management look? Are you at the point at which a lack of systems and processes is holding the firm back? Are you personally up to the challenge of building the business, or would the company be better off if you stepped aside in favor of experienced managers?

Summing up

- Growth challenges the founding management team, whose members may lack the skills, experience, or temperament for leading a larger, more complex organization

- The work of Michael Roberts describes four modes of management: real-time management of content, management of behavior, management of results, and management of context. The founder and management team must recognize which mode is appropriate under which circumstances and must know when to change from one approach to another.

- A few entrepreneurs have successfully adapted with the growth of their companies. Others must either change themselves (often a difficult prospect), change their roles by bringing in professional management, or cash in their equity and move on to new challenges.

12.

Keeping the Entrepreneurial Spirit Alive

People associate entrepreneurial ventures with innovation. And they are usually right. A successful entrepreneur brings something new to the marketplace—a unique product or service that differentiates the company, gives it a competitive advantage, and even perhaps changes the world in some important way. Entrepreneurial innovation may take the form of a technical advance, such as a thin-screen computer monitor with much higher performance, or a welcome new service, such as smartphone-based taxi hailing. The innovation may also be something that customers never see, such as a breakthrough manufacturing process that slashes time and cost from the manufacturing process. Henry Ford's assembly line accomplished this in the twentieth century; process innovations that enable manufacturers to produce smaller and more complex semiconductor chips at lower cost are a modern equivalent.

Newness that customers view favorably is usually the entrepreneur's wedge for fitting into a profitable market niche. It is difficult to think of successful entrepreneurial firms that aren't good at innovating.

Established companies, in contrast, are often viewed as slow in identifying and exploiting opportunities and as too rigid to innovate. That perception contradicts evidence of innovation in some established companies. Both Honda and Toyota introduced the hybrid automobile to the market—perhaps the single greatest innovation in automotive technology in the previous half century. This feat was not merely technical but matched a real need for substantial emissions reductions and fuel conservation. Corning, a 160-year-old firm, has produced innovation decade after decade, most recently with thin, lightweight, and exceptionally durable glass for smartphones and other electronics. Similarly, 3M continues to uphold its decades-long reputation as a serial innovator.

But for every Honda, Toyota, Corning, and 3M, there are dozens of large firms for which innovation is a forgotten art. When they need innovation, they buy it through acquisition or licensing agreements—and usually from entrepreneurial companies.

Business founders risk losing the entrepreneurial spirit and the ability to innovate as their startup companies grow. This chapter takes a hard look at why many small firms lose their entrepreneurial spark as they succeed. It offers some practical remedies for offsetting this risk.

The challenges

Why are large, established firms less adept at innovation than entrepreneurial firms are? There are three plausible answers: size, the desire to serve existing customers, and complacency. All three reasons are challenges that the entrepreneurial enterprise must confront and defeat as it grows.

The size problem

Size requires specialization of functions, creates communication and coordination problems between functions, and requires management systems —review boards and approval requirements—that often frustrate creative people and impede the pace of idea development. The problems that the founding team solved informally over coffee now require formal meetings involving many people with divergent views. The more people who are involved, the longer it takes to agree on the simplest things. And agreements are more likely to be compromises than optimal solutions.

The existing-customers problem

Businesses understand the importance of customers and the importance of serving and retaining them; *customer-focused* has become almost a buzzword today. When an enterprise serves its existing customers diligently, it faces two consequences that can impede innovation:

- **Existing customers often discourage substantial innovation.** For example, a major technical advance in computing can jeopardize the investments customers have made in existing hardware and systems. Consequently, these customers often urge their vendors to continue supplying them with parts and incremental upgrades—in effect, to stay in their old businesses. Some call this phenomenon the "tyranny of served markets." Companies that slavishly give customers what they want concentrate on incremental innovations to existing products, leaving the invention of truly breakthrough products to their rivals. Ironically, if you keep giving your customers what they want, they will eventually abandon you and switch to more innovative rivals.

- **Management shifts its focus to operations.** The job of serving customers profitably requires operational excellence. As the business grows, the leadership team's attention is increasingly absorbed by people issues, marketing, finance, operations, customer service, and so forth. Innovation can easily slip off the radar.

Complacency

Success begets complacency and self-satisfaction. It tricks people into believing that if they simply continue doing what they are doing, all will be well. Author and scholar Richard Pascale described this phenomenon many years ago as the paradox of success. Success, in his view, plants the seeds of eventual failure.

When faced with a new competing technology, for example, many successful companies have the impulse to invest still further in the technology that made them successful in the first place. This impulse applied, for example, when steamships challenged makers of sailing ships, when Edison's electric lighting systems challenged the gas illumination companies in the late 1800s, and when jet engines challenged piston-driven aircraft engines in the late 1940s. The established companies threatened by these innovations continued to invest in and marginally improve their mature technologies even as the new ones were becoming better and cheaper by the month.

When you launch a new company, your organization is initially untroubled by the problems of size, the tyranny of served markets, and complacency. Success and growth, however, have a way of undermining that advantage. As your organizational infrastructure expands to support growing customer and user bases, your innovative spirit can be gradually dissipated. The challenge to the founding team, then, is to keep the innovative spirit alive as the organization matures.

Fortunately, success and growth are not incompatible with the entrepreneurial spirit, as we saw with Toyota, Corning, and other established companies that continue to innovate. But what can the leadership do to ensure the continued vitality of that spirit? This section contains some practical advice for staying aggressive, innovative, and responsive to market conditions.

Preserve an innovation-friendly culture

The impact of organizational culture on creativity and idea generation is well understood. In the absence of a supportive culture, creativity and innovation will not germinate and grow.

Authors Michael Tushman and Charles O'Reilly explain that in the culture at IBM before CEO Lou Gerstner took over, innovation fell on infertile soil. The culture was, in their words, "characterized by an inward focus, extensive procedures for resolving issues through consensus and 'push back,' arrogance bred by previous success, and a sense of entitlement on the part of some employees that guaranteed jobs without a quid pro quo." If your company's culture is taking on these characteristics, then creativity and innovation are unlikely to flourish. Worse, the most innovative people will become discouraged and dispirited, and they will begin looking for other opportunities.

These questions will help you determine whether your company is losing its creative edge:

- Is our current success making us self-satisfied and complacent?

- Are we inwardly focused?

- Do we punish risk takers who fail?

- Are creative people and new ideas unwelcome or unappreciated in this company?

- Do we fail to reward acts of creativity?

- Do we handle new ideas too bureaucratically?

- Are hierarchy and its symbols creeping into our culture?

If you answered yes to any of these questions, your organizational culture needs a serious evaluation and an adjustment. Three places to look are your physical environment, risk taking and learning, and incentives and rewards.

Enrich the physical environment

A work space that invites face-to-face interactions and chance encounters, especially one filled with many types of creative stimuli, can encourage people to make new connections and to think more broadly about problem solving and finding new opportunities. Casual conversations and spontaneous meetings can spark innovative ideas in unexpected ways. Part of the power of these interactions—which often occur around coffee machines or water coolers and in other public areas such as copy rooms or kitchens—may come from their spontaneity. Note where people already gather informally, and make these areas more inviting places to linger. Add comfortable chairs that encourage people to sit and converse. One company designed staircases wide enough for people to stop and chat. Another placed beanbag chairs in conference rooms to create a more casual atmosphere. Bring in snacks every week or two, and invite your team to take a break just to talk.

Place tools for creativity and communication in unexpected spots. Some organizations leave whiteboards, markers, and flip charts in informal meeting spaces—in the kitchen, for example. These tools inspire people to capture and sketch out ideas during a spontaneous discussion. Other companies distribute crayons and white paper on conference room tables to encourage doodling and making diagrams, enabling a mode of thought that's different from the usual verbal discussion.

Find opportunities for play using games and other stress relievers. Play serves a serious function: when employees are clattering a ball around a foosball table, they may also be subconsciously unwinding a sticky work problem. Giving the conscious mind a break from the problem at hand allows a person to later return to work refreshed—perhaps with a new approach or a unique solution.

Keep in mind, though, that like your diverse team, your organization has many different ways of working and thinking. Beyond these open, collaborative spaces, create areas for quiet work and reflection: a company library where silence is expected or meeting rooms where doors can shut out distractions.

Encourage risk and learning

In addition to considering your company's physical environment, look at its psychological setting. Creative problem solving and inventive thinking will flourish only in an organization that welcomes them. Innovation should be viewed as a normal part of business.

Encourage individuals within your company to take risks. Innovative progress and risk are inseparable. One new idea could easily fail, but another could have great benefits. An organization that recognizes this dynamic must communicate that reasonable risks aren't only acceptable, but are necessary to keep the company moving forward.

Encourage knowledge sharing across the organization. Tightly controlling information limits the opportunity for people's knowledge to combine and intersect in ways that can spur innovation and creative thinking. Make opportunities for your employees to share information and bring new ideas to the fore. Encourage communities of interest, groups of people across the organization with similar passions, to exchange ideas. Urge employees to gain insight from external sources by attending professional meetings and conferences, visiting customers, and meeting experts. The more knowledge that's exchanged and brought into your organization, the more likely it is to be used in creative ways.

Establish a reward system

Inspire idea champions. Network with influential people within your organization, and make sure they see especially creative efforts. Attention from organizational leadership signals to an individual, a team, and the rest of the company that a project is important. And that attention can be a powerful motivator for continued creative work. Executives who stand behind good ideas can provide not only moral support but also protection and resources to new endeavors. Such support—and the rewards that come with it—can further motivate employees to bring their creative ideas to life.

Most people naturally associate the word *reward* with money or bonuses. Such extrinsic rewards—which include additional pay, a vacation, or even special recognition—appeal to a person's desire to attain a goal that is distinct from the work itself. But these external awards aren't the only way to motivate your employees to continue their inventive efforts. Intrinsic rewards can appeal to a person's desire for self-actualization or challenge, to a deep interest and involvement in the work, or to an individual's curiosity or sense of enjoyment.

Four types of intrinsic and extrinsic rewards can support and encourage your employees to continue their inventive efforts:

1. **Recognition:** A sense of making progress is a powerful motivator. Publicly acknowledge an individual or a group with an announcement or award. For example, ask a high-level executive to share his

or her appreciation for what a team is doing. Or publicly recognize people who have worked outside their preferred style or function.

2. **Control:** Involve an individual or a group in a decision that affects them. Grant them the autonomy to solve problems on their own. For example, after a successful customer engagement event, invite your team members to choose a new marketing opportunity to think about next. Or give them increasingly challenging projects to tackle that pique their interests.

3. **Celebration:** Applaud a successful venture by throwing a small party. Toast a new product's launch, or take your employees out to dinner after successfully launching a redesigned website.

4. **Rejuvenation:** Offer time off or time away from a given task. Give team members extra vacation days for breaking your company's core cereal brand into a new international market. Or send individuals to industry conferences so that they can develop their skills, build relationships, and come back to work renewed and energized.

You can stimulate *and* sustain your team's creative energy—and help people make progress every day—with a thoughtfully constructed system of rewards and support in an atmosphere of openness. A culture that builds creative momentum can help you lead your team to generate and implement new solutions to the tough challenges you face.

Establish vision and strategic direction

If innovative people lose sight of where the company should be heading, they are likely to generate and pursue ideas that don't fit, that eat up resources, and that eventually will be rejected before commercialization. A loss of vision thus costs money and dissipates the energy of idea generators.

As a company grows, keep it focused on its mission. PayPal and LinkedIn founder Reid Hoffman expands on this idea: "Almost every blitzscaling org that I have seen up close has a lot of internal unhappiness. Fuzziness about roles and responsibilities, unhappiness about the lack of a clearly defined sandbox to operate in. 'Oh my God, it's chaos, this place is a mess.' The thing that keeps these companies together—whether it's PayPal, Google, eBay, Facebook, LinkedIn, or Twitter—is the sense of excitement about what's happening and the vision of a great future."

This vision can help the innovative team focus. Because both creative energy and money are scarce commodities, it makes sense to encourage your team to generate ideas within the boundaries defined by your company strategy. For example, if your e-commerce site focuses on active women's professional apparel, encourage ideas that fall within the boundaries of "better connections with our customers" and "fast and accurate order fulfillment." Within those strategy-related boundaries, new ideas for improving customer intelligence, order processing, and logistics should be welcomed. If you set the boundaries right, your company's creative energies will naturally focus themselves in areas with the greatest payoff potential.

And don't forget your competitors: always be thinking about who is going to be coming after your space and how. Cannibalize yourself before someone else can do it. For example, to avoid cannibalizing its highly successful line of iPods, Apple could have held off on introducing the iPhone or avoided including iPod features in its new product. And certainly, the established iPod line lost revenue once the iPhone was introduced. But Apple as a whole benefited.

Be personally involved with innovation

As your company grows, operational issues will begin to eat up your time. This is natural. But don't allow operational humdrum to detach you from the innovation on which your future depends. Some of the best and most successful executives have been happiest and most effective when they were in the R&D lab rubbing elbows with bench scientists and technicians. Leaders cannot make good decisions about R&D if they operate in a vacuum or think of innovation as a mysterious force. They must understand the technical issues facing their organizations and the portfolio of ideas and projects that are in the pipeline at any given time.

So stay very close to sources of innovation within your company as it grows. Visit the research people regularly. Have lunch with project teams. Get to know key people one-on-one. Understand the technical hurdles that stand between appealing ideas and their commercialization. Staying close to innovative activities has several benefits:

- It sends a powerful signal to employees that innovation matters.

- It provides entrepreneurial leaders with opportunities to articulate the strategic direction of the enterprise and the boundaries within which innovation should be pursued.

- It keeps you up-to-date on technological advances, customer trends, and market trends.

Continually improve the idea-to-commercialization process

Chances are that the innovative idea that spawned your company was conceived and developed informally. You didn't have approval committees and proposal documentation and approval processes to deal with. The growth that follows success, however, makes such processes both necessary and useful. Indeed, companies that continue to innovate and grow have a process for generating ideas, experimenting with them, evaluating promising ideas, and recognizing which have commercial potential, followed by development and commercialization. You will need such a process, too; otherwise, your innovative efforts will be ad hoc, arbitrary, and a waste of resources. A good innovation process does the following:

- Generates a sufficient number of good ideas

- Is free of the bottlenecks that impede development and frustrate innovators

- Is free of politics

- Encourages calculated risk taking

- Is not arbitrary

- Creates cheap failures

- Channels resources to the worthiest projects

- Involves people who understand the company's capabilities, its strategy, and its customers

Like the shaping of organizational culture, developing and improving the innovation process is a job for founders and the leadership team. And it's one of the most important jobs they will ever handle.

Apply portfolio thinking

Many entrepreneurial firms, particularly in the tech space, are launched with only one or two products in process. That makes organizational life simple: all resources, brainstorming, and marketing can be concentrated on those one or two things. As these companies succeed and grow, however, they may have dozens of funded projects in play at any given time. Some may be low-risk, short-term projects that aim to incrementally improve an existing product. Others may represent radically new concepts that aim to create new markets. Still others may fall between these two extremes.

Because incremental and radical projects entail substantial differences in risk levels, time frames, and potential payoffs, it's helpful to think of them in terms of a portfolio. Portfolio thinking helps you see a set of ongoing projects in terms of risk-versus-return characteristics. And when you understand those characteristics, you can shape and manage the portfolio to achieve the right balance of risk and potential return.

As a first step toward portfolio thinking, create a visual map of your ongoing projects like the one in figure 12-1. Here, the horizontal axis indicates the maturity or newness of market or technology factors. The vertical axis indicates rising levels of technical challenge, uncertainty, and economic opportunity. Each circle in the matrix represents a project, and the size of each circle indicates the magnitude of the resources currently dedicated to it.

FIGURE 12-1

Innovation portfolio

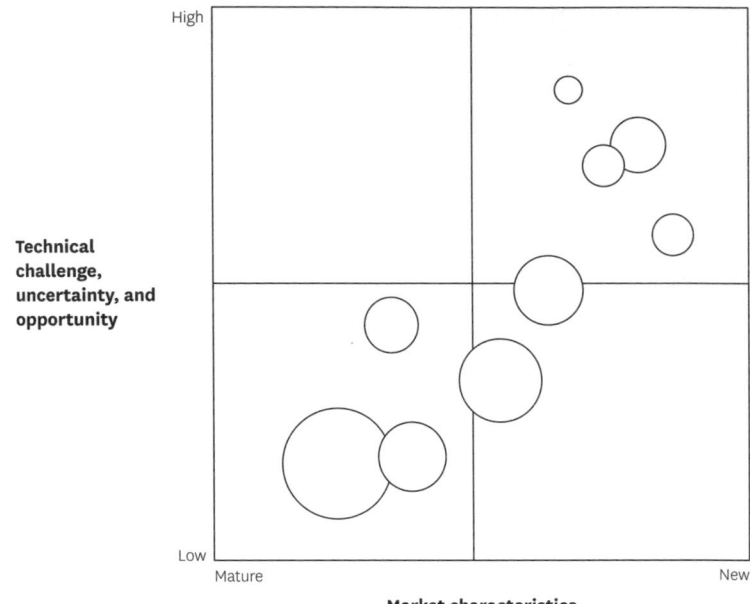

In the map shown here, the biggest projects are cautious. They have mature technical and market characteristics. As a result, these projects are among the least technically challenging and involve the least risk and potential opportunity for the company. In contrast, the small projects in the upper-right quadrant involve higher technical risk and address new markets, but they also hold the prospect for greater economic opportunity for the company.

Try constructing a similar map for your company. When you've mapped out your current projects, what does it tell you? If most projects and re-sources are located in the lower-left quadrant, your company is being very risk-averse and may be doing too little to address future opportunities, new technologies, and new markets. On the other hand, if most projects

Tips for making good innovation decisions

Keeping the entrepreneurial spirit alive means continually pushing into uncharted terrain with R&D projects, market initiatives, and human resource investments. Each of these areas involves making decisions without perfect information, under conditions of uncertainty. Here are a few tips that can help you make those decisions as well as possible:

- Exclude friends and "yes people" from your leadership team and board of directors. You need solid advice and blunt, honest feedback as you consider investment in an innovative idea.

- Surround yourself with people who have complementary skills and different approaches to analyzing issues and making decisions. Listen to their suggestions and arguments, even when you disagree. These other voices can help you avoid walking off a cliff.

- Learn when to cut your losses. You cannot win the game if you don't play. But don't play every game to the end. Like a good poker player, recognize when you're pouring resources into a losing hand, and have the courage to walk away with your losses.

- Double-check your assumptions. What looks rosy can be a disaster if those assumptions are not realistic.

and resources are in the upper-right quadrant, your firm is being very aggressive, perhaps dangerously so.

What would constitute a suitable risk-to-reward balance for your company? As the entrepreneurial leader, can you articulate that balance to your employees and investors?

As you consider your choices, consult the box "Tips for making good innovation decisions."

Hire people who have entrepreneurial attitudes

The most important decisions an entrepreneur makes as the company grows involve hiring. Growth creates a need for new employees, but what types of people are most likely to be successful innovators?

Look for people who think beyond their own roles and who look to the organization and beyond. They should understand the patterns of your industry, internalize your strategy, and connect this insight with their own work. People who are narrowly interested in applying their technical skills will rarely produce the practical innovations you need.

New hires in general should have the following qualities:

- Be comfortable with change.

- View unmet needs as opportunities.

- Adopt appropriate time horizons.

- Be comfortable with failure.

- Have an experimental mindset.

- Enjoy collaborative work.

- Think and act like entrepreneurs.

Some observers say that those with a liberal arts background can be a particularly good fit for innovative roles. People with such backgrounds are used to dealing with big ideas, complexity, ambiguity, writing, and communications.

People being hired as supervisors or managers should be comfortable with the idea of participative management. Anything else will lead to the kind of hierarchical, bureaucratic environment that kills the entrepreneurial spirit.

Create an ambidextrous organization

Leaders of fast-growing entrepreneurial companies quickly find themselves being tugged in two directions. On the one hand, you need to focus on the innovations required to sustain growth. On the other, you must run an operationally effective organization. How can you possibly do both?

The source of the challenge is not hard to understand. Success in the current business is usually driven by certainty, efficiency, and cost control. The future business, conversely, depends on an innovation process that is uncertain, inefficient, and costly. Few executives can operate successfully in these two different worlds. Most become absorbed with one world, to the detriment of the other. In most cases, the immediate problems of the business dominate their time and attention, leaving the future business to be treated as a stepchild.

Tushman and O'Reilly suggest that leaders create "ambidextrous" organizations—that is, organizations that can "get today's work done more effectively and anticipate tomorrow's discontinuities." These are seemingly contradictory capabilities, but ambidextrous enterprises can excel in the present even as they create the future.

How to do this? Innovation experts from Clayton Christensen to Vijay Govindarajan suggest creating separate areas of your organization to foster discontinuous innovation. As Govindarajan explains, you should not distract those doing today's work at high performance levels with the work of innovation. And similarly, according to Christensen, those working on innovation need to have different goals, values, and processes from those of the core business.

Summing up

- Growth challenges the entrepreneurial spirit. Size creates specialization of functions, communication problems, and control systems that frustrate creativity and idea development.

- Once a company has customers, the tyranny of served markets can block a company's capacity to innovate.

- The success that accompanies growth often leads to complacency, which is antithetical to the entrepreneurial spirit.

- Establish the strategic direction within which innovation should take place.

- Entrepreneurial leaders can keep the spirit alive if they (1) preserve an innovation-friendly culture, (2) establish a strategic direction, (3) remain personally involved with innovation, (4) continually improve the idea-to-commercialization process, (5) apply portfolio thinking to their innovative efforts, (6) hire people with entrepreneurial attitudes, and (7) create an ambidextrous organization that is effective at both getting today's work done (operations) and anticipating the future.

PART FIVE

Looking to the Future

13.

Harvest Time

Some entrepreneurs pass on their businesses to family members. The majority, however, eventually look for an opportunity to harvest the monetary value they have created—value that is locked up in the enterprise. This chapter examines the motivations that lead to an exit, the primary mechanisms for using an exit to harvest the company's value, and the methods used to determine the right value for the business.

Why entrepreneurs cash out

There are probably as many reasons for harvesting an investment as there are entrepreneurs. Retirement is one reason. An offer "too good to refuse" is yet another. Most investment harvesting, however, tends to be motivated by one or another of the following reasons:

- **A need to diversify wealth:** Successful entrepreneurs can easily get into a position in which most of their wealth is dangerously concentrated in one basket. Their net worth could easily be wiped out by a change in technology, the emergence of powerful competitors, or some other business setback. Harvesting gives the entrepreneur an opportunity to diversify personal wealth.

- **The business has reached the end of its line:** Some successful entrepreneurs sense where the wind is blowing, and sometimes they sense an ill wind. More specifically, they realize that their business has gone about as far as it can go, at least under their leadership. They recognize that continued growth would require a new level of investment that they are not interested in making. In other cases, they can feel the competitive environment turning against them, as when the owner of several hardware stores finds that the business must now go head-to-head with a national chain having enormous buying power.

- **The owner's urge to begin anew:** Some entrepreneurs are motivated by the challenge of creating something out of almost nothing. They love the early phase of business building. But when operational concerns begin to absorb most of their time, they are happy to move on.

Harvesting mechanisms

When you have decided to cash out, the next step is to determine which harvesting method is most timely and appropriate. This section examines the most common harvesting methods as well as their advantages and shortcomings. (See the box "Shearing versus selling" if you are interested in something less than full harvesting, that is, if you only want to liquefy some of your capital.)

Initial public offering

We described the role of the IPO in harvesting entrepreneurial investments in chapter 9. When a public market for a firm's shares has been established, its founders as well as its private investors can, within certain regulatory restrictions, sell some or all of their shares. Those restrictions, however, may hold up share sales by insiders for some period and may put a cap on the number of shares that the holder of restricted shares can sell in any one-month period (SEC Rule 144). (For information on SEC Rule 144, see appendix D.)

The investment banker underwriting the deal will also require key pre-IPO shareholders to sign a lockup agreement barring them from selling their shares during a specific period after the company goes public. This lockup, which may last up to six months, ensures that insiders will not dump their shares onto the market, causing losses for the public investors who stepped forward to buy shares of the IPO.

Few firms ever qualify for an IPO in any case; they are either too small or too limited in their potential, or they are in a moribund industry that doesn't attract investor interest. Even those that qualify have plenty of reasons to avoid the harvesting IPO route: deal-making costs, public scrutiny of the firm's operations, reporting requirements, and so forth. These reasons may not trouble private investors (e.g., venture capitalists); their primary interest is often to quickly cash out, lock in a high rate of return, and move on to the next opportunity.

Perhaps the best case for harvesting via an IPO is the higher price that is often obtained through this means than through others. This is particularly true when investor appetite for new shares is high.

Mergers and acquisitions

Many more harvests are accomplished through mergers and acquisitions than through IPOs. Each year, thousands of companies join with others in some form of strategic merger. Perhaps as many are snapped up by other companies that seek to capture their patents, product lines, or manufacturing capabilities or something else.

Because the typical entrepreneur has no experience with the complex transactions of mergers and acquisitions, you should enlist experienced legal and financial advisers to help with any proposed deal. The transactions are particularly complicated when neither of the participants is a public company whose share value can be determined from actual public trading. In these cases, valuations must be conducted.

In general, give careful attention to the following three issues as you approach a merger or acquisition deal:

- **How the deal is valued:** Different valuation methods produce different results.

- **How payment will be structured:** Payment may be in the form of cash, some mix of cash and the stock of the acquiring company, or debt. In a merger, the entrepreneur may end up with the stock of a newly formed company. Cash is the ideal form of payment because all other forms tie up the entrepreneur's capital in the other company for some period. But not all stock-in-payment deals are bad. For example, Sabeer Bhatia received 2.7 million shares of Microsoft when he sold his company, Hotmail, to the software giant. The shares of other acquiring companies may be less solid.

- **The relationship between the selling entrepreneur and the merged or acquired company:** Many deals provide for some period of managerial involvement by the seller. The seller may even welcome this arrangement. Approach these arrangements with care, however, because the acquirer is unlikely to give you the free hand you enjoyed in running the business that was once yours.

Employee stock ownership plan

An employee stock ownership plan (ESOP) is another harvesting option for a company that lacks a public market for its shares. An ESOP is a formal plan under which corporate shares are acquired by the plan on behalf of employees, for whom it is a tax-qualified retirement plan. In effect, the ESOP acts as a market for the owner's shares, purchasing those shares gradually over a period of years. Consider this hypothetical example:

> *Macmillan Metal Works was a closely held corporation with eighty full-time employees. Howard Macmillan, the founder, owned all the shares. Most of his family's wealth was tied up in the company, and Howard had few means of getting it out other than selling the*

enterprise. Howard learned from his attorney that an ESOP could
meet several of his goals at once: provide a retirement plan for his
employees, give employees an ownership interest in the business,
and allow him to gradually cash out his shares.

The attorney set up a plan, and Howard hired a business ap-
praiser to develop a valuation for company shares. Using this
valuation, he sold two thousand shares that year to the plan.
Qualified employees were then committed to purchasing specified
numbers of shares each year, with Macmillan Metal Works con-
tributing part of the purchase price. The sales proceeds, of course,
went to Howard Macmillan, who used the cash to diversify his
investment assets.

The ESOP harvest approach has disadvantages. Company shares must
be valued through an independent business appraisal every year, a process
that can be costly for a small company. What's more, the employee members of the plan will one day own a majority of the shares, something that
you as the founder may not like.

Another disadvantage involves the employees themselves. ESOPs are
not always a good thing for them. Tying up part or all of their retirement
funds in the shares of a single company (their employer) puts them in a
doubly nondiversified position. A serious setback for the company could
result in both a loss of employment and a loss of retirement fund value. The
huge personal losses suffered by employees of Enron Corporation in the
early 2000s exemplify what can happen when employees have both their
net worth and their current income tied up in a single enterprise.

Selling to management

Senior managers represent another potential set of buyers if you are seeking to harvest your investment. These senior managers understand the
company and the industry. They know the cash-generating potential of the
business as well as anyone. So it is not surprising when an employee group
offers to buy the company from the founding owner. These cases are often
referred to as management buyouts.

In many cases, the buyer group can use the assets of the company as collateral for loans they need to finance the purchase. After the purchase is made, the buyers find themselves with a very high debt-to-equity ratio—sometimes 10:1—and staggeringly large interest payments. Typically, management responds by selling the firm's operating units that are either underperforming or that don't fit management's new strategy. Managers also sell the corporate aircraft and nonessential property to pay down large chunks of the debt immediately. At the same time, the new owners increase the amount of free cash by reducing employee head counts, cutting expenses, and reducing inventories.

This type of transaction is called a leveraged buyout, an approach that was practiced widely during the 1980s, often by outside "raiders" who recognized that the separate parts of a company could be sold for much more than the company's total market value.

Most of the leveraged-buyout deals of the 1980s relied on substantial outside debt capital in the form of high-yield, or junk, bonds, an approach that is seldom available to today's buyer groups. Consequently, the selling owner today may have to act as lender, taking a collateral-backed note in payment for his or her share of the company. The owner's harvest in these cases is spread out over many years of principal and interest payments by the buying group.

Although they get much less press these days, leveraged buyouts still accounted for $70.5 billion in US company sales transactions in 2016. In general, the best candidates for these buyouts are companies with high levels of predictable free cash flow, few requirements for capital spending, little debt, and substantial nonessential assets.

Selling to a new owner

While selling your business to current management ensures that the company will remain in the hands of those experienced in running it, another option is to sell your business to a completely new owner. Business brokers who specialize in businesses of your size can help connect you with qualified buyers—typically these brokers work with businesses valued up to $20 million. They work on a commission that you'll pay mostly when the

Shearing versus selling

Selling is a way for you to get a substantial amount of capital out of your company, particularly when you want to walk away and do something else with your life. For many owners, however, walking away isn't the issue; nor is receiving all their capital at once a primary goal. Some owners are content to periodically withdraw some of their capital to improve their living standards, to gain retirement income, or to diversify. If this is your goal, you could pocket whatever cash flow is not needed to maintain or expand your business.

Successful ventures generate more cash flow than the amount they need to maintain a steady state condition. Growth-oriented owners reinvest that excess cash in the business: to expand the sales force, to acquire or develop new product lines, to open new retail locations, and so forth. But if you want to liquefy some of your capital, you can pocket this excess cash instead of reinvesting it. This "shearing" of company cash flow will limit your company's ability to finance continued growth through internally generated cash. But for some owners, growth may no longer matter; their companies may be as large as they can comfortably handle. And if you do want continued growth, you may be able to substitute debt capital for internally generated cash flow. In that case, you will get part of your equity capital, and your business will experience a change in its debt-to-equity ratios.

deal is finalized. Most brokers are members of professional groups that you can approach for broker listings, for example, the International Business Brokers Association, the Association for Corporate Growth, the Alliance of Merger & Acquisition Advisors, or the Association of Professional Merger and Acquisitions Advisors.

When you sell, you will need to decide (and negotiate with your buyer) whether you are selling the company's assets or its stock. Selling the assets means that the buyer is getting just the physical elements of the business: its employees, its buildings, its equipment, and intangibles like trademarks and goodwill. Things like liability, however, stay with you: if an employee you hired files a lawsuit, you may be liable. Selling the stock may therefore be more beneficial to you; it means that the company itself shifts to the new owner's responsibility.

Timing matters

No matter which method of harvesting you use, you need to select the proper time. The only exception to the strategies mentioned here is the ESOP, which features the sale of stock over many years, in both good times and bad.

What applies to the IPO market applies also to other forms of harvesting: the mood of investors—and business buyers—swings like a pendulum between optimism and fear. Buyers who are giddy with optimism will pay much more for a business than they will during periods of fear. Be alert to the mood of investors in timing the sale of shares or of the entire business.

What's it worth?

With the exception of the shearing method, valuation is at the heart of each harvesting mechanism described in this chapter. Valuation attempts to answer a fundamental question: "What is this company really worth?" If you cannot answer that question, you will be in a poor position to negotiate a deal.

Values for an IPO

The share value in an IPO is generally a function of what the marketplace of investors will accept and what the future of the company appears to hold. Thus, the deal's underwriter will look at the mood of investors, the price of comparable public corporate shares relative to earnings, the company's current and anticipated financial performance, proprietary technology, and growth potential. In light of this less-than-scientific process, the underwriter will suggest an issuing price per share, one that is slightly discounted to the anticipated trading level of the shares. That discount is meant to put initial investors in a profitable position when trading begins.

More-rigorous valuation methods

Other harvesting mechanisms rely on more rigorous methods of evaluating the worth of the company. Although appendix C explains these methods and their strengths and weaknesses in some detail, we'll summarize them here as well. The two most reliable valuation approaches are the earnings-based method and the discounted cash-flow method (see the box "Working with a business appraiser" for recommendations about who should conduct a valuation of your business).

Earnings-based valuation

The earnings-based method multiplies one or another earnings figure from the income statement by some number. For example, a valuation specialist might find that similar companies in the same industry are selling at roughly five times their earnings before interest and taxes (EBIT).

A more exacting approach adds back any depreciation or amortization charges that reduced income statement earnings, because those are noncash expenses. This more exacting figure is called EBITDA (earnings before interest and taxes plus depreciation and amortization).

The idea in both cases is to attach the multiple to the cash flows actually available to the owner. Thus, if EBIT for an entrepreneurial firm were $2 million and if similar companies in the industry were selling for five times that multiple, the value of the firm would be $10 million.

The multiple used in these valuations shouldn't appear from outer space. Rather, it should correspond with what other investors have paid recently for the EBIT of comparable companies that were on the sales block. So be very careful about the multiple you use, because it can make a huge difference in the estimated value of your company. You should also understand that multiples, as with price-earnings ratios for company stock, float up and down with the moods and expectations of investors. When an industry is out of favor and when investors are pessimistic about future prospects, its multiple will slide downward. The opposite happens when an industry is in favor or when prospects for earnings growth are favorable. The lesson to the selling entrepreneur is to sell when investors are giddy with optimism.

Discounted cash-flow (DCF) valuation

The key drawback of this multiple-of-earnings method is that it is not forward-looking. It bases value on current earnings, not on future ones. Thus, a firm with rapidly growing earnings would probably be short-changed by this type of valuation.

The remedy is to consider the firm's value in terms of its stream of future cash flows. It is that stream of future earnings, after all, that investors are buying. As described by Tom Copeland, Tim Koller, and Jack Murrin, authors of what many consider the bible of valuation, "The DCF approach captures all the elements that affect the value of the company in a comprehensive yet straightforward manner."

The DCF valuation method requires a forecast of cash flows extending several years into the future and the application of time-value-of-money calculations. It discounts those cash flows to their present value. Professional help is usually needed to implement these requirements.

Working with a business appraiser

Business valuation isn't likely to be the entrepreneur's area of expertise. Nor is it an issue that matters more than once or a few times during a business career. Nevertheless, valuation's impact on the outcome of harvesting is huge. Consequently, the entrepreneur should learn as much as possible about this technical field—or at least enough to work with a professional business appraiser and make intelligent decisions.

Summing up

- Entrepreneurs seek to harvest their investments for several reasons. Key among them are to diversify their wealth, to take the business to a higher level, or to try something new.

- Although it is available to very few enterprises, an IPO can give the entrepreneurial team liquidity over time.

- For most companies, selling the company through an acquisition is a more likely harvesting mechanism than is an IPO. In an acquisition, the entrepreneurs should pay close attention to how the deal is valued, how payment will be structured (cash, stock, debt), and how any ongoing relationship with the acquiring entity or merger partner will be defined.

- An ESOP is a tax-qualified retirement plan that purchases owner shares over a period of years. In effect, the owner sells to the employees.

- In many cases, the members of a business's management group will join together to buy out the founder-owner. They can do so through a leveraged buyout or through a debt arrangement with the seller.

- One popular approach to business valuation multiplies earnings before interest and taxes (EBIT) times a number called a multiple. The multiple should correspond with what other investors have paid recently for the EBIT of comparable companies.

- The discounted cash-flow (DCF) approach to valuation provides a better measure of company value because it is future oriented.

Understanding Financial Statements

What does your company own, and what does it owe to others? What are its sources of revenue, and how has it spent its money? How much profit has it made? What is the state of your company's financial health? This appendix helps you answer those questions by explaining the three essential financial statements: the balance sheet, the income statement, and the cash-flow statement. The appendix also helps you understand some of the managerial issues implicit in these statements and broadens your financial know-how through a discussion of two important concepts: financial leverage and the financial structure of the firm.

If you have a business degree or senior management experience, you may already know as much as you need to know about these topics. But many entrepreneurs have neither. For example, Ken Olsen, the legendary founder of Digital Equipment Corporation in the late 1950s, knew all about electrical engineering and programming, and he had terrific ideas for building a new generation of computers. But he knew next to nothing about financial statements, which the venture capitalists (VCs) wanted him to include in his business plan. According to entrepreneurial lore, Olsen went to the public library, borrowed a copy of Paul Samuelson's famous economics textbook, found an example of a balance sheet and income statement, and used them as models for his projected figures. The VCs were impressed and gave him the money he needed to develop his business.

If you're already knowledgeable about financial statements, you can skip this appendix. But the ability to read and interpret financial statements is essential for the enterprising businessperson. So if you're more like Olsen, this appendix gives you an introduction to the fundamentals. For more details, we recommend the *HBR Guide to Finance Basics for Managers*.

Why financial statements?

Financial statements are the essential documents of business. Managers use them to assess performance and identify areas that require their intervention. Shareholders use them to keep tabs on how well their capital is being managed. Outside investors use them to identify opportunities. And lenders and suppliers routinely examine financial statements to determine the creditworthiness of the companies with which they deal.

Publicly traded companies are required by the Securities and Exchange Commission (SEC) to produce financial statements and make them available to everyone as part of the full-disclosure requirement the SEC places on publicly owned and traded companies. Companies not publicly traded are under no such requirement, but their private owners and bankers expect financial statements nevertheless.

Financial statements—the balance sheet, the income statement, and the cash-flow statement—follow the same general format from company to company. And even though specific line items may vary with the nature of a company's business, the statements are usually similar enough to allow you to compare one business's performance against another's.

The balance sheet

Many people go to a doctor once a year to get a checkup—a snapshot of their physical well-being at a particular time. Similarly, companies prepare balance sheets as a way of summarizing their financial positions at one point in time, usually at the end of the month, the quarter, or the fiscal year.

In effect, the balance sheet describes the assets controlled by the business and shows how those assets are financed—with the funds of creditors (liabilities), with the capital of the owners, or with both. A balance sheet reflects the following basic accounting equation:

Assets = Liabilities + Owners' Equity

Assets in this equation are what a company invests in so that it can conduct business. Examples include cash and financial instruments, inventories of raw materials and finished goods, land, buildings, and equipment. Assets also include money owed to the company by customers and others—an asset category referred to as accounts receivable.

Now look at the other side of the equation, starting with liabilities. To acquire its necessary assets, a company often borrows money or promises to pay suppliers for various goods and services. Moneys owed to creditors are called liabilities. For example, a company that makes smartphone cases may acquire $1 million worth of plastic for molding from a supplier, with payment due in thirty days. In doing so, the company increases its inventory assets by $1 million and increases its liabilities—in the form of accounts payable—by an equal amount. The equation stays in balance. Similarly, if the same company were to borrow $100,000 from a bank, the cash infusion would increase its assets by $100,000 and its liabilities by the same amount.

Owners' equity, also known as shareholders' or stockholders' equity, is what is left after total liabilities are deducted from total assets. Thus, a company that has $3 million in total assets and $2 million in liabilities would have owners' equity of $1 million.

$$\text{Assets} - \text{Liabilities} = \text{Owners' Equity}$$

$$\$3,000,000 - \$2,000,000 = \$1,000,000$$

If $500,000 of this same company's uninsured assets burned up in a fire, its liabilities would remain the same, but its owners' equity—what's left after all claims against the assets are satisfied—would be reduced to $500,000:

$$\text{Assets} - \text{Liabilities} = \text{Owners' Equity}$$

$$\$2,500,000 - \$2,000,000 = \$500,000$$

Thus, the balance sheet "balances" a company's assets and liabilities. Notice, for example, that the total assets equal total liabilities and owners' equity in the balance sheet of Amalgamated Hat Rack, our sample company (table A-1). The balance sheet also shows how much the company has invested in assets and where the money is invested. Further, the balance sheet indicates how much of those monetary investments in assets comes from creditors (liabilities) and how much comes from owners (equity). Analysis of the balance sheet can give you an idea of how efficiently a company is using its assets and how well it is managing its liabilities.

Balance-sheet data is most helpful when compared with the same information from one or more previous years. Consider the balance sheet of Amalgamated Hat Rack. First, this statement represents the company's financial position at a moment in time: December 31, 2017. A comparison of the figures for 2016 against those for 2017 shows that Amalgamated is moving in a positive direction: it has increased its owner's equity by $397,500.

Assets

You should understand some details about this financial statement. The balance sheet begins by listing the assets most easily converted to cash: receivables, inventory, and prepaid expenses. These are called current assets, generally, those that can be converted into cash within one year.

Next, the balance sheet tallies other assets that are tougher to convert to cash—for example, buildings and equipment. These are called plant

TABLE A-1

Amalgamated Hat Rack balance sheet as of December 31, 2017

	2017	2016	Increase (Decrease)
Assets			
Cash and marketable securities	$652,500	486,500	166,000
Accounts receivable	555,000	512,000	43,000
Inventory	835,000	755,000	80,000
Prepaid expenses	123,000	98,000	25,000
Total current assets	2,165,500	1,851,500	314,000
Gross property, plant, and equipment	2,100,000	1,900,000	200,000
Less: Accumulated depreciation	333,000	290,500	(42,500)
Net property, plant, and equipment	1,767,000	1,609,500	157,500
Total assets	$3,932,500	3,461,000	471,500
Liabilities and owners' equity			
Accounts payable	$450,000	430,000	20,000
Accrued expenses	98,000	77,000	21,000
Income tax payable	17,000	9,000	8,000
Short-term debt	435,000	500,000	(65,000)
Total current liabilities	1,000,000	1,016,000	(16,000)
Long-term debt	750,000	660,000	90,000
Total liabilities	1,750,000	1,676,000	74,000
Contributed capital	900,000	850,000	50,000
Retained earnings	1,282,500	935,000	347,500
Total owners' equity	2,182,500	1,785,000	397,500
Total liabilities and owners' equity	$3,932,500	$3,461,000	$471,500

assets or, more commonly, fixed assets (because it is hard to change them into cash).

Because most fixed assets, except land, depreciate—or become less valuable—over time, the company must reduce the stated value of these fixed assets by something called accumulated depreciation. Gross property, plant, and equipment minus accumulated depreciation equals the current book value of property, plant, and equipment.

Some companies list goodwill among their assets. If a company has purchased another company for a price above the fair market value of its assets, that so-called goodwill is recorded as an asset. This is, however, strictly an accounting fiction. Goodwill may also represent intangible things such as brand names or the acquired company's excellent reputation. These may have real value. So too can other intangible assets, such as patents.

Finally, we come to the last line of the asset section of the balance sheet. Total assets represent the sum of current and fixed assets.

Liabilities and owners' equity

Now let's consider the claims against those assets, beginning with a category called current liabilities. These liabilities represent the claims of creditors and others that typically must be paid within a year; they include short-term IOUs, accrued salaries, accrued income taxes, and accounts payable. This year's repayment obligation on a long-term loan is also listed under current liabilities.

Subtracting current liabilities from current assets gives you the company's net working capital. Net working capital is the amount of money the company has tied up in its current (short-term) operating activities. Just how much is adequate for the company depends on the industry and the company's plans. In the balance sheet shown in table A-1, Amalgamated has $1,165,500 in net working capital.

Long-term liabilities are typically bonds and mortgages—debts that the company is contractually obliged to repay, with respect to both interest and principal.

According to the aforementioned accounting equation, total assets must equal total liabilities plus owners' equity. Thus, subtracting total liabilities from total assets, the balance sheet arrives at a figure for the owners' equity. Owners' equity comprises retained earnings (net profits that accumulate on a company's balance sheet after any dividends are paid) and contributed capital (capital received in exchange for shares).

Historical values

The values represented in many balance-sheet categories may not correspond to their actual market values. Except for items such as cash, accounts receivable, and accounts payable, the measurement of each classification will rarely be equal to the actual current value or cash value shown. This is because accountants must record most items at their historic cost. If, for example, XYZ's balance sheet indicated land worth $700,000, that figure would represent what XYZ paid for the land way back when. If the land was purchased in downtown San Francisco in 1992, you can bet that it is now worth immensely more than the value stated on the balance sheet.

So why do accountants use historic instead of market values? The short answer is that it represents the lesser of two evils. If market values were mandated, then every public company would be required to get a professional appraisal of every one of its properties, warehouse inventories, and so forth—and would have to do so every year. And how many people would trust those appraisals? So we're stuck with historic values on the balance sheet.

Managerial issues

Although the balance sheet is prepared by accountants, it represents several important issues for managers.

Working capital

Business owners pay substantial attention to the level of working capital, which naturally expands and contracts with sales activities. Too little working capital can put a company in a bad position: the company may be unable to pay its bills or to take advantage of profitable opportunities. Too much working capital, on the other hand, reduces profitability, because that capital has a carrying cost; it must be financed in some way, usually through interest-bearing loans.

Inventory is one component of working capital—unless yours is a service business that has no inventory. Like working capital, inventory must be balanced between too much and too little. Having lots of inventory on hand allows a company to fill customer orders without delay and provides a buffer against potential production stoppages and strikes. The flip side of plentiful inventory is the cost of financing and the risk of deterioration in the market value of the inventory itself. Every excess widget in the stockroom adds to the company's financing costs, and that reduces profits. And every item that sits on the shelf may become obsolete or less salable as time goes by—again, with a negative impact on profitability.

The personal-computer business provides a clear example of how excess inventory can wreck the bottom line. Some analysts estimate that the value of finished-goods inventory melts away at a rate of approximately 2 percent per day because of technical obsolescence in this fast-moving industry.

Financial leverage

You have probably heard someone say, "It's a highly leveraged situation." Do you know what "leveraged" means in the financial sense? Financial leverage refers to the use of borrowed money in acquiring an asset. We say that a company is highly leveraged when the percentage of debt on its balance sheet is high relative to the capital invested by the owners. For example, suppose that you paid $400,000 for an asset, using $100,000 of your own money and $300,000 in borrowed funds. For simplicity, we'll ignore loan payments, taxes, and any cash flow you might get from the investment. Four years go by, and your asset has appreciated to $500,000. You decide to sell. After paying off the $300,000 loan, you end up with $200,000 in your pocket (your original $100,000 plus a $100,000 profit). That's a gain of 100 percent on your personal capital, even though the asset increased in value by only 25 percent. Financial leverage made this possible. In contrast, if you had financed the purchase entirely with your own funds ($400,000), then you would have ended up with only a 25 percent gain.

Financial leverage creates an opportunity for a company to gain a higher return on the capital invested by its owners. In the United States and most other countries, tax policy makes financial leverage even more attractive by allowing businesses to deduct the interest paid on loans. But leverage can cut both ways. If the value of an asset drops (or fails to produce the anticipated level of revenue), then leverage works against its owner. Consider what would have happened in our example if the asset's value had dropped by $100,000, that is, to $300,000. The owner would have lost the entire $100,000 investment after repaying the initial loan of $300,000.

Financial structure of the firm

The potential downside of financial leverage is what keeps CEOs from maximizing their debt financing. Instead, they seek a financial structure that creates a realistic balance between debt and equity on the balance sheet. Although leverage enhances a company's potential profitability as long as things go right, managers know that every dollar of debt increases the riskiness of the business—both because of the danger just cited and because high debt results in high interest payments, which must be paid in good times and bad. Many companies have failed when business reversals or recessions reduced their ability to make timely payments on their loans.

When creditors and investors examine corporate balance sheets, they look carefully at the debt-to-equity ratio. They factor the riskiness of the balance sheet into the interest they charge on loans and the return they demand from a company's bonds. Thus, a highly leveraged company may have to pay 14 percent on borrowed funds instead of the 10 to 12 percent paid by a less leveraged competitor. Investors also demand a higher rate of return for their stock investments in highly leveraged companies. They will not accept high risks without an expectation of commensurately large returns.

The income statement

The income statement indicates the results of operations over a specified period. Those last two words are important. Unlike the balance sheet, which is a snapshot of the enterprise's position at a point in time, the income statement indicates cumulative business results within a defined time frame. Because it tells you whether the company is making a profit—that is, whether it has positive or negative net income (net earnings)—the income statement is often referred to as the profit-and-loss statement, or P&L. It shows a company's profitability at the end of a particular time—typically at the end of the month, the quarter, or the company's fiscal year. In addition, the income statement tells you how much money the company spent to make that profit—from which you can determine the company's profit margin.

As we did with the balance sheet, we can represent the contents of the income statement with a simple equation:

$$\text{Revenues} - \text{Expenses} = \text{Net Income (or Net Loss)}$$

An income statement starts with the company's revenues: the amount of money that results from selling products or services to customers. A company may have other revenues as well. These are often from investments or interest income from its cash holdings. Various costs and expenses—from the costs of making and storing goods, to depreciation of plant and equipment, to interest expense and taxes—are then deducted from revenues. The bottom line—what's left over—is the net income, or net profit or net earnings, for the period of the statement.

Consider the meaning of various line items on the income statement for Amalgamated Hat Rack (table A-2). The cost of goods sold is what it cost Amalgamated to manufacture its hat racks. This figure includes the cost of raw materials, such as lumber, as well as the cost of turning them into finished goods, including direct labor costs. By deducting the cost of goods sold from sales revenue, we get a company's gross profit—the roughest estimation of the company's profitability.

The next major category of cost is operating expenses. These expenses include administrative employee salaries, rents, and sales and marketing costs, as well as other costs of business not directly attributed to the cost of manufacturing a product. The lumber for making hat racks would not be included here; the cost of the advertising and the salaries of Amalgamated administrative employees would be included.

Depreciation is counted on the income statement as an expense, even though it involves no out-of-pocket payments. As described earlier, depreciation is a way of estimating the "consumption" of an asset, or the diminishing value of equipment, over time. A laptop, for example, loses about one-fifth of its value each year. Thus, the company would not expense the

TABLE A-2

Amalgamated Hat Rack income statement

	For the period ending December 31, 2017
Retail sales	$2,200,000
Corporate sales	1,000,000
Total sales revenue	3,200,000
Less: Cost of goods sold	1,600,000
Gross profit	1,600,000
Less: Operating expenses	800,000
Less: Depreciation expenses	42,500
Earnings before interest and taxes (EBIT)	757,500
Less: Interest expense	110,000
Earnings before income taxes	647,500
Less: Income taxes	300,000
Net income	$347,500

full value of a laptop in the first year of its purchase but rather would decrease its value as it is actually used over a span of five years. The idea behind depreciation is to recognize the diminished value of certain assets.

By subtracting operating expenses and depreciation from the gross profit, we get operating earnings. These earnings are often called earnings before interest and taxes, or EBIT.

We're now down to the last reductions in the path that revenues follow on their way to the bottom line. Interest expense is the interest charged on loans a company has taken out. Income tax—tax levied by the government on corporate income—is the final charge.

What revenues are left are referred to as net income, or earnings. If net income is positive—as it is in the case of Amalgamated—we have a profit, what the for-profit company lives for.

Making sense of the income statement

As with the balance sheet, our analysis of a company's income statement is greatly aided when presented in a multiperiod format. By using several time

TABLE A-3

Amalgamated Hat Rack multiperiod income statement, 2015–2017

	FOR THE PERIOD ENDING DECEMBER 31		
	2017	2016	2015
Retail sales	$2,200,000	2,000,000	1,720,000
Corporate sales	1,000,000	1,000,000	1,100,000
Total sales revenue	3,200,000	3,000,000	2,820,000
Less: Cost of goods sold	1,600,000	1,550,000	1,400,000
Gross profit	1,600,000	1,450,000	1,420,000
Less: Operating expenses	800,000	810,000	812,000
Less: Depreciation expenses	42,500	44,500	45,500
Earnings before interest and taxes (EBIT)	757,500	595,500	562,500
Less: Interest expense	110,000	110,000	150,000
Earnings before income taxes	647,500	485,500	412,500
Less: Income taxes	300,000	194,200	165,000
Net income	$347,500	291,300	247,500

points, we can spot trends and turnarounds. Most annual reports make multiperiod data available, often going back five or more years. Amalgamated's income statement in multiperiod form is depicted in table A-3.

In this multiyear format, we observe that Amalgamated's annual retail sales have grown steadily, and its corporate sales have stagnated and even declined slightly. Operating expenses have stayed about the same, however, even as total sales have expanded. That's a good sign that management is holding the line on the cost of doing business. The company's interest expense has also declined, perhaps because it has paid off one of its loans. The bottom line, net income, has shown healthy growth.

The cash-flow statement

The cash-flow statement, the last of the three essential financial statements, is the least used and understood. This statement details the reasons that the amount of cash (and cash equivalents) changed during the accounting period. More specifically, it reflects all changes in cash as affected by operating activities, investments, and financing activities. Like the bank statement you receive for your checking account, the cash-flow statement tells how much cash was on hand at the beginning of the period and how much was on hand at the end. It then describes how the company acquired and spent cash in a particular period. The uses of cash are recorded as negative figures, and sources of cash are recorded as positive figures.

If you're a manager in a large corporation, changes in the company's cash flow typically don't have an impact on your day-to-day functioning. Nevertheless, it's a good idea to stay up-to-date with your company's cash-flow projections, because they may come into play when you prepare your budget for the upcoming year. For example, if cash is tight, you will probably want to be conservative in your spending. Alternatively, if the company is flush with cash, you may have opportunities to make new investments. If you're a manager in a small company (or its owner), you're probably keenly aware of your cash-flow situation and feel its impact almost every day.

The cash-flow statement is useful because it indicates whether your company is turning accounts receivable into cash—and that ability is ultimately what will keep your company solvent. Solvency is the ability to pay bills as they come due.

As we did with the other statements, we can conceptualize the cash-flow statement in terms of a simple equation:

$$\text{Cash Flow from Profit} + \text{Other Sources of Cash} - \text{Uses of Cash} - \text{Change in Cash}$$

Again using the Amalgamated Hat Rack example, we see that in its year 2017 cash-flow statement, the company generated a positive cash flow of $166,000 (table A-4). The statement shows that cash flows from operations ($291,000), from investing activities (-$200,000), and from financing ($75,000) produced $166,000 in additional cash.

TABLE A-4

Amalgamated Hat Rack cash-flow statement for the year ending December 31, 2017

Net income	$347,500
Operating activities	
Accounts receivable	(43,000)
Inventory	(80,000)
Prepaid expenses	(25,000)
Accounts payable	20,000
Accrued expenses	21,000
Income tax payable	8,000
Depreciation expense	42,500
Total changes in operating assets and liabilities	(56,500)
Cash flow from operations	291,000
Investing activities	
Sale of property, plant, and equipment	267,000*
Capital expenditures	(467,000)
Cash flow from investing activities	(200,000)
Financing activities	
Short-term debt decrease	(65,000)
Long-term borrowing	90,000
Capital stock	50,000
Cash dividends to stockholders	—
Cash flow from financing activities	75,000
Increase in cash during year	$ 166,000

* Assumes sale price was at book value; the company had yet to start depreciating this asset.

The cash-flow statement doesn't measure the same thing as the income statement. If there is no cash transaction, then it cannot be reflected on a cash-flow statement. Notice, however, that net income at the top of the cash-flow statement is the same as the bottom line of the income statement; it's the company's profit. Through a series of adjustments, the cash-flow statement translates this net income into a cash basis.

The statement's format reflects the three categories of activities that affect cash. Cash can be increased or decreased because of (1) operations; (2) the acquisition or sale of assets, that is, investments; or (3) changes in debt or stock or other financing activities. Let's consider each activity in turn, starting with operations:

- Accounts receivable and finished-goods inventory represent items the company has produced but for which it hasn't yet received payment. Prepaid expenses represent items the company has paid for but has not yet consumed. These items are all subtracted from cash flow.

- Accounts payable and accrued expenses represent items the company has already received or used but for which it hasn't yet paid. Consequently, these items add to cash flow.

Now consider investments, which include the following:

- Gains realized from the sale of plant, property, and equipment. In other words, these gains are realized from converting investments into cash.

- Cash that the company uses to invest in financial instruments and plant, property, and equipment. The latter investments are often shown as capital expenditures.

The cash-flow statement shows that Amalgamated has sold a building for $267,000 and has made capital expenditures of $175,000, for a net addition to cash flow of $92,000.

Cash flow versus profit

Many people think of profits as cash flow. Don't make this mistake. For a particular period, profit may or may not contribute positively to cash flow. For example, if this year's profit derives from a huge sale made in November, the sale may be booked as revenues in the fiscal period, thus adding to profit. But if payment for that sale is not received until the next accounting period, it goes on the books as an account receivable, and that reduces cash flow.

Finally, we come to cash-flow changes from financing activities. Amalgamated has raised money by increasing its short-term debt, by borrowing in the capital markets, and by issuing capital stock, thereby increasing its available cash flow. The dividends that Amalgamated pays ($50,000), however, must be paid out of cash flow and thus represent a decrease in cash flow.

There's a lot more to financial statements and their interpretation than we can provide in this short primer, but you now have a basis for learning more. The statements generated by your small startup will be fairly simple in any case, and you can learn more as you work with your accountant or financial officer, and as your company grows.

Breakeven Analysis

Whether they are planning their new business or deciding whether to offer new products or services, entrepreneurs need to know the point at which they will begin making money. Breakeven analysis is a handy tool for this purpose. It can tell you how much (or how much more) you need to sell to pay for a fixed investment—in other words, at what point you will break even. With that information in hand, you can look at market demand and competitors' market shares to determine whether it's realistic to expect to sell that much. Breakeven analysis can also help you think through the impact of changing price and volume relationships.

More specifically, the breakeven calculation helps you determine the volume at which the total after-tax contribution from a product line or an investment covers its total fixed costs. But before you can calculate this value, you need to understand the components that go into it.

Making the calculation

To calculate breakeven, you must first understand three accounting concepts: fixed costs, variable costs, and contribution margin.

- *Fixed costs:* These costs stay mostly the same, no matter how many units of a product or service are sold—costs such as insurance, management salaries, and rent or lease payments. For example, the rent on the production facility will remain the same whether the company makes ten thousand or twenty thousand units, and so will the cost of insurance.

- *Variable costs:* These costs change with the number of units produced and sold; examples include utilities, labor, and the costs of raw materials. The more units you make, the more you consume these items. Sales commissions are another variable cost.

- *Contribution margin:* This is the amount of money that every sold unit contributes to paying for fixed costs. It is defined as net unit revenue minus variable (or direct) costs per unit.

With these concepts, we can make the calculation. We are looking for the solution to this straightforward equation:

Breakeven Volume = Fixed Costs ÷ Unit Contribution Margin

Here's how we do it. First, find the unit contribution margin by subtracting the variable costs per unit from the net revenue per unit. Then divide the total fixed costs, or the amount of the investment, by the unit contribution margin. The quotient is the breakeven volume, that is, the number of units that must be sold if all fixed costs are to be covered.

Let's consider a hypothetical situation. Amalgamated Hat Rack is planning to sell its new plastic wall-mounted hat rack for $75 per unit. The company's variable cost per unit is $22. It will spend $100,000 (a fixed cost) for the plastic extruder that will make these hat racks. Thus

$75 (Price per Unit) − $22 (Variable Cost per Unit)

= $53 (Unit Contribution Margin)

Therefore

$$\$100,000 \text{ (Total Investment Required)} \div$$
$$\$53 \text{ (Unit Contribution Margin)} = 1,887 \text{ Units}$$

The preceding calculations indicate that Amalgamated must sell 1,887 hat racks to break even on its $100,000 investment.

At this point, Amalgamated must decide whether the breakeven volume is achievable: Is it realistic to expect to sell 1,887 additional hat racks, and if so, how quickly?

A breakeven complication

Our hat rack breakeven analysis represents a simple case. It assumes that costs are distinctly fixed or variable, that costs and unit contributions will not change as a function of volume (i.e., that the sale price of the item under consideration will not change at different levels of output, rent will stay the same whether one thousand or ten thousand units are produced and sold).

These assumptions may not hold in your more complicated world. Up to a certain level of production, your rent may be fixed and then increase by 50 percent as you rent a secondary facility to handle expanded output. Labor costs may in reality be a hybrid of fixed and variable. And as you push more of your product into the market, you may have to offer price discounts, which will reduce contribution per unit. You must adjust the breakeven calculation to accommodate these untidy realities.

Operating leverage

Your goal as an entrepreneur, of course, is not to break even but to make a profit. After you've covered all your fixed costs with the contributions of many unit sales, every subsequent sale contributes directly to profits. As we observed earlier,

Unit Net Revenue – Unit Variable Cost = Contribution to Profit

You can see at a glance that the lower the unit variable cost, the greater the contribution to profits. In the pharmaceutical business, for example, the unit cost of cranking out and packaging a bottle of a new drug may be less than $1. Yet if the company can sell each bottle for $100, a whopping sum of $99 contributes to corporate profits after sales have gotten beyond the breakeven point! The trouble is that the pharmaceutical company may have invested $400 million up front in fixed product-development costs just to get the first bottle out the door. It will have to sell many bottles of the new medication just to break even. But when it does, profits can be extraordinary.

The relationship between fixed and variable costs is often described in terms of operating leverage. Companies whose fixed costs are high relative to their variable costs are said to have high operating leverage. The pharmaceutical business, for example, generally operates with high operating leverage.

Now consider the opposite: low operating leverage. Here, fixed costs are low relative to the total cost of producing each unit of output. A consulting business is a good example of one that functions with low operating leverage. The firm has a minimal investment in equipment and other fixed expenses. The bulk of its costs are the fees it pays its consultants, which vary depending on the actual hours they bill to the firm.

Operating leverage is a great thing after a company passes its breakeven point, but it can cause substantial losses if breakeven is never achieved. In other words, it's risky. Managers accordingly give much thought to finding the right balance between fixed and variable costs.

Appendix C

Valuation: What Is Your Business Really Worth?

What is your business worth? This is a question that most entrepreneurs must eventually answer because they are either buying an existing business or selling one of their own. And answering it correctly is extremely important. If you pay too much for a business, your rate of return will be disappointing. Similarly, if you underestimate the value of an entity you are selling, you will shortchange yourself without knowing it.

Valuing an ongoing business—large or small—is neither easy nor exact. In most cases, it is the domain of experts. But as an entrepreneur, you should be familiar with the various valuation approaches used by those experts and understand the strengths and weaknesses of these techniques. We'll discuss these approaches here.

But before we get started, consider these cautions. The true value of a business is never completely certain, because of two problems. First, different valuation methods consistently fail to produce the same outcome, even when meticulously calculated. Second, the product of valuation methods is only as good as the data and the estimates we bring to them, and the numbers are often incomplete, unreliable, or based on projections. For example, one method depends heavily on estimates of future cash flows, and even in the very best cases, these estimates will only be close. In the worst cases, they will stray far from the mark.

Another consideration is that a company is worth different amounts to different parties. Different prospective buyers are likely to assign different values to the same set of assets. For example, if you were a book collector who already owned first editions of every Hemingway novel except *For Whom the Bell Tolls*, then that book would be much more valuable to you than it would be to another collector who owned only one or two first-edition Hemingways. The reason? For you, the acquisition would complete a set, whose value is greater than the sum of the individual volumes considered separately. Businesses look on acquisitions with a similar perspective. The acquisition of a small high-tech company, for example, might provide the acquirer with the technology it needs to leverage its other operations. This difference in how parties value an asset explains, in part, why many firms are purchased for more than the market value of their existing shares.

Also keep in mind that, as we've said, valuation is the province of specialists. Among other reasons, a small and closely held business typically turns to professional appraisers when its value must be established for a sale or when it needs to determine the value of its shares when an ESOP is used. When large public firms or their business units are the subjects of a valuation, executives generally turn to a variety of full-service accounting, investment banking, or consulting firms. Many of these vendors have departments devoted entirely to mergers and acquisitions, in which valuation issues are a central focus. A well-rounded entrepreneur cannot be an expert in these matters, but you should understand the nature of various valuation methods along with their strengths and weaknesses.

Valuation problems often arise in the context of closely held businesses—that is, businesses with only a few owners—or in the sale of an operating unit of a public company. In neither case are there publicly traded ownership shares. Public markets for ownership, such as NASDAQ or the New York Stock Exchange, make value more transparent. Everyday buying and selling in these markets establishes a company's per-share price. And that price, multiplied by the number of outstanding shares, often provides a basis for a fair approximation of a company's value at a point in time. But this basis is not available in the absence of public trading.

Asset-based valuations

One way to value an enterprise is to determine the value of its assets. There are four approaches to asset-based valuations: equity book value, adjusted book value, liquidation value, and replacement value.

Equity book value

Equity book value, the simplest valuation approach, uses the balance sheet as its primary source of information. Here's the formula:

$$\text{Equity Book Value} = \text{Total Assets} - \text{Total Liabilities}$$

To test this formula, consider the balance sheet of Amalgamated Hat Rack Company, which we encountered in appendix A. Table A-1 showed total assets of $3,932,500 and total liabilities of $1,750,000 for 2017. The difference—the equity book value—is $2,182,500. Notice that equity book value is the same as total owners' equity. In other words, if you reduce the balance-sheet (or book) value of the business's assets by the amount of its debts and other financial obligations, you have its equity value.

This equity-book-value approach is easy and quick. And it is common for executives in a particular industry to roughly calculate their company's value in the context of equity book value. For example, one owner might contend that their company is worth at least book value in a sale because that was the amount that they invested in the business.

But equity book value is not a reliable guide for businesses in many industries. Assets are placed on the balance sheet at their historical costs, which may not represent their value today. The value of balance-sheet assets may be unrealistic for other reasons as well. Consider Amalgamated's assets:

- Accounts receivable could be suspect if many accounts are uncollectible.

- Inventory reflects historic cost, but inventory may be worthless or less valuable than its stated balance-sheet value because of spoilage or obsolescence. Or some inventory may be undervalued.

- Property, plant, and equipment depreciation should also be closely examined—particularly for land. If Amalgamated's property was put on the books in 1995—and if it happens to be in the heart of San Francisco—then its real market value may be ten or twenty times the 1995 figure.

The preceding hypotheticals are only a few examples of why book value is not always true market value.

Adjusted book value

The weaknesses of the quick-and-dirty equity-book-value approach have led some to adopt adjusted book value, which attempts to restate the value of balance-sheet assets to realistic market levels. Consider the influence of adjusted book value in a leveraged buyout of a major retail store chain. At the time of the analysis, the store chain had an equity book value of $1.3 billion. After its inventory and property assets were adjusted to their appraised values, however, the enterprise's value leaped to $2.2 billion—an increase of 69 percent.

When asset values are adjusted, appraisers must determine the real value of any listed intangibles, such as goodwill and patents. Goodwill is usually an accounting fiction created when one company buys another at a premium to book value—that is, at a price higher than book value. The premium must be put on the balance sheet as goodwill. But to a potential buyer, the intangible asset may have no value.

Liquidation value

Liquidation value is similar to adjusted book value. It attempts to restate balance-sheet values in terms of the net cash that would be realized if assets were disposed of in a quick sale and all company liabilities were paid off or otherwise settled. This approach recognizes that many assets, especially inventory and fixed assets, usually fetch less than they would if the sale were made more deliberately.

Replacement value

Some people use replacement value to obtain a rough estimate of value. This method simply estimates the cost of reproducing the business's assets. Of course, a buyer may not want to replicate all the assets included in the sale price of a company. In this case, the replacement value represents more than the value that the buyer would place on the company.

The various asset-based valuation approaches described here generally share some strengths and weaknesses. On the positive side, asset-based methods are easy and inexpensive to calculate. They are also easy to understand. On the negative side, both equity book value and liquidation value fail to reflect the actual market value of assets. And all these approaches fail to recognize the intangible value of an ongoing enterprise, which derives much of its wealth-generating power from human knowledge, skill, and reputation.

Earnings-based valuation

Another approach to valuing a company is to capitalize its earnings. This involves multiplying one or another income-statement earnings figure (e.g., earnings before income tax) by some figure. Some earnings-based methods, however, are more sophisticated.

Earnings multiple

For a publicly traded company, the current share price multiplied by the number of outstanding shares indicates the market value of the company's equity. Add to this the value of the company's debt, and you have the total value of the enterprise. In other words, the total value of the company is the equity of the owners plus any outstanding debt. Why add the debt? Consider your own home. When you go to sell your house, you don't set the price at the level of your equity in the property. Rather, its value is the total of the outstanding debt and your equity interest. Similarly, the value of a company is the shareholders' equity plus the liabilities. This is often referred to as the enterprise value.

For a public company whose shares are priced by the market every business day, pricing the equity is straightforward. But what about a closely held corporation, whose share price is generally unknown because such a firm does not trade in a public market? We can reach a value estimate by using the known price-earnings multiple (often called the P/E ratio) of similar enterprises that are publicly traded. The P/E-multiple approach to share value begins with this formula:

$$\text{Share Price} = \text{Current Earnings} \times \text{Multiple}$$

We calculate the multiple from comparable publicly traded companies as follows:

$$\text{Multiple} = \text{Share Price} \div \text{Current Earnings}$$

Thus, if XYZ Corporation's shares are trading at $50 per share and its current earnings are $5 per share, then the multiple is 10. In stock market parlance, we'd say that XYZ is trading at ten times earnings.

We can use this multiple approach to price the equity of a nonpublic corporation if we can find one or more similar enterprises with known P/E multiples. Finding such companies is a challenge, because no two enterprises are exactly alike. Because of the uniqueness of every business, valuation experts recognize their work as part science and part art.

To examine this method further, let's return to our sample firm. Because Amalgamated Hat Rack is a closely held firm, we have no readily available benchmark for valuing its shares. But let's suppose that we did identify a publicly traded company (or, even better, several companies) similar to Amalgamated in most respects—in terms of both industry and size. We'll call one of these firms Acme Corporation. And let's suppose that Acme's P/E multiple is 8. Let's also suppose that our crack researchers have discovered that another company, this one private and in the same industry as Amalgamated, was recently acquired at roughly the same multiple: 8. This gives us confidence that our multiple of 8 is in the ballpark.

With this information, let's revisit Amalgamated's income statement presented in appendix A (table A-2), where we find that its net income (earnings) is $347,500. Plugging the relevant numbers in to the following formula, we estimate Amalgamated's value:

Earnings × Appropriate Multiple = Equity Value

$347,500 × 8 = $2,780,000

Remember that this is the value of the company's equity. To find the total enterprise value of Amalgamated, we must add the total of its interest-bearing liabilities. Table A-1 in appendix A shows that the company's interest-bearing liabilities (short-term and long-term debt) for 2017 are $1,185,000. Thus, the value of the entire enterprise is as follows:

Enterprise Value = Equity Value + Value of Interest-Bearing Debt

$3,955,000 = $2,780,000 + $1,175,000

The effectiveness of the multiple approach to valuation depends partly on the reliability of the earnings figure. The most recent earnings might, for example, be unnaturally depressed by a onetime write-off of obsolete inventory or pumped up by the sale of a subsidiary company. For this reason, you have to factor out random and nonrecurring items. Similarly, you should review expenses to determine that they are normal—neither extraordinarily high nor extraordinarily low. For example, inordinately low maintenance charges over a period would pump up near-term earnings but would result in extraordinary expenses in the future for deferred maintenance. Similarly, nonrecurring windfall sales can also distort the earnings picture.

In small, closely held companies, you need to pay particular attention to the salaries of the owner-managers and the members of their families. If these salaries have been unreasonably high or low, an adjustment of earnings is required. You should also assess the depreciation rates to determine their validity and, if necessary, to make appropriate adjustments to reported earnings.

Earnings before interest and taxes (EBIT) multiple

The reliability of the multiple approach to valuation just described depends on the comparability of the firm or firms used as proxies for the target company. In the Amalgamated example, we relied heavily on the observed earnings multiple of Acme Corporation, a publicly traded company whose business is similar to Amalgamated's. Unfortunately, these two companies could produce equal operating results and yet indicate much different bottom-line profits to their shareholders.

How is this possible? The answer is twofold. The two companies show different bottom lines because of how they are financed and because of taxes. If a company is heavily financed with debt, its interest expenses will be large, and those expenses will reduce the total dollars available to the owners at the bottom line. Similarly, one company's tax bill might be much higher than the other's for some reason that has little to do with its future wealth-producing capabilities. And taxes reduce bottom-line earnings.

Consider the hypothetical scenario in table C-1. Notice that the two companies produce the same earnings before interest and taxes (EBIT). But because Acme uses more debt and less equity in financing its assets,

TABLE C-1

Hypothetical income statements of Amalgamated Hat Rack and Acme Corporation

	Amalgamated	Acme
Earnings before interest and taxes	$757,500	$757,500
Less: Interest expense	$110,000	$350,000
Earnings before income tax	$647,500	$407,400
Less: Income tax	$300,000	$187,000
Net income	$347,500	$220,500

its interest expense is much higher ($350,000 versus $110,000). This dramatically reduces its earnings before income taxes compared with that of Amalgamated. Even though each pays an equal percentage in income taxes, Acme ends up with substantially lower bottom-line earnings.

This earnings variation between two otherwise comparable enterprises would produce different equity values. You can circumvent the problem by using EBIT instead of bottom-line earnings in the valuation process. Some practitioners go one step further and use the EBITDA (EBIT plus depreciation and amortization) multiple. Depreciation and amortization are noncash charges against bottom-line earnings—accounting allocations that tend to create differences between otherwise similar firms. By using EBITDA in the valuation equation, you avoid this potential distortion.

Discounted cash-flow method

The earnings-based methods just described are based on historical performance—what happened last year. But past performance is no assurance of future results. If you were making an offer to buy a local small business, chances are that you'd base your offer on its ability to produce profits in the years ahead. Similarly, if your company were hatching plans to acquire Amalgamated Hat Rack, it would be less interested in what Amalgamated earned in the past than in what it is likely to earn in the future under new management.

We can direct our earnings-based valuation toward the future by using a more sophisticated valuation method: discounted cash flow (DCF). The DCF valuation method accounts for the time value of money (concepts beyond the scope of this volume but described in many books on finance). DCF determines value by calculating the present value of a business's future cash flows, including its terminal value. Because those cash flows are available to both equity holders and debt holders, DCF can reflect the value of the enterprise as a whole or can be confined to the cash flows left available to shareholders.

The DCF method has numerous strengths:

- It recognizes the time value of future cash flows.

- It is future oriented and estimates future cash flows in terms of what the new owner could achieve.

- It accounts for the buyer's cost of capital.

- It does not depend on comparisons with similar companies—comparisons that are bound to be different in various dimensions (e.g., earnings-based multiples).

- It is based on real cash flows instead of accounting values.

On the downside, the DCF method assumes that future cash flows, including the terminal value, can be estimated with reasonable accuracy. This is rarely the case for cash-flow estimates made far into the future.

Clearly, the information given here will not make you an expert valuation practitioner, but with a little reflection, it should put you in a better position to deal with those practitioners in negotiating the sale of your own company or the purchase of another.

Summing up

The important but difficult subject of business valuation can be summarized in three types of approaches:

- **Asset-based:** This valuation approach includes the use of equity book value, adjusted book value, liquidation value, or replacement value. In general, these methods are easy to calculate and to understand but have notable weaknesses. Except for replacement and adjusted book methods, they fail to reflect the actual market values of assets; they also fail to recognize the intangible value of an ongoing enterprise, which derives much of its wealth-generating power from human knowledge, skill, and reputation.

- **Earnings-based:** This valuation approach includes the price-earnings method, the EBIT method, and the EBITDA method. The earnings-based approach is generally superior to asset-based methods, but it depends on the availability of comparable businesses whose P/E multiples are known.

- **Discounted-cash-flow-based:** This method includes the time value of money. The DCF method has many advantages, the most important being its future-looking orientation. The method estimates future cash flows in terms of what a new owner could achieve. It also recognizes the buyer's cost of capital. The major weakness of the method is the difficulty inherent in producing reliable estimates of future cash flows.

In the end, these approaches to valuation are bound to produce different outcomes. Even the same method applied by two experienced professionals can produce different results. For this reason, most appraisers use more than one method in approximating the true value of an asset or a business.

Appendix D

Selling Restricted and Control Securities: SEC Rule 144

The trading of common stock acquired before an IPO is restricted by the US Securities and Exchange Commission (SEC). Several rules govern how that restriction can be lifted. Here is the SEC's own description of its key rule governing restricted shares.

When you acquire restricted securities or hold control securities (see the next section for definitions), you must find an exemption from the SEC's registration requirements to sell them in a public marketplace. Rule 144 allows public resale of restricted and control securities if various conditions are met. This overview tells you what you need to know about selling your restricted or control securities. It also describes how to have a restrictive legend removed.

What are restricted and control securities?

Restricted securities are securities acquired in unregistered, private sales from the issuing company or from an affiliate of the issuer. Investors typically receive restricted securities through private placement offerings, Regulation D offerings, employee stock ownership plans, as compensation for professional services, or in exchange for providing seed money or startup capital to the company. Rule 144(a)(3) identifies which sales produce restricted securities.

Control securities are those held by an affiliate of the issuing company. An affiliate is a person, such as an executive officer, a director, or a large shareholder, in a relationship of control with the issuer. *Control* means the power to direct the management and policies of the company in question, whether through the ownership of voting securities, by contract, or otherwise. If you buy securities from a controlling person or an affiliate, you take restricted securities, even if they were not restricted in the affiliate's hands.

If you acquire restrictive securities, you will almost always receive a certificate stamped with a "restrictive" legend. The legend indicates that the securities may not be resold in the marketplace unless they are registered with the SEC or are exempt from the registration requirements. Certificates for control securities usually are not stamped with a legend.

What are the conditions of Rule 144?

If you want to sell your restricted or control securities to the public, you can meet the applicable conditions set forth in Rule 144. The rule is not the exclusive means for selling restricted or control securities, but it provides a safe-harbor exemption to sellers. The rule's five conditions are summarized below:

1. **Holding period:** Before you may sell any restricted securities in the marketplace, you must hold them for a certain period. If the company that issued the securities is a "reporting company" in that it is subject to the reporting requirements of the Securities

Exchange Act of 1934, then you must hold the securities for at least six months. If the issuer of the securities is not subject to the reporting requirements, then you must hold the securities for at least one year. The relevant holding period begins when the securities were bought and fully paid for. The holding period only applies to restricted securities. Because securities acquired in the public market are not restricted, there is no holding period for an affiliate who purchases securities of the issuer in the marketplace. But the resale of an affiliate's shares as control securities is subject to the other conditions of the rule.

Additional securities purchased from the issuer do not affect the holding period of previously purchased securities of the same class. If you purchased restricted securities from another nonaffiliate, you can tack on that nonaffiliate's holding period to your holding period. For gifts made by an affiliate, the holding period begins when the affiliate acquired the securities and not on the date of the gift. In the case of a stock option, including employee stock options, the holding period begins on the date the option is exercised and not the date it is granted.

2. **Current public information:** There must be adequate current information about the issuing company publicly available before the sale can be made. For reporting companies, this condition generally means that the companies have complied with the periodic reporting requirements of the Securities Exchange Act of 1934. For nonreporting companies, this means that certain company information, including information about the nature of its business, the identity of its officers and directors, and its financial statements, is publicly available.

3. **Trading volume formula:** If you are an affiliate, the number of equity securities you may sell during any three-month period cannot exceed the greater of 1 percent of the outstanding shares of the same class being sold, or if the class is listed on a stock exchange, the greater of 1 percent or the average reported weekly trading volume

during the four weeks preceding the filing of a notice of sale on Form 144. Over-the-counter (OTC) stocks, including those quoted on the OTC Bulletin Board and the Pink Sheets, can only be sold using the 1 percent measurement.

4. **Ordinary brokerage transactions:** If you are an affiliate, the sales must be handled in all respects as routine trading transactions, and brokers may not receive more than a normal commission. Neither the seller nor the broker can solicit orders to buy the securities.

5. **Filing a notice of proposed sale with the SEC:** If you are an affiliate, you must file a notice with the SEC on Form 144 if the sale involves more than five thousand shares or the aggregate dollar amount is greater than $50,000 in any three-month period.

If I am not an affiliate of the issuer, what conditions of Rule 144 must I comply with?

If you are not (and have not been for at least three months) an affiliate of the company issuing the securities and have held the restricted securities for at least one year, you can sell the securities without regard to the conditions in Rule 144 discussed above. If the issuer of the securities is subject to the Exchange Act reporting requirements and you have held the securities for at least six months but less than one year, you may sell the securities as long as you satisfy the current public-information condition.

Can the securities be sold publicly if the conditions of Rule 144 have been met?

Even if you have met the conditions of Rule 144, you can't sell your restricted securities to the public until you've gotten the legend removed from the certificate. Only a transfer agent can remove a restrictive legend. But the transfer agent won't remove the legend unless you've obtained the consent of the issuer—usually in the form of an opinion letter from the issuer's counsel—that the restrictive legend can be removed. Unless this happens, the transfer agent lacks the authority to remove the legend and permit execution of the trade in the marketplace.

To have the legend removed, an investor should contact the company that issued the securities, or the transfer agent for the securities, to ask about the procedures for removing a legend. Removing the legend can be a complicated process requiring you to work with an attorney who specializes in securities law.

What if a dispute arises over whether I can remove the legend?

If a dispute arises over whether a restrictive legend can be removed, the SEC will not intervene. Removal of a legend is a matter solely in the discretion of the issuer of the securities. State law, not federal law, covers disputes about the removal of legends. Thus, the SEC will take no action in any decision or dispute about removing a restrictive legend.

Glossary

ACCELERATOR A time-limited cohort program for early-stage businesses that comes with equity investment.

ACCOUNTS PAYABLE A category of balance-sheet liabilities representing moneys owed by the company.

ACCOUNTS RECEIVABLE A category of balance-sheet assets representing moneys owed to the company by customers and others.

ACID-TEST RATIO The ratio of so-called quick assets (cash, marketable security, and accounts receivable) to current liabilities. Unlike the current ratio, inventory is left out of the calculation.

ADJUSTED BOOK VALUE A refinement of the book-value method of valuation that attempts to restate the value of certain assets on the balance sheet according to realistic market values.

AMORTIZATION A noncash expense that effectively reduces the balance-sheet value of an intangible asset over its presumed useful life.

ANGEL INVESTOR A high-net-worth individual, usually a successful businessperson or professional, who provides early-stage capital to a startup business in the form of debt, ownership capital, or both.

ASSETS The balance-sheet items in which a company invests so that it can conduct business. Examples include cash and financial instruments, inventories of raw materials and finished goods, land, buildings, and equipment.

Assets also include moneys owed to the company by customers and others—an asset category referred to as accounts receivable.

BALANCE SHEET A financial statement that describes the assets owned by the business and shows how those assets are financed—with the funds of creditors (liabilities), the equity of the owners, or both. Also known as the statement of financial position.

BOND A debt security usually issued with a fixed interest rate and a stated maturity date. The bond issuer has a contractual obligation to make periodic interest payments and to redeem the bond at its face value on maturity.

BOOTSTRAP FINANCING A form of startup financing in which the founders rely on their own personal financial resources and those of friends, family, employees, and suppliers to launch the business.

BREAKEVEN ANALYSIS A form of analysis that helps determine how much (or how much more) a company needs to sell to pay for the fixed investment—in other words, at what point the company will break even on its cash flow.

BUSINESS MODEL A conceptual description of an enterprise's revenue sources, cost drivers, investment size, and success factors and how they work together.

BUSINESS PLAN A document that explains a business opportunity, identifies the market to be served, and provides details about how the entrepreneurial organization plans to pursue it. Ideally it describes the unique qualifications that the management team brings to the effort, defines the resources required for success, and forecasts results over a reasonable time horizon.

CAPITAL MARKETS The financial markets in which long-term debt instruments and equity securities—including private placements—are issued and traded.

CASH-FLOW STATEMENT A financial statement that details the reasons for changes in cash (and cash equivalents) during the accounting period. More specifically, it reflects all changes in cash as affected by operating activities, investments, and financing activities.

C CORPORATION In the United States, an entity chartered by the state and treated as a person under the law. The C corporation can have an infinite number of owners. Ownership is evidenced by shares of company stock. The entity is managed on behalf of shareholders—at least indirectly—by a board of directors.

COLLATERAL An asset pledged to the lender until the loan is satisfied.

COMMERCIAL PAPER A short-term financing instrument used primarily by large, creditworthy corporations as an alternative to short-term bank borrowing. Most paper is sold at a discount to its face value and is redeemable at face value on maturity.

COMMON STOCK (or COMMON SHARES) A security that represents a fractional ownership interest in the corporation that issued it.

COST OF GOODS SOLD On the income statement, what it costs a company to produce its goods and services. This figure includes raw materials, production, and direct labor costs.

CURRENT ASSETS Assets that are most easily converted to cash: cash equivalents such as certificates of deposit and US Treasury bills, receivables, and inventory. Under generally accepted accounting principles, current assets are those that can be converted into cash within one year.

CURRENT LIABILITIES Liabilities that must be paid in one year or sooner; these typically include short-term loans, salaries, income taxes, and accounts payable.

CURRENT RATIO Current assets divided by current liabilities. This ratio is often used as a measure of a company's ability to meet currently maturing obligations.

DEBT RATIO The ratio of debt to either assets or equity in a company's financial structure.

DEPRECIATION A noncash expense that effectively reduces the balance-sheet value of an asset over its presumed useful life.

DISCOUNTED CASH FLOW (DCF) A method based on the time value of money, it calculates value by finding the present value of a business's future cash flows.

DUE DILIGENCE With respect to a public offering of securities, the investigation of facts and statements of risk made in the issuer's registration statement.

EBIT A measure of a firm's profits that calculates its earnings before interest and taxes.

EMPLOYEE STOCK OWNERSHIP PLAN (ESOP) In the United States, a formal plan under which corporate shares are acquired by the plan on behalf of employees, for whom it is a tax-qualified retirement plan.

ENTERPRISE VALUE The value of a company's equity plus its debt.

EQUITY BOOK VALUE The value of total assets less total liabilities.

EQUITY CAPITAL Capital contributed to a business that provides rights of ownership in return.

EXECUTIVE SUMMARY In a business plan, a short section that compellingly explains the opportunity, shows why it is timely, describes how the company plans to pursue it, outlines the entrepreneur's expectation of results, and includes a thumbnail sketch of the company and the management team.

FINANCIAL LEVERAGE *See* "leverage."

FIXED ASSETS Assets that are difficult to convert to cash—for example, buildings and equipment. Sometimes called plant assets.

FIXED COSTS Costs that are incurred by the business and stay about the same, no matter how many goods or services are produced.

GOODWILL An intangible balance-sheet asset. If a company has purchased another company for a price above the fair market value of its assets, that "goodwill" is recorded as an asset. Goodwill may also represent intangible things such as the acquired company's excellent reputation, its brand names, or its patents, all of which may have real value.

GROSS PROFIT Sales revenues less the cost of goods sold. The roughest measure of profitability. Also called gross margin.

INCOME STATEMENT A financial statement that indicates the cumulative results of operations over a specified period. Also referred to as the profit-and-loss statement, or P&L.

INCUBATOR A development program for new businesses. Incubators usually either operate as a nonprofit or charge a venture for rent (coworking space is shared with other young companies). Work with an incubator is not limited to the early stages of a venture's development; some incubators specialize in later-phase growth.

INITIAL PUBLIC OFFERING (IPO) A corporation's first offering of its shares to the public.

INVENTORY The supplies, raw materials, components, and so forth that a company uses in its operations. It also includes work in process—goods in various stages of production—as well as finished goods waiting to be sold or shipped.

IPO *See* "initial public offering."

LEVERAGE The degree to which the activities of a company are supported by liabilities and long-term debt as opposed to owners' capital contributions.

LEVERAGED BUYOUT The purchase of a company using a significant amount of borrowed funds in addition to the buyer's own equity. Their equity is thus "leveraged" to provide more capital for the purchase. The company's cash flow provides the collateral for the loans and is used to repay them over time.

LIABILITY A claim against a company's assets.

LIMITED-LIABILITY CORPORATION (LLC) A hybrid form of company structure, combining benefits of both a partnership and a corporation.

LIMITED PARTNERSHIP A hybrid form of organization having both limited and general partners. The general partner (there may be more than one) assumes management responsibility and unlimited liability for the business and must have at least a 1 percent interest in profits and losses. The limited partner (or partners) has no voice in management and is legally liable only for the amount of his or her capital contribution plus any other debt obligations specifically accepted.

MINIMUM VIABLE PRODUCT In product development, an initial offering with limited features that allows developers to test their assumptions about what customers value, how the product performs in the market, and so forth.

NET INCOME The "bottom line" of the income statement. Net income is revenues less expenses less taxes. Also referred to as net earnings or net profits.

NET WORKING CAPITAL Current assets less current liabilities; the amount of money a company has tied up in short-term operating activities.

NETWORK EFFECTS A phenomenon in which a product's value for users increases as the number of users of that product increases.

OPERATING EARNINGS On the income statement, gross margin less operating expenses and depreciation. Often called earnings before interest and taxes, or EBIT.

OPERATING EXPENSES On the balance sheet, a category that includes administrative expenses, employee salaries, rents, sales and marketing costs, as well as other costs of business not directly attributed to the cost of manufacturing a product.

OPERATING LEVERAGE The extent to which a company's operating costs are fixed instead of variable. For example, a company that relies heavily on machinery and very few workers to produce its goods has a high operating leverage.

OWNERS' EQUITY What, if anything, is left over after total liabilities are deducted from total assets. Owners' equity is the sum of capital contributed by owners plus their retained earnings. Also known as shareholders' equity.

PARTNERSHIP A business entity with two or more owners. In the United States, it is treated as a proprietorship for tax and liability purposes. Earnings are distributed according to the partnership agreement and are treated as personal income for tax purposes. Thus, like the sole proprietorship, the partnership is simply a conduit for generating income for its partners.

PITCH DECK A slide presentation created to describe a new business venture to potential investors.

PIVOT A substantive adjustment to a startup's strategy, business model, or offering, often in response to market feedback or testing.

PLATFORM (ALSO "MULTISIDED PLATFORM") A business that brings together producers and consumers and facilitates exchanges and interactions, often in reference to digital businesses such as eBay, Uber, and Alibaba, but also describing the models of companies like malls and temp agencies.

PREFERRED STOCK An equity-like security that pays a specified dividend and has a superior position to common stock in case of distributions or liquidation.

PRESENT VALUE The monetary value today of a future payment discounted at some annual compound interest rate.

PRICE-EARNINGS MULTIPLE The price of a share of stock divided by earnings per share.

PRIVATE PLACEMENT The sale of company stock to one or a few private investors instead of to the public.

PROFIT Financial gain, calculated as the difference between revenue and expenses.

PROFIT-AND-LOSS STATEMENT (P&L) *See* "income statement."

PROFIT MARGIN The percentage of every dollar of sales that makes it to the bottom line. Profit margin is net income after tax divided by net sales. Sometimes called the return on sales.

PRO FORMA FINANCIAL STATEMENT Financial statement (balance sheet or income statement) containing hypothetical or forecast data.

PROSPECTUS A formal document that provides full disclosure to potential investors about the company, its business, its finances, and the way it intends to use the proceeds of its securities issuance. In its preliminary form, it is known as a red herring.

RED HERRING *See* "prospectus."

REPLACEMENT VALUE A valuation approach that estimates the cost of reproducing an asset, rather than the more common reliance on an asset's book value.

RETAINED EARNINGS Annual net profits that accumulate on a company's balance sheet after dividends are paid.

REVENUE The amount of money that results from selling products or services to customers.

ROAD SHOW A series of meetings between company officials and prospective investors, usually held in major cities around the country in conjunction with a forthcoming issue of corporate securities. The investors can put questions to the CEO or CFO about the company and the intended offering of securities.

ROUNDS (FUNDING) One way of defining the stage of a startup's growth. The seed stage is the first funding round, when the venture first borrows capital to finance growth, typically from family or friends. The Series A round is the next stage, often involving angel investors. Finally, the Series B round takes the company to scale and often involves venture capital.

S CORPORATION In the United States, a closely held corporation whose tax status is the same as the partnership's but whose participants enjoy the liability protections granted to corporate shareholders. In other words, it is a conduit for passing profits and losses directly to the personal income tax returns of its shareholders, whose legal liabilities are limited to the amount of their capital contributions.

SEED INVESTMENT *See* "rounds (funding)."

SERIAL ENTREPRENEUR An individual who has started multiple businesses over time.

SERIES (FUNDING) *See* "rounds (funding)."

SOLE PROPRIETORSHIP A business owned by a single individual. In the United States, this owner and the business are one and the same for tax and legal liability purposes. The proprietorship is not taxed as a separate entity. Instead, the owner reports all income and deductible expenses for the business on Schedule C of his or her personal income tax return.

STRATEGY A plan that will differentiate the enterprise and give it a competitive advantage.

TIMES-INTEREST-EARNED RATIO Earnings before interest and taxes divided by interest expense. Creditors use this ratio to gauge a company's ability to make future interest payments in the face of fluctuating operating results.

VARIABLE COSTS Costs that rise or fall with the volume of output.

VENTURE CAPITALIST (VC) A high-risk investor who seeks an equity position in a startup or an early-growth company having high potential. In return for capital, the VC typically takes a significant percentage ownership of the business and a position on its board.

WARRANT A security that gives the holder the right to purchase common shares of the warrant-issuing company at a stated price for a stated period. The stated price is generally set higher than the current valuation of the shares.

WORKING CAPITAL *See* "net working capital."

Further Reading

Part 1: Preparing for the Journey

Articles

Andreessen, Marc, and Adi Ignatius. "In Search of the Next Big Thing," *Harvard Business Review*, May 2013 (product #R1305G). Cofounder and partner of VC firm Andreessen Horowitz talks about the challenges of entrepreneurship today.

Bhidé, Amar. "The Questions Every Entrepreneur Must Answer," *Harvard Business Review*, November–December 1996 (product #96603). A classic article: entrepreneurs tend to have a bias for action, but they should also step back and ask themselves about their personal goals as well as the company's strategy.

Butler, Timothy. "Hiring an Entrepreneurial Leader," *Harvard Business Review*, March–April 2017 (product #1702E). A Harvard Business School professor describes new research that shows what makes the most successful entrepreneurial leaders.

Valencia, Jordana. "How Founders Can Recognize and Combat Depression." HBR.org, February 17, 2017. Entrepreneurs are 30 percent more likely to experience depression than their nonentrepreneurial counterparts; this article discusses how to address it—and how to avoid it to begin with.

Books

Ruback, Richard S., and Royce Yudkoff. *HBR Guide to Buying a Small Business* (HBR Guide Series). Boston: Harvard Business Review Press, 2016. If you want to run your own company but don't want to start it from scratch, consider buying an existing small business.

Part 2: Defining Your Enterprise

Articles

Blank, Steve. "Why the Lean Start-Up Changes Everything." *Harvard Business Review*, May 2013 (product #1305C). Introducing an experimental approach to creating a new business.

Brown, Tim. "Design Thinking." *Harvard Business Review*, June 2008 (product #R0806E). How to imbue innovation with a human-centered approach.

Hagiu, Andre, and Simon Rothman. "Network Effects Aren't Enough." *Harvard Business Review*, April 2016 (product #R1604D). How to avoid the pitfalls of platform businesses with rapid growth.

Kavadias, Stelios, et al. "The Transformative Business Model." *Harvard Business Review*, October 2016 (product #R1610H). How an innovative business model can change your industry and build your business.

Ladd, Ted. "The Limits of the Lean Start-Up Method." HBR.org, March 7, 2016. The lean startup method can work, but there are other things to keep in mind.

Ovans, Andrea. "What Is a Business Model?" HBR.org, January 23, 2015. A primer on business models and how thinking about the concept has evolved over the last two decades.

Magretta, Joan. "Why Business Models Matter." *Harvard Business Review*, May 2002 (product #R0205F). What a business model is, how it differs from strategy, and why it's important.

McGrath, Rita Gunther. "Transient Advantage." *Harvard Business Review*, June 2013 (product #R1306C). Why sustainable competitive advantage is no longer a viable goal, and what smart companies can do to stay ahead of the competition.

Sahlman, William A. "How to Write a Great Business Plan." *Harvard Business Review*, July–August 1997 (product #97409). A classic article by a seasoned scholar with deep experience in new ventures describes what financiers look for in a business plan. He explains that most plans waste too much ink on numbers and devote too little space to the information that truly matters to experienced investors: the people who will run the venture, the opportunity and its economic underpinnings, the context of the venture, and the risk-versus-reward situation.

Thomke, Stefan, and Donald Reinertsen. "Six Myths of Product Development." *Harvard Business Review*, May 2012 (product #R1205E). Product development is different from manufacturing and needs to be managed in a new way.

Van Alstyne, Marshall W., et al. "Pipelines, Platforms, and the New Rules of Strategy." *Harvard Business Review*, April 2016 (product #R1604C). Platform businesses such as online marketplaces and exchanges are in the spotlight for their impressive growth. How do they achieve such impressive growth, and how does their structure change what we know about strategy?

Books

Harvard Business Review. *Creating Business Plans* (HBR 20-Minute Manager Series). Boston: Harvard Business Review Press, 2014. The fundamentals of crafting a business plan.

Osterwalder, Alexander. *Business Model Generation: A Handbook for Visionaries, Game Changers, and Challengers*. New York: Wiley, 2010. A guide for entrepreneurs looking to experiment and iterate on their business models.

Ries, Eric. *The Lean Startup: How Today's Entrepreneurs Use Continuous Innovation to Create Radically Successful Businesses*. New York: Crown, 2011. The book that first introduced lean entrepreneurship in detail.

Sheen, Raymond, with Amy Gallo. *HBR Guide to Building Your Business Case* (HBR Guides Series). Boston: Harvard Business Review Press, 2015. For entrepreneurs and innovators in large organizations alike, a guide to crafting an appealing business case document.

Part 3: Financing Your Business

Articles

Anderson, Chris. "How to Give a Killer Presentation." *Harvard Business Review*, June 2013 (product #R1306K). The curator of TED talks gives a primer on how to hook your audience.

Mulcahy, Diane. "Six Myths About Venture Capitalists." *Harvard Business Review*, May 2013 (product #R1305E). A clear-eyed view of the VC ecosystem for entrepreneurs.

Mullins, John. "Use Customer Cash to Finance Your Start-Up." *Harvard Business Review*, July–August 2013 (product #F1307A). Many scalable, tech-oriented startups are finding ways to get early funding from their customers—and to avoid having to seek outside capital.

Zider, Bob, and Hal R. Varian. "How Venture Capital Works." *Harvard Business Review*, November–December 1998 (product #98611). A classic on the model that drives venture capitalists.

Books

Baehr, Evan, and Evan Loomis. *Get Backed: Craft Your Story, Build the Perfect Pitch Deck, and Launch the Venture of Your Dreams.* Boston: Harvard Business Review Press, 2016. A handbook for writing a pitch deck—and presenting it to potential funders.

Berinato, Scott. *Good Charts: The HBR Guide to Making Smarter, More Persuasive Data Visualizations.* Boston: Harvard Business Review Press, 2016. How to create the most persuasive data visualizations for your business plan or pitch deck.

Bussgang, Jeffrey, *Mastering the VC Game: A Venture Capital Insider Reveals How to Get from Start-Up to IPO on Your Terms.* New York: Portfolio, 2011. Learn more about the venture-capitalist ecosystem so that you can gain the right partner for your business.

Duarte, Nancy. *HBR Guide to Persuasive Presentations* (HBR Guides Series). Boston: Harvard Business Review Press, 2012. Master the art and science of high-stakes pitches, from a deck that tells a simple, compelling story to an authentic speaking style that conveys your competence.

Harvard Business Review. *HBR Guide to Finance Basics for Managers* (HBR Guides Series). Boston: Harvard Business Review Press, 2012. What you need to know about the numbers.

Part 4: Scaling Up

Articles

Bower, Joseph L., and Clayton M. Christensen. "Disruptive Technologies: Catching the Wave." *Harvard Business Review*, January–February 1995 (product #95103). The seminal article on disruptive innovation.

Christensen, Clayton M., and Michael Overdorf. "Meeting the Challenge of Disruptive Change." *Harvard Business Review*, March 2000 (product #R00202).

How established organizations can stay innovative and avoid being disrupted by new entrants.

Churchill, Neill C., and Virginia L. Lewis. "Five Stages of Small Business Growth." *Harvard Business Review*, May 1983 (product #83301). This classic describes the path from startup to established business, addressing the common problems arising at specific stages in their development.

Govindarajan, Vijay. "Great Innovators Create the Future, Manage the Present, and Selectively Forget the Past." HBR.org, March 31, 2016. How to go beyond being an ambidextrous organization—executing for today and innovating for tomorrow—to also get beyond the values and beliefs that keep you tied to the past.

Hoffman, Reid, and Tim Sullivan. "Blitzscaling." *Harvard Business Review*, April 2016 (product #R1604B). How to manage the spectacularly rapid growth experienced by some startup wunderkinds.

Zook, Chris, and James Allen. "Reigniting Growth." *Harvard Business Review*, March 2016 (product #R1603F). Using the "founder's mentality" to keep growing even as a more established company.

Books

Christensen, Clayton M. *The Innovator's Dilemma*, 2nd ed. Boston: Harvard Business Review Press, 2013. A more detailed look at Christensen's theory of disruptive innovation.

Part 5: Looking to the Future

Articles

Wasserman, Noam. "The Founder's Dilemma." *Harvard Business Review*, February 2008 (product #R0802G). A classic article that asks founders, Do you want to be rich, or do you want to be king?

Sources

Introduction

Blank, Steve. "Why the Lean Start-Up Changes Everything." *Harvard Business Review*, May 2013.

Brown, Morgan Brown. "Airbnb: The Growth Story You Didn't Know." https://growthhackers.com/growth-studies/airbnb.

Bygrave, William D., ed. *The Portable MBA in Entrepreneurship*, 2nd ed. New York: J. Wiley & Sons, 1997.

McIntyre, Douglas A. "Airbnb Reaches $25.5 Billion Valuation," *24/7 Wall St.* November 21, 2015, http://247wallst.com/services/2015/11/21/airbnb-reaches-25-5-billion-valuation.

Texiera, Thales S., and Morgan Brown. "Airbnb, Etsy, Uber: Growing from One Thousand to One Million Customers," Case 516-108. Boston: Harvard Business School, June 7, 2016.

What's ahead

Gordon Mills, Karen, and Brayden McCarthy. "The State of Small Business Lending: Innovation and Technology and the Implications for Regulation." Working paper 17-042. Boston: Harvard Business School, 2016.

Chapter 1: Is Starting a Business Right for You?

Ideas and drive

Gergen, Christopher, and Gregg Vanourek. "Vision(ary) Entrepreneur," HBR.org, August 14, 2008.

People skills

Baehr, Evan, and Evan Loomis. *Get Backed: Craft Your Story, Build the Perfect Pitch Deck, Launch the Venture of Your Dreams*. Boston: Harvard Business Review Press, 2015.

Isenberg, Daniel. "Entrepreneurial Passion." HBR.org, January 6, 2010.

Onyemah, Vincent, Martha Rivera Pesquera, and Abdul Ali. "What Entrepreneurs Get Wrong." *Harvard Business Review*, May 2013.

Ruback, Richard S., and Royce Yudkoff. *HBR Guide to Buying a Small Business* (HBR Guide Series). Boston: Harvard Business Review Press, 2017.

Work style

Kuemmerle, Walter. "A Test for the Fainthearted," *Harvard Business Review*, May 2012.

Financial savvy

HBS Working Knowledge. "Skills and Behaviors That Make Entrepreneurs Successful." Harvard Business School, June 6, 2016.

Entrepreneurial background

Bricklin, Dan. "Natural-Born Entrepreneur," *Harvard Business Review*, September 2001, 53–59.

Chapter 2: Shaping an Opportunity

Evaluating the opportunity

Hagiu, Andrei, and Simon Rothman. "Network Effects Aren't Enough." HBR.org, April 2016.
Timmons, Jeffry A. *New Venture Creation*, 6th ed. Burr Ridge, IL: McGraw Hill-Irwin, 2004.
———. "Opportunity Recognition." In *The Portable MBA in Entrepreneurship*, 2nd ed. Edited by William D. Bygrave. New York: J. Wiley & Sons, 1997.
Vermeulen, Freek. "What So Many Strategists Get Wrong About Digital Disruption." HBR.org, January 3, 2017.

Chapter 3: Building Your Business Model and Strategy

Ovans, Andrea. "What Is a Business Model?" HBR.org, January 23, 2015.

Defining your business model

Blank, Steve. "Why the Lean Start-Up Changes Everything." *Harvard Business Review*, May 2013.
Fallon, Nicole. "Accelerator Programs 101: How to Apply and What to Expect." *Business News Daily*, June 5, 2015.
Gilad, Benjamin. "How a Food-Ordering App Broke into a Crowded Market." *Harvard Business Review*, November 25, 2015.
Hamermesh, Richard G., and Paul W. Marshall, "Note on Business Model Analysis for the Entrepreneur." Class note 9-802-048. Boston: Harvard Business School Publishing, 2002.
Hathaway, Ian. "What Startup Accelerators Really Do." HBR.org, March 1, 2016.
Magretta, Joan. "Why Business Models Matter." *Harvard Business Review*, May 2002.
Ovans, Andrea. "What Is a Business Model?" HBR.org, January 23, 2015.
Salz, Peggy Anne. "The Changing Economics of App Development." HBR.org, November 4, 2015.

Statista. "Number of Apps Available in Leading App Stores as of March 2017." www.statista.com/statistics/276623/ number-of-apps-available-in-leading-app-stores.

Defining your strategy

Andreessen, Marc, and Adi Ignatius. "In Search of the Next Big Thing." *Harvard Business Review*, May 2013.

Hagiu, Andrei, and Simon Rothman. "Network Effects Aren't Enough." HBR.org, April 2016.

Henderson, Bruce. "The Origin of Strategy." *Harvard Business Review*, November–December 1989.

Johnson, Mark W., Clayton M. Christensen, and Henning Kagermann. "Reinventing Your Business Model." *Harvard Business Review*, December 2008.

Ladd, Ted. "The Limits of the Lean Startup Method." HBR.org, March 7, 2016.

McGrath, Rita Gunther. "Transient Advantage." *Harvard Business Review*, June 2013.

Osborne, Alfred E. Memo to writer, March 21, 2004.

Porter, Michael E. "What Is Strategy?" *Harvard Business Review*, November–December 1996.

Sullivan, Tim. "Blitzscaling." *Harvard Business Review*, April 2016.

Chapter 4: Organizing Your Company

C corporations

Lundeen, Andrew, and Kyle Pomerleau. "Corporations Make Up 5 Percent of Businesses but Earn 62 Percent of Revenues." *Tax Foundation*, November 25, 2014, taxfoundation.org/corporations-make-5-percent-businesses-earn-62-percent-revenues.

The limited-liability company

US Small Business Administration. "Starting & Managing: Limited Liability Company." Accessed July 12, 2017, https://www.sba.gov/starting-business/ choose-your-business-structure/limited-liability-company.

Chapter 5: Writing Your Business Plan

How business plans are changing

Baehr, Evan, and Evan Loomis. *Get Backed: Craft Your Story, Build the Perfect Pitch Deck, Launch the Venture of Your Dreams.* Boston: Harvard Business Review Press, 2015.

Blank, Steve. "No Plan Survives First Contact with Customers: Business Plans Versus Business Models." *Steve Blank* (blog), April 8, 2010, steveblank.com/ 2010/04/08/no-plan-survives-first-contact-with-customers-%E2%80%93 -business-plans-versus-business-models.

Nivi, Babak. "How to Write an Elevator Pitch." *Harvard Business Review*, April 1, 2009.

Sahlman, William A. "How to Write a Great Business Plan." *Harvard Business Review*, July–August 1997.

Key elements

Sahlman, William A. "How to Write a Great Business Plan." *Harvard Business Review*, July–August 1997.

Style

Berinato, Scott. *Good Charts: The HBR Guide to Making Smarter, More Persuasive Data Visualizations*. Boston: Harvard Business Review Press, 2016.
Duarte, Nancy. *HBR Guide to Persuasive Presentations*. Boston: Harvard Business Review Press, 2012.
Strunk Jr., William and E. B. White. *The Elements of Style*, 3rd ed. New York: Macmillan, 1979.

Chapter 6: Startup-Stage Financing

Types of business and their life cycles

Blank, Steve. "Why the Lean Start-Up Changes Everything." *Harvard Business Review*, May 2013.
Delgado, Mercedes, and Karen G. Mills. "A New Categorization of the US Economy: The Role of Supply Chain Industries in Performance." Preliminary white paper, May 23, 2016.
Gordon Mills, Karen, and Brayden McCarthy. "The State of Small Business Lending: Innovation and Technology and the Implications for Regulation." Working paper 17-042. Boston: Harvard Business School, 2016.
Hall, Alan E. "Don't Abandon Crowdfunding—Manage It." HBR.org, May 10, 2012.
Hathaway, Ian. "What Startup Accelerators Really Do." HBR.org, March 1, 2016.
Isenberg, Daniel. "The Road to Crowdfunding Hell." HBR.org, April 23, 2012.
Kauffman Firm Survey. "The Capital Structure Decisions of New Firms." Kauffman Foundation, April 17, 2009, www.kauffman.org/what-we-do/research/kauffman-firm-survey-series/the-capital-structure-decisions-of-new-firms.
Kauffman Foundation. "Changing Capital: Emerging Trends in Entrepreneurial Finance." Kauffman Foundation, October 24, 2016, www.kauffman.org/what-we-do/research/2016/changing-capital-emerging-trends-in-entrepreneurial-finance.
Mollick, Ethan. "The Unique Value of Crowdfunding Is Not Money—It's Community." HBR.org, April 21, 2016.
Oculus Rift. "Oculus Rift: Step into the Game." Kickstarter project page. Accessed July 8, 2017, www.kickstarter.com/projects/1523379957/oculus-rift-step-into-the-game.
Ruback, Richard S., and Royce Yudkoff. *HBR Guide to Buying a Small Business* (HBR Guide Series). Boston: Harvard Business Review Press, 2017.
Wiens, Jason, and Jordan Bell-Masterson. "How Entrepreneurs Access Capital and Get Funded." *Entrepreneurship Policy Digest*, Kauffman Foundation, June 2, 2015, www.kauffman.org/what-we-do/resources/entrepreneurship-policy-digest/how-entrepreneurs-access-capital-and-get-funded.

Chapter 7: Growth-Stage Financing

Debt

Federal Reserve Bank of Boston. "Small Business Credit Survey." Federal Reserve
Bank of Boston, 2015, https://www.newyorkfed.org/medialibrary/media/small
business/2015/Report-SBCS-2015.pdf.

Gordon Mills, Karen, and Brayden McCarthy. "The State of Small Business Lending: Innovation and Technology and the Implications for Regulation." Working
paper 17-042. Boston: Harvard Business School, 2016.

Wiens, Jason, and Jordan Bell-Masterson. "How Entrepreneurs Access Capital and
Get Funded." *Entrepreneurship Policy Digest*, Kauffman Foundation, June 2,
2015, www.kauffman.org/what-we-do/resources/entrepreneurship-policy
-digest/how-entrepreneurs-access-capital-and-get-funded.

Financing growth at eBay

Bunnell, David, with Richard Luecke. *The eBay Phenomenon: Business Secrets
Behind the World's Hottest Internet Company*. New York: Wiley, 2000.

eBay. 2001 annual report to SEC.

Chapter 8: Angel Investment and Venture Capital

Angel investors

Baehr, Evan, and Evan Loomis. *Get Backed: Craft Your Story, Build the Perfect
Pitch Deck, Launch the Venture of Your Dreams*. Boston: Harvard Business
Review Press, 2015.

Harvard Business Review. "How Venture Capitalists Really Assess a Pitch." *Harvard Business Review*, May–June 2017.

Mirabile, Christopher. "Strength in Numbers: Working with Angel Group." *Inc.*,
January 6, 2015.

Mulcahy, Diane. "Six Myths About Venture Capitalists." *Harvard Business Review*,
May 2013.

Ortmans, Jonathan. "The Rise of Angel Investing." Kauffman Foundation,
March 28, 2016, www.kauffman.org/blogs/policy-dialogue/2016/march/
the-rise-of-angel-investing.

Sohl, Jeffrey. "The Angel Investor Market in 2015: A Buyers' Market." Center for
Venture Research, May 25, 2015.

Torres, Nicole. "What Angel Investors Value Most When Choosing What to Fund."
HBR.org, August 6, 2015.

Venture capital

Hague, Katherine. "6 Questions Every Founder Should Ask Before They Raise
Capital." O'Reilly, March 8, 2016, www.oreilly.com/ideas/6-questions-every
-founder-should-ask-before-they-raise-capital.

Hallett, Rachel. "These Are the Industries Attracting Venture Capital." World
Economic Forum, February 13, 2017, www.weforum.org/agenda/2017/02/
these-are-the-industries-attracting-the-most-venture-capital.

Harvard Business Review. "For Founders, Preparation Trumps Passion." *Harvard Business Review*, July–August 2015.

———. "How Venture Capitalists Really Assess a Pitch." *Harvard Business Review*, May–June 2017.

Hathaway, Ian. "What Startup Accelerators Really Do." HBR.org, March 1, 2016.

Mulcahy, Diane. "Six Myths About Venture Capitalists." *Harvard Business Review*, May 2013.

Chapter 9: Going Public

Weighing the decision to go public

Jones, Howard, and Rüdiger Stucke. "A Cheaper Way to Do IPOs." *Harvard Business Review*, November 2013.

Wasserman, Elizabeth. "How to Prepare a Company for an Initial Public Offering." *Inc.*, February 1, 2010.

The making of an IPO candidate

Andreessen, Marc, and Adi Ignatius. "In Search of the Next Big Thing." *Harvard Business Review*, May 2013.

Blowers, Stephen C., Peter H. Griffith, and Thomas L. Milan. *The Ernst & Young LLP Guide to the IPO Value Journey*. New York: Wiley, 1999.

The role of the investment bank

Wasserman, Elizabeth. "How to Prepare a Company for an Initial Public Offering." *Inc.*, February 1, 2010.

Chapter 10: Sustaining Entrepreneurial Growth

Hoffman, Reid, and Tim Sullivan. "Blitzscaling." *Harvard Business Review*, April 2016.

The impact of growth

Airbnb. "Airbnb Summer Travel Report: 2015." Accessed July 12, 2017, http://blog.atairbnb.com/wp-content/uploads/2015/09/Airbnb-Summer-Travel-Report-1.pdf.

Hoffman, Reid, and Tim Sullivan. "Blitzscaling." *Harvard Business Review*, April 2016.

Lien, Tracy. "Uber Is on Growth Fast Track, Leaked Document Shows." *Los Angeles Times*, August 21, 2015.

Growth strategy

Anthony, Scott, and Evan I. Schwartz. "What the Best Transformational Leaders Do." HBR.org, May 8, 2017.

Chopra, Sunil, and Murali Veeraiyan. "Movie Rental Business: Blockbuster, Netflix, and Redbox." Case KEL616. Evanston, IL: Kellogg School of Management, Northwestern University, 2010.

Scaling up your organization

Hoffman, Reid, and Tim Sullivan. "Blitzscaling." *Harvard Business Review*, April 2016.

Chapter 11: Leadership for a Growing Business

Bhidé, Amar. "Building the Self-Sustaining Firm." Class note 395-200. Boston: Harvard Business School Publishing, 1995.

The right leadership approach for your size

Roberts, Michael J. "Managing Transitions in the Growing Enterprise." Class note 393-107. Boston: Harvard Business School Publishing, 1993.

Is it time to change the guard?

Andreessen, Marc, and Adi Ignatius. "In Search of the Next Big Thing." *Harvard Business Review*, May 2013.

Baehr, Evan, and Evan Loomis. *Get Backed: Craft Your Story, Build the Perfect Pitch Deck, Launch the Venture of Your Dreams.* Boston: Harvard Business Review Press, 2015.

Flamholtz, Eric G., and Yvonne Randle. *Growing Pains: Transitioning from an Entrepreneurship to a Professionally Managed Firm*, revised edition. San Francisco: Jossey-Bass, 2000.

Hill, Linda A., and Maria Farkas. "Meg Whitman at eBay, Inc. (A)," Case 401-024. Boston. Harvard Business School, 2000; revised November 2005.

MacPherson, Kerrie. "Who Advises the Entrepreneur?" HBR.org, October 22, 2013.

Mulcahy, Diane. "Six Myths About Venture Capitalists." *Harvard Business Review*, May 2013.

Chapter 12: Keeping the Entrepreneurial Spirit Alive

Govindarajan, Vijay, and Srikanth Srinivas. "The Innovation Mindset in Action: 3M Corporation." HBR.org, August 6, 2013.

Pisano, Gary P. "You Need an Innovation Strategy." *Harvard Business Review*, June 2015.

Preserve an innovation-friendly culture

Harvard Business Review. *Innovative Teams* (20-Minute Manager Series). Boston: Harvard Business Review Press, 2015.

Tushman, Michael L., and Charles A. O'Reilly III. *Winning Through Innovation: A Practical Guide to Leading Organizational Change and Renewal.* Boston: Harvard Business School Press, 1997.

Establish vision and strategic direction

Hoffman, Reid, and Tim Sullivan. "Blitzscaling." *Harvard Business Review*, April 2016.

Green, Sarah. "Why You Should Cannibalize Your Company: [An Interview with James Allworth]." HBR.org, November, 21 2012.

Hire people who have entrepreneurial attitudes

Bell, Katherine. "The Three-Box Approach to Business Model Reinvention: Putting the Idea into Practice." HBR.org, September 19, 2011.

Christensen, Clayton M., and Michael Overdorf. "Meeting the Challenge of Disruptive Change." *Harvard Business Review*, March–April 2000.

Golsby-Smith, Tony. "Want Innovative Thinking? Hire from the Humanities." HBR.org, March 31, 2011.

Tushman, Michael L., and Charles A. O'Reilly III. *Winning Through Innovation: A Practical Guide to Leading Organizational Change and Renewal*. Boston: Harvard Business School Press, 1997.

Chapter 13: Harvest Time

Harvesting mechanisms

Peterson, Richard. "U.S. Leveraged Buyout Deal Value Advances in 2016." *S&P Global: Market Intelligence*, October 20, 2016, http://marketintelligence.sp global.com/blog/u-s-leveraged-buyout-deal-value-advances-in-2016.

Ruback, Richard S., and Royce Yudkoff. *HBR Guide to Buying a Small Business* (HBR Guide Series). Boston: Harvard Business Review Press, 2017.

Wall Street Journal. "Ways to Cash Out of Your Business." *Wall Street Journal*, accessed July 12, 2017.

Copeland, Tom, Tim Koller, and Jack Murrin. *Valuation: Measuring and Managing the Value of Companies*, 2nd edition. New York: John Wiley & Sons, 1994.

Appendix A: Understanding Financial Statements

Harvard Business Review. *HBR Guide to Finance Basics for Managers* (HBR Guides Series). Boston, Harvard Business Review Press, 2012.

Appendix C: Valuation

Robert, Michael J. "Valuation Techniques." Class note 9-384-185. Boston: Harvard Business School Publishing, revised August 18, 1988.

Index

The most important management ideas all in one place.

We hope you enjoyed this book from *Harvard Business Review*. For the best ideas HBR has to offer turn to HBR's 10 Must Reads Boxed Set. From books on leadership and strategy to managing yourself and others, this 6-book collection delivers articles on the most essential business topics to help you succeed.

HBR's 10 Must Reads Series

The definitive collection of ideas and best practices on our most sought-after topics from the best minds in business.

- Change Management
- Collaboration
- Communication
- Emotional Intelligence
- Innovation
- Leadership
- Making Smart Decisions

- Managing Across Cultures
- Managing People
- Managing Yourself
- Strategic Marketing
- Strategy
- Teams
- The Essentials

hbr.org/mustreads

Buy for your team, clients, or event.
Visit hbr.org/bulksales for quantity discount rates.

The One Primer You Need to Develop Your Management Skills

If you enjoyed reading the **HBR Entrepreneur's Handbook**, turn to the **HBR Manager's Handbook Ebook + Tools** for step-by-step advice and downloadable tools on the 17 skills you need to stand out.

Packed with templates, worksheets, videos, and more, the **HBR Manager's Handbook Ebook + Tools** provides best practices on topics, ranging from understanding financial statements and the fundamentals of strategy to emotional intelligence and building your employees' trust. Keep this guide with you throughout your career and be a more impactful leader in your organization.

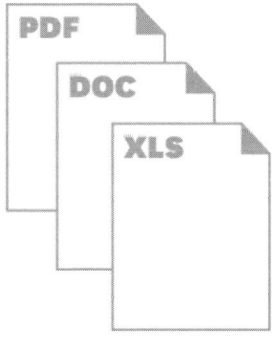

hbr.org/books